TIME ANNUAL 2005

By the Editors of TIME

TIME
ANNUAL

2005

By the Editors of TIME

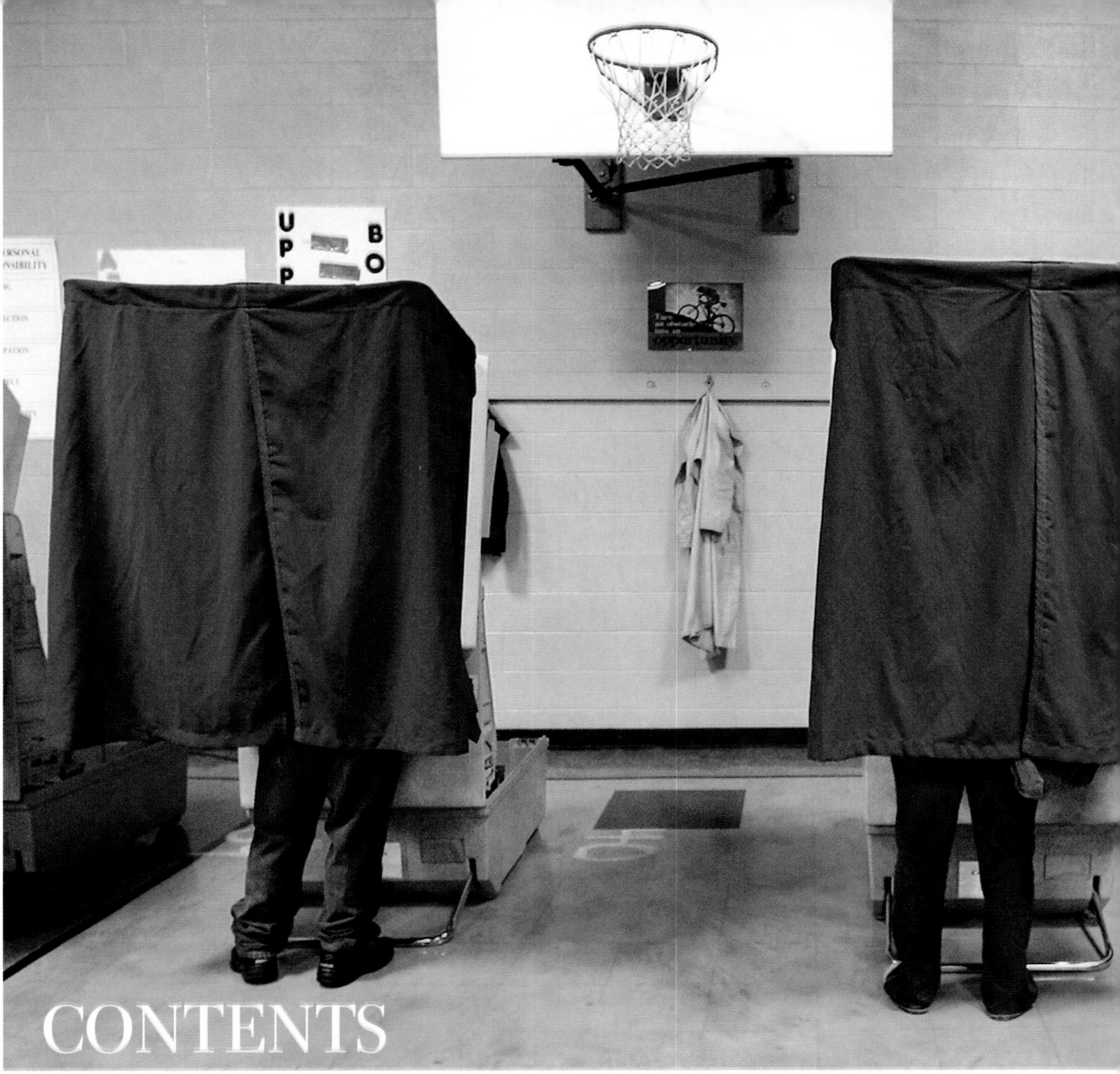

CONTENTS

The Year in Review

Election 2004

Person of the Year

Nation

World

TIME ANNUAL 2005

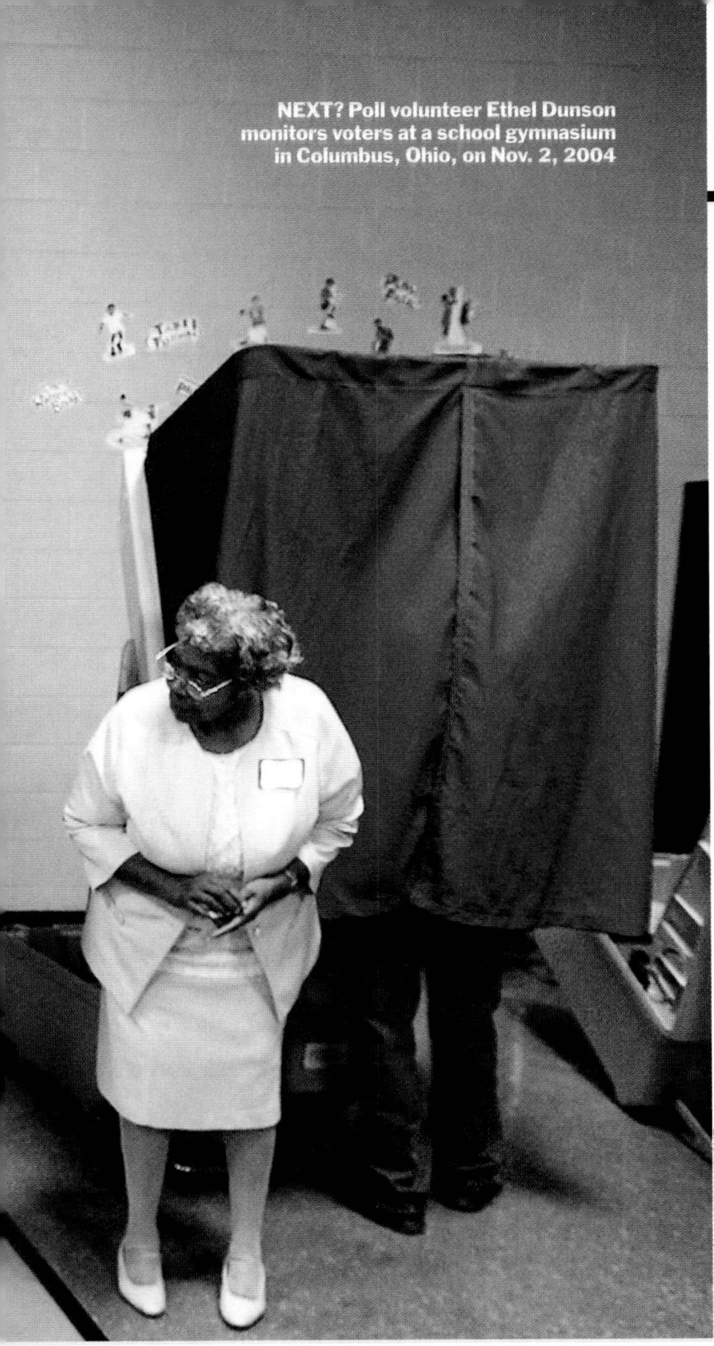

NEXT? Poll volunteer Ethel Dunson monitors voters at a school gymnasium in Columbus, Ohio, on Nov. 2, 2004

LAURA RAUCH AP/WIDE WORLD

Credits: FRONT COVER, from top, left to right: Patrick Baz—AFP/Getty Images; Brooks Kraft—Corbis; The White House; Garrett W. Ellwood—©NBAE 2004 via Getty Images; J. Pat Carter—AP/Wide World; Steve Liss; Stephen Danelian—Corbis Outline; Charles Rex Arbogast—AP/Wide World; Ciclops—Space Science Institute/JPL/NASA. BACK COVER, from top, left to right: Timothy A. Clary—AFP/Getty Images; Steve Schilling—USGS; Kelly A. Swift—Retna; Mark Baker—AP/Wide World

TIME ANNUAL 2005

EDITOR Kelly Knauer
DESIGNER Ellen Fanning
PICTURE EDITOR Patricia Cadley
RESEARCH DIRECTOR/WRITER Matthew McCann Fenton
COPY EDITOR Bruce Christopher Carr

TIME INC. HOME ENTERTAINMENT
PRESIDENT Rob Gursha
VICE PRESIDENT, NEW PRODUCT DEVELOPMENT Richard Fraiman
EXECUTIVE DIRECTOR, MARKETING SERVICES Carol Pittard
DIRECTOR, RETAIL & SPECIAL SALES Tom Mifsud
DIRECTOR OF FINANCE Tricia Griffin
MARKETING DIRECTOR Ann Marie Doherty
PREPRESS MANAGER Emily Rabin
BOOK PRODUCTION MANAGER Jonathan Polsky
PRODUCT MANAGER Kristin Walker
ASSISTANT PRODUCT MANAGER Candice Ogarro

SPECIAL THANKS TO:
Bozena Bannett, Alex Bliss, Bernadette Corbie, Robert Dente, Anne-Michelle Gallero, Peter Harper, Suzanne Janso, Robert Marasco, Natalie McCrea, Brooke McGuire, Margarita Quiogue, Mary Jane Rigoroso, Steven Sandonato

THE WORK OF THE FOLLOWING TIME STAFF MEMBERS AND CONTRIBUTORS IS FEATURED IN THIS VOLUME:
Kathleen Adams, Christopher Allbritton, Melissa August, Perry Bacon Jr., Harriet Barovick, Hannah Beech, Brian Bennett, Lisa Beyer, Laura Bradford, Timothy J. Burger, Massimo Calabresi, James Carney, Jeff Chu, Howard Chua-Eoan, John Cloud, Adam Cohen, Wendy Cole, Matthew Cooper, Richard Corliss, Simon Crittle, Bruce Crumley, Lisa Takeuchi Cullen, Pat Dawson, Jeanne DeQuine, Sally B. Donnelly, Andrea Dorfman, John F. Dickerson, Michael Duffy, Daniel Eisenberg, Simon Elegant, Philip Elmer-DeWitt, Michael Elliott, Steven Erlanger, Stephan Faris, Christopher John Farley, Matthew Forney, Stefanie Friedhoff, Nancy Gibbs, Helen Gibson, Frederic Golden, Andrew Goldstein, Christine Gorman, James Graff, Peter Hawthorne, Paul Gray, Karl Taro Greenfeld, Sean Gregory, Lev Grossman, Anita Hamilton, Ghulam Hasnain, Syed Talat Hassain, Rita Healy, John Heilemann, Marc Hequet, Avery Holton, Susan Jakes, Daniel Kadlec, James Kelly, Naeemah Khabir, Barbara Kiviat, Jeffrey Kluger, Joshua Kucera, Richard Lacayo, John Larkin, Michael D. Lemonick, Belinda Luscombe, Jessica Lynch, Donald Macintyre, Malcolm Macpherson, Scott MacLeod, Rian Malan, J.F.O. McAllister, Terry McCarthy, Johanna McGeary, Tim McGirk, Marguerite Michaels, Siobhan Morrissey, Jodie Morse, J. Madeleine Nash, Michele Orecklin, Peta Owens-Liston, Tim Padgett, Priscilla Painton, Alice Park, Andrew Perrin, Alex Perry, James Poniewozik, Eric Pooley, Andrew Purvis, Paul Quinn-Judge, Josh Quittner, Romesh Ratnesar, Matt Rees, Jessica Reaves, Amanda Ripley, Simon Robinson, Daffyd Roderick, Wilson Rothman, Nir Rosen, Eric Roston, Andrea Sachs, Richard Schickel, Elaine Shannon, Nelly Sindayen, Joel Stein, Richard Stengel, Sonja Steptoe, Ron Stodghill II, Stewart Stogel, Chris Taylor, Jason Tedjasukmana, Cathy Booth Thomas, Mark Thompson, Jyoti Thottam, Karen Tumulty, Josh Tyrangiel, Jill Underwood, David Van Biema, Vivienne Wait, Douglas C. Waller, Claudia Wallis, Michael Ware, Cindy Waxer, Michael Weisskopf, Leigh Anne Williams, Huang Yong, Kim Yooseung, Adam Zagorin, Yuri Zarakhovich, Richard Zoglin

SPECIAL THANKS TO:
Ken Baierlein, Barbara Dudley Davis, Richard Duncan, Jackson Dykman, Ed Gabel, Arthur Hochstein, Edward L. Jamieson, Kevin Kelly, Joe Lertola, Michele Stephenson, Lamarr Tsufura, Lon Tweeten, Cornelis Verwaal, Miriam Winocour

Published by TIME Books
Time Inc. • 1271 Avenue of the Americas • New York, NY 10020

First Edition • ISSN: 1097-5721 ISBN: 1-932273-53-0
TIME Books is a trademark of Time Inc.

We welcome your comments and suggestions about TIME Books. Please write to us at:
TIME Books • Attention: Book Editors • PO Box 11016 • Des Moines, IA 50336-1016

If you would like to order any of our hardcover Collector's Edition books, please call us at 1-800-327-6388 (Monday through Friday, 7 a.m.—8 p.m., or Saturday, 7 a.m.—6 p.m., Central time)

PRINTED IN THE UNITED STATES OF AMERICA

Images

08•20•04

Nowhere to Run, Nowhere to Hide

Americans were famously divided in 2004, as politicians, commentators and the pages of TIME kept reminding us. Yet there was one emotion that bridged the gaps, gathering red states and blue states, gays and straights, NASCAR fans and PBS buffs into one nation, indivisible: respect for the Americans serving in Iraq. Like the two U.S. Army soldiers above, taking cover in Najaf in August, they were far from home and surrounded by hostiles; their mission was questioned by many and undermined by a few at Abu Ghraib. Yet they hung tough, profiles in courage.

07•08•04

Traveling in the Best of Circles

In a year that brought fresh momentum (as well as a few speed bumps) to America's exploration of space, no sight was more moving than the view of Saturn and its rings provided by the two-part planetary probe Cassini-Huygens. Cassini, the smallish main craft (it is 22 ft. long and weighs 4,700 lbs.) went into orbit around Saturn on June 30, where it will stay for four years, during which time it is expected to complete 76 loops of the ringed planet, recording its activities with a dozen different cameras and instruments. Cassini has already returned revelatory images of some of Saturn's 31 moons, including the largest of them, Titan. Attached to Cassini is the Huygens module, a 705-lb. conical probe scheduled to be dropped into Titan's skies in mid-January 2005.

Photograph by Ciclops/Science Space Institute/J.P.L./NASA

07•04•04

Tall Order

"All politics is local," former Speaker of the House Tip O'Neill used to say, and even a campaign for the highest office in the land leads through driveways, backyards and grade schools all around the country. It doesn't get much more red-white-and-blue than this picture of candidate John Kerry, which was taken at an event billed as a "4th of July Family Barbecue" in—where else?—Independence, Iowa. Kerry, who would officially become the Democratic nominee in a few weeks at the party convention in Boston, stands 6-ft. 4-in., but he still needed a bit of a boost on this occasion. The Massachusetts Senator faced another steep challenge in trying to unseat incumbent President George W. Bush; when he failed to do so, Kerry said in his concession speech, "In an American election, there are no losers, because whether or not our candidates are successful, the next morning we all wake up as Americans."

GLUBA

Photograph for TIME by Callie Shell—Aurora

08 • 23 • 04

Three Amigos

Draw, podnuh! President George W. Bush strikes a classic gunslinger's pose in this memorable picture by veteran TIME photographer Christopher Morris, taken on Mr. Bush's ranch in Crawford, Texas. Flanking the Commander in Chief are the two men who helped him craft America's aggressive stance against international terrorism, Vice President Dick Cheney and Secretary of Defense Donald Rumsfeld. When the President won re-election in the fall, many members of his first-term Cabinet stepped aside, but both Cheney and Rumsfeld remained firmly in place. Readers had strong reactions to the photo when it first appeared in TIME. "Did the photographer pose them as cowboys inadvertently or on purpose?" asked one. Cameraman Morris replied that he didn't pose his subjects; a gunfighter stance may just come with the territory in the Lone Star State.

Photograph by Christopher Morris—VII for TIME

05•04•04

A Rallying Cry in Saddam's Shadow

This palace in Tikrit is one of the many showplaces that Saddam Hussein built as a monument to his power; now it is a tactical-operations center for U.S. forces, who have their own name for the crowded information hive: the Pit. General John Abizaid, chief of the U.S. military's Central Command (Centcom), is the man in the middle, addressing his soldiers on a visit to this city in the heart of the troubled, pro-Saddam Sunni triangle in May, only a week after pictures of torture at the Abu Ghraib prison were released and captured U.S. civilian Nicholas Berg was decapitated. Rallying the troops, Abizaid told them that back home, Americans "see pictures of burning humvees, they see pictures of abused prisoners at Abu Ghraib, and they see all the negative things that happen. But the positive things that happen day after day—the only people who really know about that are you."

Photograph for TIME by Christopher Morris—VII

Undated

The Shame Of Abu Ghraib

The images the world may remember longest from 2004 were actually taken in autumn 2003. Sadly, these photos are also among the most repulsive and shocking in American history. Taken inside the Abu Ghraib prison in Baghdad, long used as a torture chamber by Saddam Hussein, they show U.S. troops humiliating and abusing Iraqi detainees while gleefully mocking their captives. The photographs—documents in an ongoing Pentagon inquiry—were shown by CBS News on American television in April and soon were seen around the world. The damage to American prestige was incalculable: President George W. Bush called the pictures "abhorrent." The U.S. soldier in this picture, Private First Class Lynndie England, is set to stand trial in January 2005. If convicted of all charges, she could face a jail sentence of 38 years. Prime Minister Tony Blair of Britain spoke for many when he said, "We went to Iraq to get rid of that type of thing, not to do it."

Photograph by Michel Matera—PNUD/Gamma

09•19•04

Wasn't That a Mighty Storm?

A cavalcade of hurricanes barreled out of the southern Atlantic during the annual storm season in late summer and fall, spreading misery across a broad swath of the Gulf of Mexico and into the U.S. mainland. While Florida was hammered by four successive blows, several Caribbean island nations, including Cuba, Grenada and Haiti, were also hit hard. In this picture, the town of Gonaïves, on Haiti's west coast, is largely submerged after Hurricane Jeanne ripped through. The nation's social fabric—already perilously frayed by a coup that deposed President Jean-Bertrand Aristide in the spring—broke down in the wake of the storm, as needy Haitians battled aid workers for water and supplies.

08 • 01 • 04

In Sudan, Hope Clings by a Thread

An aghast world watched in horror as ethnic strife turned western Sudan into a killing field, but little was done to put an end to it. Beginning in February 2003, ethnic Arab militiamen known as the Janjaweed, backed by the Sudanese government, began a reign of terror against the region's non-Arab Muslims. By summer's end, 50,000—and counting—were dead. More than 1.4 million were homeless, and thousands of women had been raped. But numbers only record the scope of the tragedy; pictures bring it to life. Veteran TIME photojournalist James Nachtwey took this photo of a Sudanese woman at a refugee camp cutting string with her teeth as she rebuilds a hut that was washed away in a storm.

Photograph for TIME by James Nachtwey—VII

Photograph by Stuart Franklin—Getty Images

08•13•04

The Olympics Return to Greece

In three letters ... wow! When the Summer Olympics kicked off in Athens, sports fans around the world were holding their breath. For months, news accounts of the preparations for the Games had accentuated the negative: the Greek hosts were poorly organized; the stadium roof was a costly white elephant; the venues wouldn't be ready in time—and what about terrorism? But on that first night, the Greeks appeared bearing gifts. For once, the opening ceremonies were truly breathtaking, a blend of classical history and modern spectacle that—like these aerial torch bearers—led us to suspend our disbelief and feel, however briefly, that sport could offer a path to transcendence.

Photograph by Bryan Chan—Los Angeles Times

06•11•04

Sunset in America: A Final Farewell

Following a state funeral at the National Cathedral in Washington, which was attended by a galaxy of former Presidents and international leaders, the body of former President Ronald Reagan was flown aboard Air Force One to California. After a sunset service, his body was interred at the Ronald Reagan Presidential Library in Simi Valley. Here, as the ceremony ends, Nancy Reagan bends to give her husband's coffin a final kiss, while sons Ron and Michael and daughter Patti lend their support.

Condoleezza Rice

THIS PICTURE OF PRESIDENT GEORGE W. Bush's National Security Adviser captures all that is fascinating about her. Arms folded, she is unapproachable. Steady of gaze, she is whip-smart, focused and calculating. Captured in profile and partially obscured, she is in the position she prefers, just offstage from history's key players. Close to the flag, she represents U.S. power and influence to the world. A black woman in a highly influential role, she is a pioneer and inspiration to millions.

Rice has always been self-effacement personified. But now she will undergo a critical metamorphosis: appointed to replace the departing Colin Powell as Secretary of State in Bush's second term, she must forsake her backstage role, acclimate herself to the spotlight and become, in Bush's phrase, "America's face to the world."

We know Rice, the former provost of Stanford University, can play the bad cop: witness her famous advice to the President concerning the U.S. allies who did not support the war in Iraq: "Punish France, ignore Germany and forgive Russia." But how will Rice, 50, fit into the diplomat's world of photo ops and politesse, where attention will be paid to the woman behind the curtain? Stay tuned ■

BROOKS KRAFT—CORBIS

Ahmad Chalabi

LIKE A FALLEN KING IN A SHAKESPEAREAN drama, Ahmad Chalabi traced tragedy's classic arc during the war in Iraq. Raised to great heights in the initial euphoria that followed the downfall of Saddam Hussein in 2003, the man who has lived as an exile from Iraq for 46 of his 59 years fancied himself the nation's future leader. But the M.I.T.-educated Chalabi ended up despised and outcast by the very people who had cultivated his great expectations, Vice President Dick Cheney, U.S. Secretary of Defense Donald Rumsfeld and their fellow hard-line neoconservatives in the Bush Administration.

In April 2003, on the day Saddam's statue was toppled, the Pentagon flew Chalabi and his 600-man militia, dubbed the Free Iraqi Forces, into southern Iraq. Chalabi's operatives helped U.S. forces track down members of Saddam's regime, and the U.S. rewarded him with a seat on the interim Iraqi Governing Council. But as U.S. stature in Iraq plummeted, so did Chalabi's fortunes. Revelations that his longtime anti-Saddam operation, the Iraqi National Congress(I.N.C.), had provided the U.S. with faulty, rose-colored prewar intelligence forced even his former Pentagon pals to back away. Nor did he find favor with his countrymen. Dogged by charges that he mishandled U.S. funds and convicted in absentia in 1991 of bank fraud in Jordan (he has always maintained his innocence), Chalabi was viewed by many Iraqis as a carpetbagger.

On May 20, five armored U.S. humvees roared up to Chalabi's house in Baghdad; his front door was broken down, his home was searched, and seven of his lieutenants were arrested. The nearby headquarters of the I.N.C. was the next target; files and computers were confiscated by U.S. agents. Chalabi, they said, was suspected of selling secrets to Iran. As of December 2004, Chalabi remained free—and, like Hamlet, free to contemplate how all occasions informed against him. ■

KARIM SAHIB—AFP/GETTY IMAGES

Howard Dean

PUBLIC FIGURES HAVE BEEN DOOMED BY SOUND bites before—those with long memories may recall George Romney claiming he had been brainwashed in Vietnam, or Ed Muskie moping in the snow in New Hampshire—but seldom has a public figure stabbed himself in the back more adeptly than did Vermont Governor Howard Dean in 2004. It was on Jan. 19, the night of the Iowa caucuses, when an overexcited Dean, trying to rally his supporters after a third-place finish, launched into a long litany of states in which he vowed he'd campaign, ending in a howl. With a single improvident slip-up, Dean annihilated his chances of becoming President: no sane viewer wanted this guy's finger anywhere near the nuclear trigger.

And that's a shame, because Dean was a gutsy, essential figure in 2004, a brave American who stood up and charged the Bush Administration with launching a war on Iraq based on faulty intelligence—charges later borne out by several independent commissions. And Dean, 57, was a political pioneer, proving one could sustain a major national campaign by galvanizing people through the Internet. Viewers who encountered him on their TV sets later in the year may have been surprised to find a thoughtful, incisive observer of the political scene, rather than the hotheaded buffoon endlessly mocked on radio and TV. But in an era of short attention spans, it's doubtful Dean will ever escape that one overcaffeinated night in Iowa. ■

TIMOTHY A. CLARY—AFP—GETTY IMAGES

Burt Rutan

THE SKY ISN'T THE LIMIT FOR BURT RUTAN: it's just the starting line—an invitation, a challenge, a beckoning field of dreams. For him, the wild blue yonder seems to appear as the Atlantic Ocean must have to Prince Henry the Navigator: a vast, promising but little-known element into which one dispatches a series of odd-looking craft, improving the quality of the vessels over time through simple trial and error. For two decades now, Rutan has delighted aviation buffs with his innovative designs. He first came to wide notice with his elegant, willowy *Voyager,* the propeller-driven aircraft that made aviation history in 1986 by flying nonstop around the world on a single tank of gas.

In 2004 Rutan, 61, made good on his most compelling vision, to break NASA's grip on the exploration of outer space and usher in a new era of private space exploration. When his many-windowed *SpaceShipOne* completed three trips into the stratosphere, two of them in a space of five days, the maverick engineer with the long sideburns proved he had the right stuff to put the space age into a time machine and bring back the gonzo flyboy days of Chuck Yeager and the Mercury astronauts. That the little rocket ship weathered severe guidance problems on two of those flights—yawing and pitching, flip-flopping like a fish—well, that only made things more interesting. Prince Henry would have understood. ■

Donald Trump

IN A BULL MARKET FOR REALITY TV, IS IT ANY surprise that the taurine Donald Trump has bucked himself to the top of the heap? For two decades the New York City real estate developer has played his role—the brash, vulgarian billionaire—to perfection. Why, it was way back in 1989 that Trump, in the first flush of fame, graced TIME's cover as a symbol of a greed-besotted era. After a rough patch in the early '90s, it seemed Trump might go away. But in 2004 the seasoned self-promoter staged a comeback in *The Apprentice*, a reality show modeled directly on *Survivor* and produced by its guru, Briton Mark Burnett. The premise: 16 aspiring businesspeople arrive in Manhattan to compete in teams for the chance to become Trump's protégé. Each week the teams complete a challenge—say, selling lemonade on the street or designing a new toy. Back in his boardroom, Trump deploys a killer catchphrase, snarling "You're fired" at a member of the losing team.

Though Trump and Burnett solemnly swear *The Apprentice* is an educational look at modern capitalism, its primary tutorial element is how damn dreamy it is to be Donald Trump. And really, this is all most of us have ever wanted to learn from him. See Donald soar over Manhattan in his private helicopter! Ogle his Versailles-like penthouse and his statuesque fiancé, Melania Knauss! Trump is the rich guy so many nonwealthy Americans love because he lives like a lottery winner. O.K., so his casino-and-hotel business declared bankruptcy in November, proving that he really isn't a supreme business strategist. Who cares about reality, anyway? ■

speedo

FACES 2004

Michael Phelps

SWIMMING IS A SPORT FOR SPECIALISTS: most athletes would be happy to qualify for the Olympic Games in one event. It is his versatility, his command of a range of strokes, that brought Michael Phelps, 19, to glory in the 2004 Games at Athens, where he paddled away with eight medals, six of them gold. Trained in the individual medley, an event that requires mastery of all four swimming strokes, Phelps possesses a phenomenal ability to compete with the best specialists in three of them: butterfly, backstroke and freestyle. In the fourth, the breaststroke, he's merely outstanding.

His talent in the pool propelled Phelps to turn pro at age 16, while he was still in high school. Even before Athens, he was an anomaly in the swimming world, a multimillionaire with endorsements from Speedo, Omega, Visa, Argent Mortgage and PowerBar; his Olympics triumph brought him more. Money isn't the goal, though: Phelps wants to make swimming matter. He sees the attention that Americans lavish on their swimmers every four years evaporate between Games, and he desperately wants what Australian swimmer Ian Thorpe has: the prestige, the celebrity and, not least of all, the marketing clout to stand, in his home country, with the best athletes.

Phelps seemed on his way: giving up his slot in a relay final to a teammate in Athens who'd done poorly in a previous race was the sort of selfless act that sports agents' dreams are made of. But his squeaky-clean image was slightly tarnished in November, when he was stopped for driving under the influence of alcohol in his native Maryland. Who knew you could swim so fast with feet of clay? ■

VERBATIM Quotes of the Year

RON EDMONDS—AP/WIDE WORLD

CHIPS OFF THE OLD THE BUSH

“Like stand up straight and keep your hair out of your eyes.”
Laura Bush, *asked what type of advice she gave her two daughters about campaigning for their father*

“Everybody’s always like, ‘Did she party?’ And I’m like, ‘She was awesome. She was really sweet. I loved her.’ ”
Hilary Duff, *teen actress and Houston native, on having had First Daughter Jenna Bush as a camp counselor*

“Run away from office is more like it.”
Kristin Gore, *daughter of former Vice President Al Gore, asked if she has any plans to run for office in the future*

CHANNEL 7—APTN—AP/WIDE WORLD

AFTERMATH

“I was in complete control of the crocodile. Robert was tucked right in my arm.”
Steve Irwin, *crocodile hunter, after criticism of a stunt in which he carried his 1-month-old baby while feeding a crocodile*

“They’re going to be heartbroken at not being heartbroken.”
Leslie Epstein, *father of Boston Red Sox general manager Theo Epstein, predicting how Boston fans would react to winning the World Series*

“He was a natural, and made it look easy. Oh, how I hated him for that.”
George H.W. Bush, *of Bill Clinton’s political skills, at the opening of Clinton’s presidential library in Arkansas*

“The events at last night’s game were shocking, repulsive and inexcusable.”
David Stern, *NBA commissioner, describing the Nov. 19 brawl between the Indiana Pacers and the Detroit Pistons*

ARTEST
91

DUANE BURLESON—AP/WIDE WORLD

THE MISSING LINK

“Those weapons of mass destruction have to be here somewhere ... Nope, no weapons over there ... Maybe under here ...”
President Bush, *at a dinner for radio and TV correspondents, as he showed slides of himself looking under furniture in the White House*

“I’m sure something will pop into my head here.”
President Bush, *when asked by* TIME *reporter John Dickerson during a TV press conference to name the biggest mistake he had made since 9/11*

“The evidence about Saddam having actual biological and chemical weapons, as opposed to the capacity to develop them, has turned out to be wrong. I acknowledge that and accept it.”
Tony Blair, *British Prime Minister, in a speech to members of his Labour Party in Brighton*

SHOULDN’T HAVE SAID THAT

“I actually did vote for the $87 billion before I voted against it.”
John Kerry, *responding to Republican campaign ads that criticized his vote against a bill to authorize $87 billion in funds for postwar Iraq*

“[It’s] the gift that kept on giving.”
Karl Rove, *George W. Bush’s top political adviser, on Kerry’s remark, after the election*

CHENEY UNCHAINED

“F___ yourself.”
Vice President Dick Cheney, *to Democratic Senator Patrick Leahy of Vermont, on the Senate floor after members gathered for their annual group photograph. Cheney added that he “felt better afterwards”*

“The first time I ever met you was when you walked onto the stage tonight.”
Vice President Dick Cheney, *to Senator John Edwards, during their debate, after criticizing his opponent’s “not very distinguished” record in the Senate*

“By the way, y’all sat next to each other at the prayer breakfast.”
Elizabeth Edwards, *the candidate’s wife, reporting what she said to Cheney when they met onstage after the debate; the men had actually met three times before*

ONE NATION, DIVISIBLE

“If you look back on the ’60s and think there was more good than harm, you’re probably a Democrat. If you think there was more harm than good, you’re probably a Republican.”
Bill Clinton, *former President, kicking off a book tour for his new autobiography,* My Life

“If you drive a Volvo and you do yoga, you are pretty much a Democrat. If you drive a Lincoln or a BMW and own a gun, you’re voting George Bush.”
Ken Mehlman, *manager of George W. Bush’s re-election campaign, characterizing the split in the electorate*

LIVE
CNN

PULLING NO PUNCHES

“[You are] hurting America … What you do is not honest. What you do is partisan hackery … You have a responsibility to the public discourse, and you fail miserably.”

Jon Stewart, *host of Comedy Central's satirical* The Daily Show, *to Tucker Carlson and Paul Begala, hosts of CNN's* Crossfire

“I've never seen a man in my life I wanted to marry. And I'm going to be blunt and plain: if one ever looks at me like that, I'm going to kill him and tell God he died.”

Jimmy Swaggart, *televangelist, discussing gay marriage on his TV show. He later apologized, saying the remarks were made in jest*

“They're like the Taliban. They're the vegetarian Taliban.”

Veronica Atkins, *widow of high-protein-diet doctor Robert Atkins, after a pro-vegetarian physicians' group obtained her late husband's medical records and released them to the press*

“If I can sell tickets to my movies like *Red Sonja* or *Last Action Hero,* you know I can sell just about anything.”

Arnold Schwarzenegger, *Governor of California, promising to lure more jobs to the state*

MATT SAYLES—AP/WIDE WORLD

“The NEA is a terrorist organization.”

Rod Paige, *Education Secretary, to Governors at a private White House meeting; he later apologized for the “poor choice of words”*

“You've got to stop beating up your women because you can't find a job because you didn't want to get an education and now you're [earning] minimum wage.”

Bill Cosby, *comic, speaking of black men, at the Rainbow/PUSH Coalition's annual conference*

“It's acceptable practice to socialize with Executive Branch officials when there are not personal claims against them. That's all I'm going to say for now. Quack, quack.”

Antonin Scalia, *Supreme Court Justice, responding to a question about a duck-hunting outing he took with Vice President Dick Cheney, a potential litigant in a future Supreme Court case*

“I don't think you give timelines to dictators.”

George W. Bush, *on dealing with the illicit nuclear-weapons programs in Iran and North Korea*

PRODUCT PLACEMENTS

HEINZ
57
HEINZ
TOMATO KETCHUP

“Heinz ketchup is America's favorite ketchup and is enjoyed by Republicans, Democrats and independents alike.”

Debora Foster, *V.P. of communications for Heinz, after a Republican politician suggested that using Heinz ketchup indicated support for John Kerry, whose wife is heir to part of the Heinz fortune*

“The bagels, just the bagels alone. You go to Toronto, they're mushy.”

Mel Brooks, *director, on why he decided to shoot his new film of* The Producers *in Brooklyn, N.Y., instead of Canada*

“This race is hotter than a Times Square Rolex.”

Dan Rather, *CBS anchor, on election night*

FAME, THOU GLITTERING BAUBLE

RICK MACKLER—GLOBE PHOTOS

“Fame is addictive. Money is addictive. Attention is addictive. But golf is second to none.”

Marc Anthony, *singer who recently wed Jennifer Lopez, on his purchase of a $22,000 set of Honma irons from Japan*

“That's cool … but I don't know who Cary Grant is.”

Frankie Muniz, *18, TV actor, after being told that a critic had described him as “the Cary Grant of child stars”*

“All of the women on *The Apprentice* flirted with me—consciously or unconsciously. That's to be expected.”

Donald Trump, *on one benefit of his TV show,* The Apprentice

“Rude, vile pigs! Do you know what that means? Rude, vile pigs! That's what all of you are!”

Elton John, *rock star, upon being greeted by pushy photographers and TV crews when he arrived in Taipei. He later posed for the cover of* ENTERTAINMENT WEEKLY *under the quote “I'm Not Cranky!”*

“People think they can all be pop stars, high-court judges, brilliant TV personalities or infinitely more competent heads of state without ever putting in the necessary work or having natural ability.”

Prince Charles, *describing an employee who charged the royal household with sex discrimination and unfair dismissal*

“I do want my life back to normal, because it's hard. It's so hard. But at the same time I'm like, Wow, I get to go to New York. I get to go to Hollywood. I get to hang out with people like Britney and Leonardo.”

Jessica Lynch, *former POW, on her life a year after her rescue*

LOUIS LANZANO—AP/WIDE WORLD

“The guy wants me to stand in line with everybody else. I'm not everybody else.”

Courtney Love, *rock star, during a court appearance in which she was forced to wait in line before she could plead guilty to disorderly conduct for hitting a fan with a microphone stand*

SECOND WIND

Weathering early exit polls that showed him losing, George W. Bush takes Florida, Ohio—and the election. How the Bush team orchestrated its nail-biting victory over Senator John Kerry and the Democrats to win four more years in office

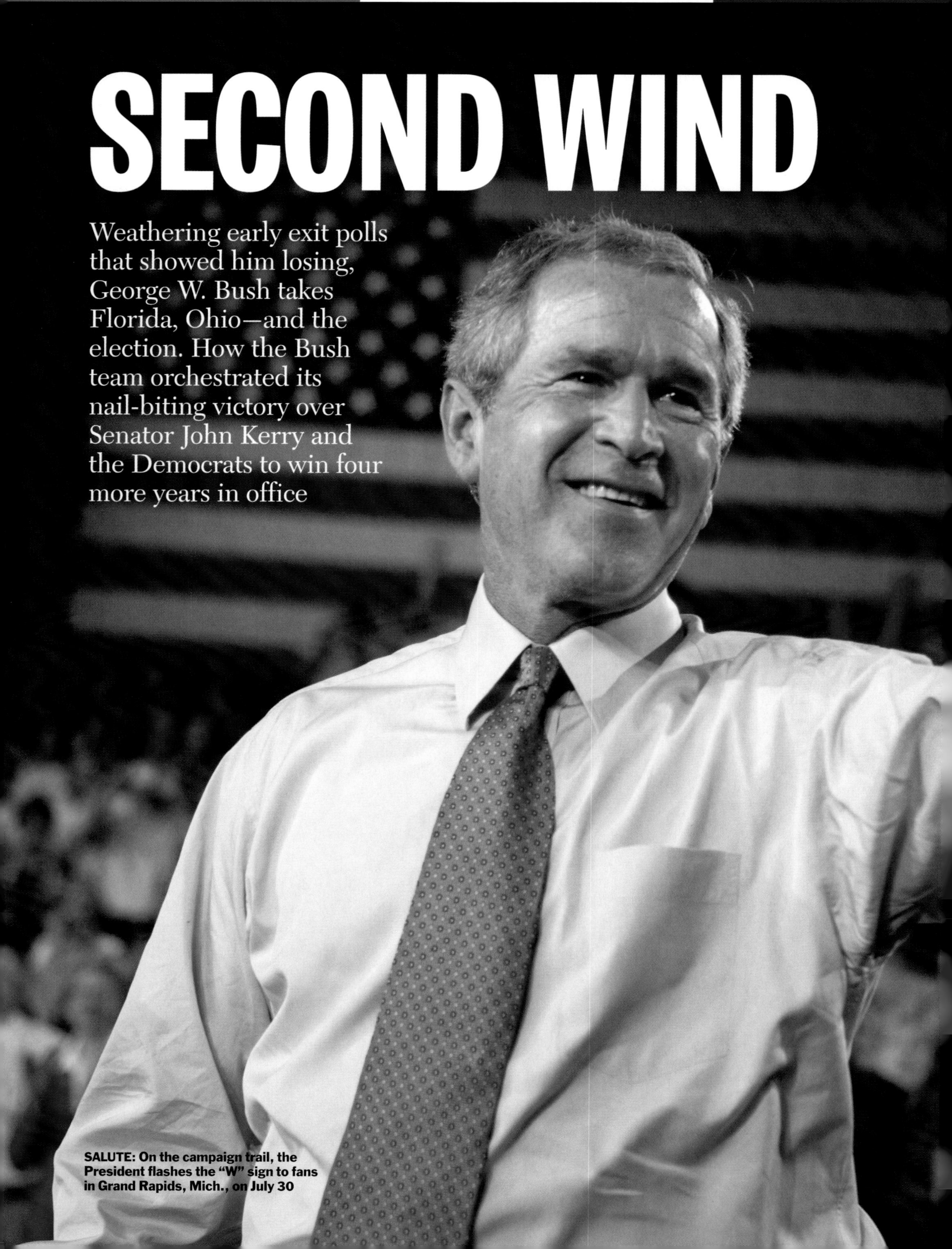

SALUTE: On the campaign trail, the President flashes the "W" sign to fans in Grand Rapids, Mich., on July 30

BROOKS KRAFT—CORBIS

AFTER MIDNIGHT OF ELECTION DAY, IN THE PREdawn hours of Nov. 3, 2004, the ghosts died in George W. Bush's White House. There was the ghost of his 2000 campaign, which Bush lost among voters but won in the court. There was the ghost of his father's last campaign, when even winning a war was not enough to earn a second term. And then there was the ghost of Election Day afternoon, when the entire Bush campaign team was haunted by the possibility that they had got it all wrong, as the first exit polls came in and nothing, but nothing, was going their way.

When it was finally over, the President who had become a radical champion of democracy's power to change the world became the living symbol of how it works. He made his decisions and moved on; the voters made theirs, in an extraordinary turnout that reflected a divisive, passionate campaign. About 120 million voted, 15 million more than in 2000, with Bush beating Massachusetts Senator John Kerry 51% to 48.5%. Bush became the first President since 1988 to win a majority of the popular vote; he gained seats in both houses of Congress; and for good measure, he knocked off not just the Democratic nominee but the party's Senate leader, South Dakota's Tom Daschle, as well.

The love-hate presidency of George W. Bush was neither an accident of ideology nor a product of these times. Asked as he left the Crawford, Texas, polling station on Tuesday, Nov. 2, about the polarized feelings he inspires in voters, Bush replied, "I take that as a compliment. It means I'm willing to take a stand." He saw his task as leading and never looking back, and only early the next morning did he learn whether enough people had decided to fall into line behind him to allow him to carry on. In a triumphant speech at the Ronald Reagan Building in D.C. that afternoon, Bush declared victory, saying, "America has spoken, and I am humbled by the trust and the confidence of my fellow citizens."

Moments earlier, John Kerry had stood before his supporters at Boston's Faneuil Hall, where his campaign began. To stamp out any delusions, he was very clear about the finality of his decision. "We cannot win this election," he said. Then, his voice breaking, he reminded his supporters that after an election, "we all wake up as Americans" and called for the healing to commence.

Kerry—the kid who was born serious, who was greeted on campus with kazoos buzzing *Hail to the Chief,* who was tagged on national TV at age 27 as a future President, who marinated in the Senate among 99 other aspiring Presidents for 19 years before launching a bid for the White House that in November 2003 saw him barely twitching at about 10% in the polls—had shown exactly the kind of toughness his opponents claimed he lacked. He emerged from a pack of 10 contenders to snag his party's nomination, beating labor's choice, Representative Dick Gephardt; Bill Clinton's choice, former General Wesley Clark; the antiwar voters' choice, Vermont Governor Howard Dean; and the

Kerry Edwards
C-SPAN
FOX NEWS
NBC
CNN
Kerry Edwards

UNITED: Kerry and Edwards brought Democrats to their feet at the conclusion of their the convention in Boston in July

moderates' choice, Senator John Edwards, who became his running mate. Kerry presided over a unified national convention, draping it in memories of his medal-winning service in Vietnam. He plainly beat the incumbent President in the first of three televised debates and easily held his own in the other two. He mortgaged his house, recast his team, renovated virtually every position he had ever taken and shook the grave dust off his suit several times before arriving at history's door. And then it closed in his face on a day when for a moment it had seemed to blow wide open.

ULTIMATELY, AN ELECTION THAT WAS SUPPOSED TO be about all the ways we are divided at least brought us together at 193,000 polling places in democracy's messy leap of faith. Turnout was huge even in states where the result was ensured. Follow-up polls suggested that the single issue that mattered most was not the Iraq war or terrorism, not the economy, but the questions of values that simmered beneath the headlines throughout the campaign—the seismic ongoing battles over abortion, gay rights and popular

A STRONGER AMER
Kerry Edwards

CALLIE SHELL—AURORA

culture that have torn America asunder in recent years.

Yet if the outcome still showed a public divided, it produced a government somewhat less so. Thanks to their sweeping victories, the Republicans ensured that the very real challenges facing Bush in a second term—from Iraq as it heads toward elections, to entitlements as they drift toward insolvency, to Supreme Court appointments and the social issues that most deeply divide the public—would be addressed by a party with a rare monopoly of power in all three branches of government and a mandate, however slim, that did not exist four years ago. The great mystery ahead: With re-election no longer the organizing principle of George Bush's presidency, what will guide his next four years, when the only judge left is history?

FOR A PRESIDENT WHO LOVES THE GAME AND KNEW this was his last campaign, Bush sounded like a man at peace at its end. "This election is in the hands of the people," he said after he voted, "and I feel very comfortable with that." On Election Day, he was host of a gin-rummy tournament on Air Force One as he headed from Crawford back to the White House to wait out the results. It was on the plane that strategist Karl Rove started calling around to get the results of early exit polls. But the line kept breaking down. The only information that came through as the plane descended was a BlackBerry message from an aide that simply read, "Not good." Not long afterward, Rove got a more detailed picture and told the President the bad news: Kerry was leading everywhere. Bush was philosophical. "Well, it is what it is," he told adviser Karen Hughes.

On the ground in Arlington, Va., that afternoon, chief strategist Matthew Dowd was walking around Bush campaign headquarters looking like a "scientist whose formulas were all wrong," said a top Bush staff member. Dowd had designed the strategy for targeting voters, and the exit polls were undermining his every theory. It would take him six long hours to crack the code. When the actual vote counts started coming in at 8 p.m., Dowd noticed that in South Carolina, Virginia and Florida the numbers were what the Republicans expected them to be; the President was outperforming the exit polls. "We've got to go talk to the press. The exit polls are wrong," Dowd said.

"WE'VE GOT TO GO TALK TO THE PRESS," SAID THE PRESIDENT'S CHIEF STRATEGIST, MATTHEW DOWD. "THE EXIT POLLS ARE WRONG."

The emotional route of Kerry's day passed Bush's somewhere near halfway, traveling from wild hope to stunned despair. After one last dawn campaign visit, a triple-witching photo op on the Iowa-Wisconsin-Minnesota border, Kerry flew back to Boston for his ritual Election Day lunch at the Union Oyster House. Superstitious, he wore his lucky Red Sox cap, carried an Ohio buckeye in one pocket and a clover in the other and refused to let his speechwriters work on election-night speeches of any flavor. But he wasn't relying entirely on voodoo. He spent the afternoon doing 38 satellite interviews over four hours in key markets.

A few hours later, as the polls closed and the results began to roll in, Bush waited them out with his parents, fam-

BUSH
CHENEY '04
CHENEY
'04
MARTINEZ
NGRESS
Kerry
Edwards
JOHN KE
BUS
CHEN
ww.George
ERIC GAY—AP/WIDE WORLD

DIVIDED WE STAND: Bush and Kerry supporters clash outside a polling place in Houston, where former President George H.W. Bush and wife Barbara cast early ballots on Oct. 18

ily and friends in the White House residence. Once it was clear that the early rumors of a Kerry sweep were all wrong, the networks were playing it very safe about calling states. In the old family dining room of the residence, Rove set up his computers. Bush called him regularly to ask about what was happening in certain precincts and districts. The candidates split two of the three swing states that both parties had predicted would dictate the outcome: Bush took Florida; Kerry took Pennsylvania.

Finally, after midnight, the President was on the phone with his communications director, Dan Bartlett, discussing Ohio. For weeks, both campaigns had suspected it could all come down to this key swing state, which no Republican has ever lost and still won the White House. Bartlett explained why the networks would be reluctant to call the race. Bush then said, "Well, they just called it," although only NBC and Fox had. The room erupted into cheers. Bartlett held out the phone so Bush could hear. "Congratulations, Mr. President," Bartlett said, "You won the presidency." But it would be nearly 15 more hours before the President could come out and say so himself.

Bush was ahead in Ohio by 130,000 votes. But about the same number of provisional ballots—given to voters whose eligibility had been challenged—remained unopened. In elections gone by, that gap would still have been enough to put the state in Bush's column, but most networks exercised uncharacteristic caution in making the call.

As the night wore on, Bush officials spoke informally to the Kerry camp, urging Kerry to concede. Kerry advisers replied that their candidate would come to his own conclusion in good time. Shortly after dawn, Kerry advisers gathered one last time to go over the Ohio math. By 9:30, their conclusion was clear: Kerry simply did not have the numbers. Campaign manager Mary Beth Cahill called Kerry at his town house. Within 10 minutes, he had called

RICK WILKING—AP/WIDE WORLD

FACE-OFF: V.P. candidates Dick Cheney and John Edwards debate on Oct. 5; neither of the two men appeared to play a major role in voters' decisions

her back to say he agreed. At 11 a.m., Kerry called Bush to concede. He congratulated the President and urged him to unify the country. Bush called Kerry "an admirable and worthy opponent."

WHAT FINALLY SWAYED THOSE NEAR MYTHICAL voters who managed to make it until Tuesday without making up their minds? The weight that voters attached to values suggests that Rove's single-minded attention to the goal of turning out 4 million more Evangelical voters than in 2000 may have paid off. And historians will have an easy time arguing that the race was always Bush's to lose; he scarcely ever ran behind, from Labor Day on. A country will seldom discharge a Commander in Chief during wartime, particularly one who had sustained a higher level of approval for longer than any modern U.S. President. He was running against a New England Senator so stiff that he creaked. And no non-Southern Democrat had won in 44 years.

So consider the obstacles Bush overcame and the rules that were broken by his victory. Since the country previously met at the polls, voters have encountered a record deficit, job losses, airport shoe searches, rising bankruptcies and bruising battles over stem-cell research and the definition of marriage. On the eve of Election Day, fully 55% of voters said the country was moving in the wrong direction. Only 49% approved of the job the President was doing, and anything below 50% is supposed to be fatal to an incumbent. A war that Bush promised would cost no more than $50 billion a year had been running at nearly three times that. He was attacked by well-organized and well-funded detractors who described him as a liar, a fraud, a drug abuser, a warmonger, an incurious zealot, an agent of the Saudis, a puppet of his goblin Vice President. And he faced an opponent with a long record of public service, a shiny record from a war Bush had avoided and a Democratic base united in the purpose of bringing this presidency it so despised to an end.

BUSH SAYS THE WAR ON TERRORISM IS NOT A CLASH OF CIVILIZATIONS, BUT HIS CAMPAIGN WAS, BY DESIGN

Bush says the war on terrorism is not a clash of civilizations, but this campaign was, by his careful design. He never really pretended to have much to say to Democrats beyond I will keep you safe. He relied largely instead on inspiring those who agreed with him already, who don't want to see gay couples kissing on the evening news, think stem-cell research has been oversold and believe abortion on demand is a sin. Even Republicans who disagreed with

Steve Gardner
Foregunner, PCF - 44
John Kerry's Boat
www.swiftvets.com

SWIFT BOAT VETERANS FOR TRUTH

SURPRISE ATTACK

Candidate John Kerry thought his status as a decorated veteran of the Vietnam War would powerfully appeal to voters. But shortly after the Democratic Convention ended, Kerry's war record came under enemy fire: in two TV ads and a best-selling book, a Texas-based group calling itself Swift Boat Veterans for Truth charged Kerry with lying and cowardice during his service in Vietnam. The Kerry campaign was slow to respond to the ads, believing they were patently false and would do little damage. Wrong: the attacks seriously undermined Kerry's image. Navy records and eyewitnesses contradicted nearly all the Swift Boat group's claims, yet after the ads had run for several weeks, a TIME survey found that 77% of registered voters had seen them or heard about them, and 35% of voters surveyed in August said they suspected there was some truth to the charges they raised.

Investigating the claims made in the ads, TIME found the charges to be largely without merit—not a surprising result, given that, of SBVT's 254 original members, only one had served on a boat Kerry commanded, and the other 10 men who had served on that boat supported Kerry's account of the events that won his medals.

As one of the so-called 527s—soft-money political groups—SBVT ran the ads without the imprimatur of the Bush campaign. Yet the biggest donor to SBVT was Houston developer Bob Perry, a major contributor to Republican causes, including President Bush's campaign, and a close friend of Bush adviser Karl Rove's.

A few weeks after the ads began running, Bush campaign counsel Benjamin Ginsberg resigned his post, acknowledging he had advised the SBVT group, although he insisted he had done nothing illegal. The founder of SBVT, retired Rear Admiral Roy Hoffmann, was John Kerry's former commander. He has been a foe of the Massachusetts Senator for decades, since Kerry first returned from Vietnam and denounced the war.

SURVEYS CONSISTENTLY FOUND THAT A MAJORITY OF VOTERS WERE READY TO FIRE BUSH

him on one or more issues—the fiscal conservatives who prefer less extravagant government spending, the civil libertarians who would like a less intrusive Patriot Act—were still prepared to side with him. Bush plainly understood that his best weapon against Kerry was less what Bush did than who he was. You may disagree with me, he said at every stop, but you know where I stand. Critics called his faith in contagious democracy naive, but the American people have always been attracted to the idea. At the very least, voters may not punish a President for placing such hope in the principles they value most.

Having said that, surveys had consistently found that a majority of voters were ready to fire Bush—provided they had an acceptable alternative. That suggests how much Bush's success owes to Kerry's failure. The Senator never needed to be as likable as Bush to win; he just needed to be plausible. His supporters saw his serial explanations of his Iraq-war position as a mark of thoroughness and subtlety; opponents were alarmed by a sense that he was guided by no core beliefs but was only searching for a politically safe place to land. Bush never missed a chance to portray Kerry as the hollow man, ever expedient, always cautious, incapable of taking a stand and sticking to it.

Bush needed to demonize Kerry to make him an unacceptable alternative. The strategy carried some risk: negative ads over the summer portrayed Kerry as such a ridiculous, windsurfing, flip-flopping fop that when the nutty cartoon version of Kerry didn't show up for the debates, Bush suffered in contrast. It was a rare miscalculation by a politician who understands well the value of low expectations. But overall, Bush succeeded in making Kerry appear an élitist emphatically defending moderation at a time when nothing less than passion would do.

The past four years have rewired our politics in ways that guaranteed this election would be a historic one, whatever the outcome. For Kerry's supporters, there is some consolation that Bush will have to take responsibility for finishing what he started in Iraq. For Bush's supporters, there is an obligation to recognize that the intense effort of the other side was as much an expression of love of country as any pledge, hymn or flag. For people on both sides, there is relief that the day affirmed the sustaining virtue of American democracy. However fierce the battle and however high the stakes, on Election Day citizens go to the polls, close a curtain and cast their vote—and then go home to honor the outcome because we have only one President at a time. ■

2004: A DIGITAL DECISION

The Internet proved its political power in the late 1990s, when the Drudge Report website played a pivotal role in the Bill Clinton–Monica Lewinsky sex scandal. But in 2004 the World Wide Web reached full political maturity, operating in multiple roles: as a fund-raising machine, as a media watchdog, as a clearinghouse for humor and satire and as a forum for voices across a wide spectrum of political opinion.

It was Governor Howard Dean of Vermont, the antiwar Democratic candidate, who first proved that he could mobilize widely scattered believers via the Internet and raise sufficient funds through their small contributions to mount a national campaign. Dean shocked veteran political operatives by raising $41 million, mainly through the Internet, by January.

Yet the Internet's most powerful effect on the campaign may have come in the form of blogs (the term, short for weblogs, refers to one-person websites that offer frequently updated commentaries on specific topics, anything from politics to sports to fashion). Bloggers positioned themselves as alternatives to the broadcast media in 2004, and several blogs had a significant impact on the election. In September, when CBS News anchor Dan Rather committed a major journalistic sin—airing charges that George W. Bush had not fulfilled his duties in the National Guard during the Vietnam War whose sources were dubious—it was bloggers who first drew attention to the clues that showed them to be suspicious. After defending the report for a week, CBS admitted the errors ; Rather later said he would step down from his anchor position in 2005—a clear victory for newfangled, one-man blogs over the massive machinery of venerable broadcast networks.

Throughout the campaign, Americans turned to satirical websites like *The Onion* for relief from the pieties of the campaign trail: one site, *jibjab.com,* produced a silly animated parody of candidates Bush and Kerry singing *This Land Is Your Land* that was widely distributed across the Web. After 2004, politics and the Internet are now partners, for better and for worse.

AMERICA 2004
BLOGGER SEA
BLOG ON: Weblog creators had reserved seats at the Democrats' convention in Boston

MARIO TAMA—GETTY IMAGES

NEW FACES IN THE U.S. SENATE

RON EDMONDS—AP/WIDE WORLD

★ BARACK OBAMA • DEMOCRAT • ILLINOIS
Obama, 43, electrified the Democratic Convention with his keynote address, then cruised to victory over last-minute G.O.P. candidate Alan Keyes in the November election, becoming only the third African American in the Senate in 100 years. The son of a Kenyan immigrant, Obama attended Columbia University and Harvard Law School, then became an Illinois state senator. "In no other country on earth is my story even possible," he said.

ERIC LANDWEHR—AP/WIDE WORLD

★ JOHN THUNE • REPUBLICAN • SOUTH DAKOTA
For three terms Tom Daschle pulled off the balancing act of being a high-profile, left-leaning Senator in right-leaning South Dakota. The majority leader was finally toppled in 2004, thanks to a big assist from the Bush White House. Giant killer Thune, 43, is a clean-living former Congressman who kept reminding voters that Daschle's positions on gay marriage, gun control and abortion were at odds with theirs.

JACK DEMPSEY—AP/WIDE WORLD

★ KEN SALAZAR • DEMOCRAT • COLORADO
Salazar, 49, appealed to Colorado farmers and ranchers, because he's one of them. His Republican rival, Peter Coors, went to Phillips Exeter Academy and Cornell University; Salazar grew up on a ranch. He favors protecting the outdoors, but unlike hard-line environmentalists, he is a staunch friend of agriculture. Ethnicity also helped; Colorado's huge and growing Hispanic population saw themselves in Salazar.

JOE RAEDLE—GETTY IMAGES

★ MEL MARTINEZ • REPUBLICAN • FLORIDA
A lawyer and longtime G.O.P. operative, Martinez, 58, became the first Cuban American elected to the U.S. Senate, winning the seat of retiring Democrat Bob Graham. The former Secretary of Housing and Urban Development ran a tough campaign, labeling his primary opponent a tool of the "radical homosexual lobby" and calling the federal agents who seized Cuban refugee Elian González in 2000 "armed thugs."

How Bush Pulled It Off

Armed with critical victories in Ohio and Florida, the President got more votes than he did in 2000, with moral values trumping the economy as a prime issue

WISCONSIN

Kerry squeezed out a narrow victory with support from **young** and **first-time voters.** A majority felt the country is safer from terrorism and approved of the war in Iraq, but also said the war is going badly

First-time voters:
Kerry 58% | Bush 41%

OHIO

Even though 55% of Ohio voters said the **job situation** is worse today than four years ago, more felt Bush could better handle the economy. Kerry made it a close race by doing well in Cleveland

Trust to handle the economy:
Kerry 38% | Bush 43%

PENNSYLVANIA

A strong turnout in Philadelphia gave Kerry enough of a boost to overcome Bush's 2-to-1 lead in **rural areas.** Kerry gained wide support from **young voters** but split the over-65 vote with Bush

Voters under 30:
Kerry 61% | Bush 39%

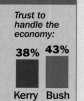

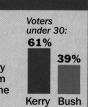

Wash. 11
Mont. 3
N.D. 3
Minn. 10
Ore. 7
Idaho 4
S.D. 3
Wis. 10
Wyo. 3
Mich. 17
Iowa 7
Neb. 5
Ill. 21
Ind. 11
Ohio 20
Nev. 5
Utah 5
Colo. 9
Kans. 6
Mo. 11
W.V
Ky. 8
Calif. 55
Okla. 7
Tenn. 11
Ariz. 10
N.M. 5
Ark. 6
S.C
Miss. 6
Ala. 9
Ga. 15
Texas 34
La. 9
Alaska 3
Fla. 27
Hawaii 4

Election results are as of 1 p.m. Nov. 3. Source: AP

Voter demographics are from the National Election Pool exit poll conducted by Edison/Mitofsky. Margin of error is ±3 percentage points for national data and ±4 percentage points for state data

TIME Graphic by Jackson Dykman and Joe Lertola

IOWA

With a lead of about 15,000 votes, Bush was on the verge of becoming the first Republican to carry Iowa since Ronald Reagan in 1984, but **broken voting machines** in two counties and uncounted provisional and absentee ballots delayed the official results

Voters who see economy as good:
Kerry 30% | Bush 69%

Small-city and rural voters:
Kerry 46% | Bush 53%

FLORIDA

The scene of the election nightmare four years ago was relatively quiet this time, with President Bush scoring a solid 5-point win. Bush increased his showing among **Hispanics, blacks and voters younger than 65.** Turnout increased by 1.4 million over 2000

Hispanics:
Kerry 44% | Bush 56%

Catholics:
Kerry 42% | Bush 57%

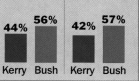

D.C

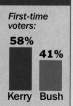

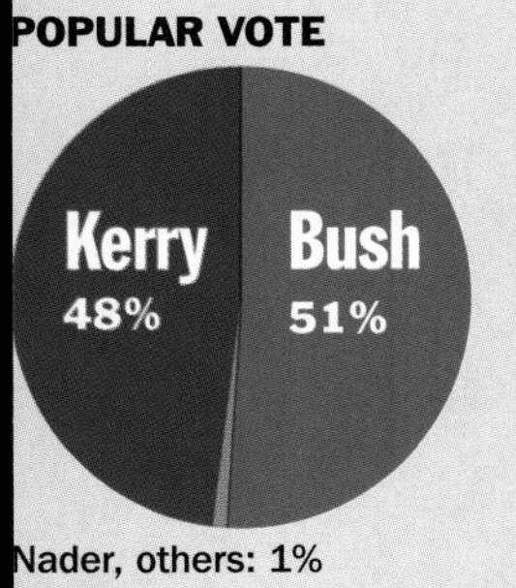
POPULAR VOTE
Kerry
48%
Bush
51%
Nader, others: 1%

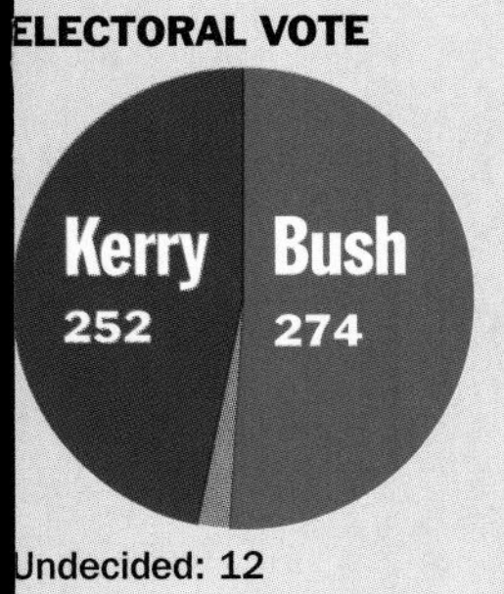
ELECTORAL VOTE
Kerry
252
Bush
274
Undecided: 12

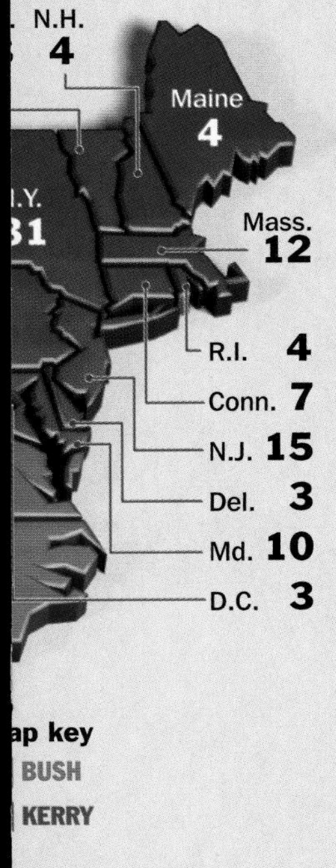
N.H.
4
Maine
4
Mass.
12
R.I. 4
Conn. 7
N.J. 15
Del. 3
Md. 10
D.C. 3
ap key
BUSH
KERRY

HOW CLOSE WAS IT?

The red states remain rock solid for Bush, giving the President an average victory margin of almost 20 points. Kerry's wins tend to be closer

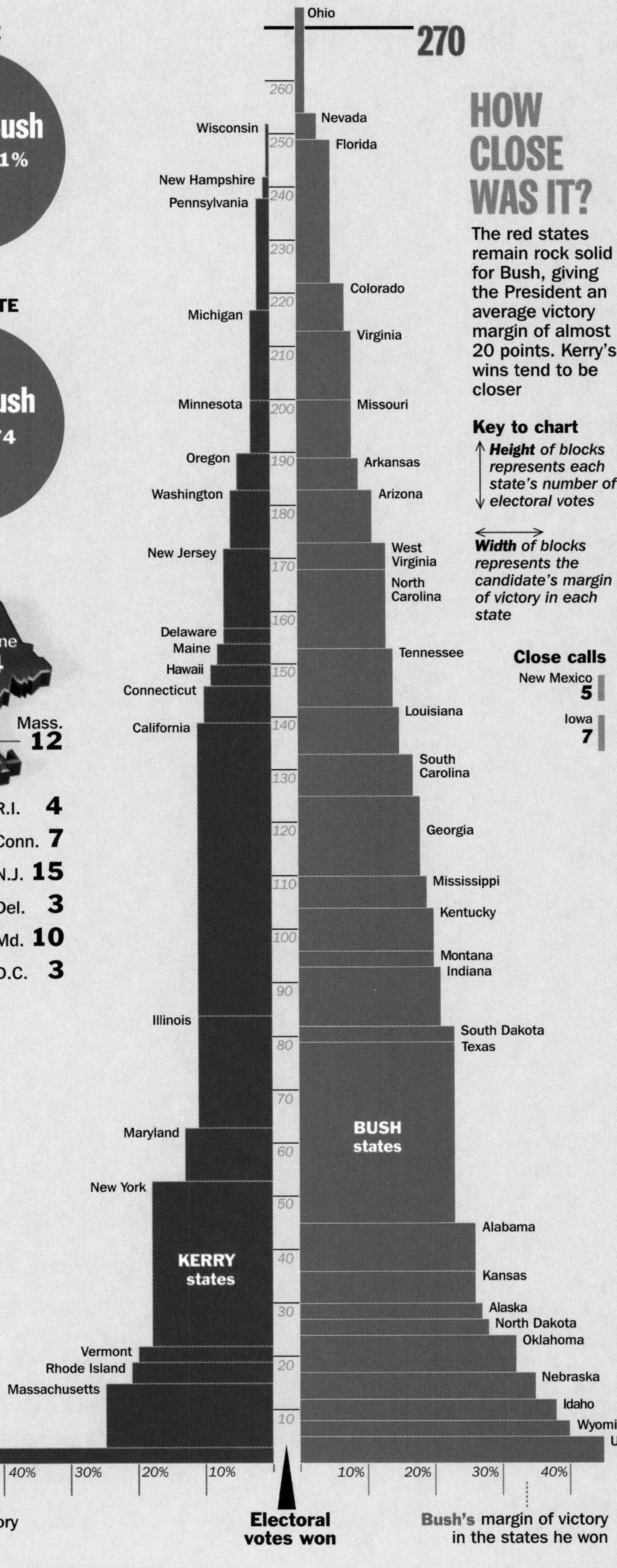
Key to chart
Height of blocks represents each state's number of electoral votes
Width of blocks represents the candidate's margin of victory in each state
Close calls
New Mexico
5
Iowa
7
Ohio
270
Nevada
Florida
Colorado
Virginia
Missouri
Arkansas
Arizona
West Virginia
North Carolina
Tennessee
Louisiana
South Carolina
Georgia
Mississippi
Kentucky
Montana
Indiana
South Dakota
Texas
BUSH states
Alabama
Kansas
Alaska
North Dakota
Oklahoma
Nebraska
Idaho
Wyoming
Utah
Wisconsin
New Hampshire
Pennsylvania
Michigan
Minnesota
Oregon
Washington
New Jersey
Delaware
Maine
Hawaii
Connecticut
California
Illinois
Maryland
New York
KERRY states
Vermont
Rhode Island
Massachusetts
260
250
240
230
220
210
200
190
180
170
160
150
140
130
120
110
100
90
80
70
60
50
40
30
20
10
60%
50%
40%
30%
20%
10%
10%
20%
30%
40%
Kerry's margin of victory in the states he won
Electoral votes won
Bush's margin of victory in the states he won

BREAKING DOWN THE NATIONAL VOTE

National exit polls found that the top issue for voters was not Iraq (15%) or the economy (20%) but moral values (22%)

WHERE BUSH HAD THE EDGE

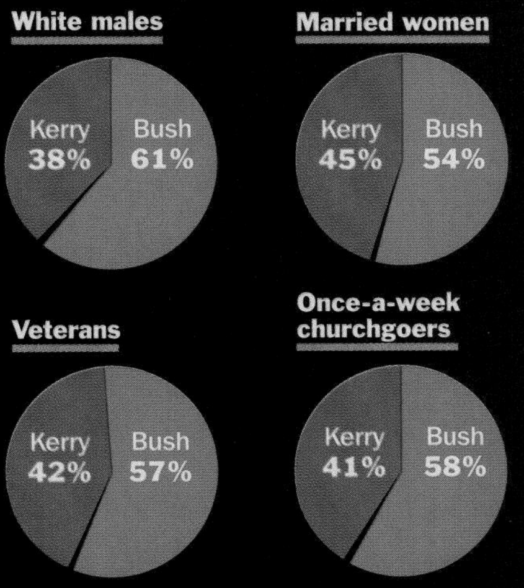
White males
Kerry
38%
Bush
61%
Married women
Kerry
45%
Bush
54%
Veterans
Kerry
42%
Bush
57%
Once-a-week churchgoers
Kerry
41%
Bush
58%

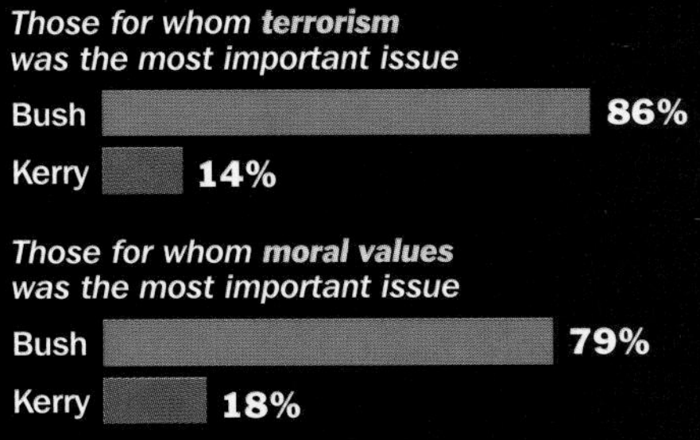
Those for whom terrorism was the most important issue
Bush 86%
Kerry 14%
Those for whom moral values was the most important issue
Bush 79%
Kerry 18%

WHERE KERRY HAD THE EDGE

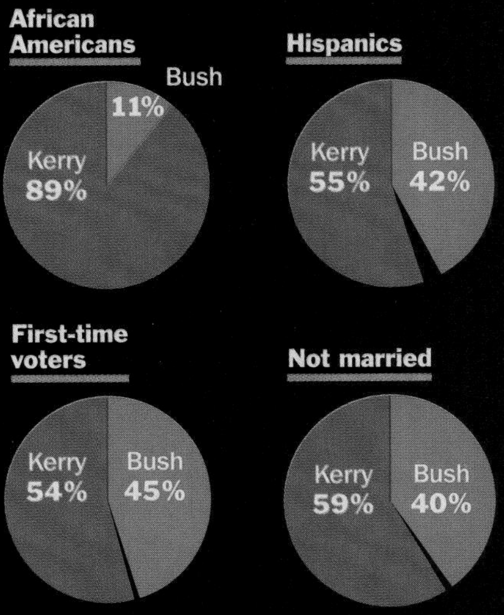
African Americans
Bush
11%
Kerry
89%
Hispanics
Kerry
55%
Bush
42%
First-time voters
Kerry
54%
Bush
45%
Not married
Kerry
59%
Bush
40%

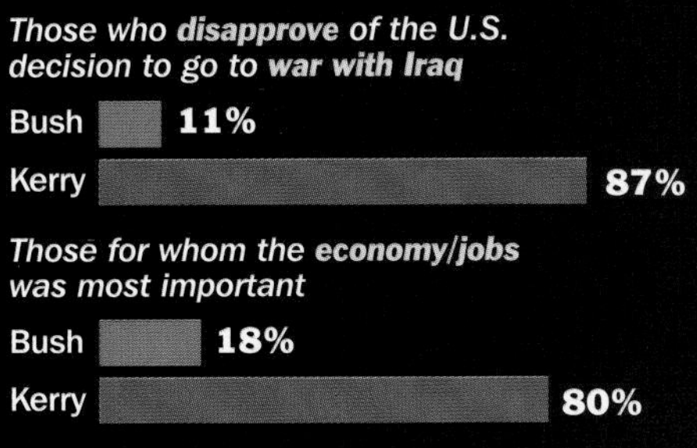
Those who disapprove of the U.S. decision to go to war with Iraq
Bush 11%
Kerry 87%
Those for whom the economy/jobs was most important
Bush 18%
Kerry 80%

Eagles rather than doves nestle in the Oval Office Christmas tree, pinecones the size of footballs are piled around the fireplace, and the President of the United States is pretty close to lounging in

Armchair One. He's wearing a blue pinstripe suit, and his shoes are shined bright enough to shave in. He is loose, lively, framing a point with his hands or extending his arm with his fingers up as though he's throwing a big idea gently across the room.

"I've had a lot going on, so I haven't been in a very reflective mood," says the man who has just replaced half his Cabinet, dispatched 12,000 more troops into battle, arm wrestled lawmakers over an intelligence bill, held his third economic summit and begun to lay the second-term paving stones on which he will walk off into history. Asked about his re-election, he replies, "I think over the Christmas holidays it'll all sink in."

As he says this, George W. Bush is about to set a political record. The first TIME poll since the election has his approval rating at 49%. Gallup has it at 53%, which doesn't sound

HIS DOMAIN

President Bush in the Oval Office in early December

Photographs for TIME by Christopher Morris—VII

bad unless you consider that it's the lowest December rating for a re-elected President in Gallup's history. That is not a great concern, however, since he has run his last race, and it is not a surprise to a President who tends to measure his progress by the enemies he makes. "Sometimes you're defined by your critics," he says. "My presidency is one that has drawn some fire, whether it be at home or around the world. Unfortunately, if you're doing big things, most of the time you're never going to be around to see them [to fruition], whether it be cultural change or spreading democracy in parts of the world where people just don't believe it can happen. I understand that. I don't expect many short-term historians to write nice things about me."

Yet even halfway through his presidency, Bush says, he already sees his historic gamble paying off. He watched in satisfaction the inauguration of Afghan President Hamid Karzai. "I'm not suggesting you're looking at the final chapter in Afghanistan, but the elections were amazing. And if you go back and look at the prognosis about Afghanistan—whether it be the decision [for the U.S. to invade] in the first place, the 'quagmire,' whether or not the people can even vote—it's a remarkable experience."

Bush views his decision to press for the transformation of Afghanistan and then Iraq—as opposed to "managing calm in the hopes that there won't be another September 11th, that the Salafist [radical Islamist] movement will somehow wither on the vine, that somehow these killers won't get a weapon of mass destruction"—as the heart of not just his foreign policy but his victory. "The election was about the use of American influence," he says. "I can remember people trying to shift the debate. I wanted the debate to be on a lot of issues, but I also wanted everybody to clearly understand exactly what my thinking was. The debates and all the noise and all the rhetoric were aimed at making very clear the stakes in this election when it comes to foreign policy."

In that respect and throughout the 2004 campaign, Bush was guided by his own definition of a winning formula. "People think during elections, 'What's in it for me?' " says communications director Dan Bartlett, and expanding democracy in Iraq, a place voters were watching smolder on the nightly news, was not high on their list. Yet "every time we'd have a speech and attempt to scale back the liberty section, he would get mad at us," Bartlett says. Sometimes the President would simply take his black Sharpie and write the word freedom between two paragraphs to prompt himself to go into his extended argument for America's efforts to plant the seeds of liberty in Iraq and the rest of the Middle East.

An ordinary politician tells swing voters what they want to hear; Bush invited them to vote for him because he refused to. Ordinary politicians need to be liked; Bush finds the hostility of his critics reassuring. Challengers run as outsiders, promising change; it's an extraordinary politician who tries this while holding the title Leader of the Free World. Ordinary Presidents have made mistakes and then sought to redeem themselves by admitting them; when Bush was told by some fellow Republicans that his fate depended on confessing his errors, he blew them off.

For candidates, getting elected is the test that counts. Ronald Reagan did it by keeping things vague: It's Morning in America. Bill Clinton did it by keeping things small, running in peaceful times on school uniforms and V chips. Bush ran big and bold and specific all at the same time, rivaling Reagan in breadth of vision and Clinton in tactical ingenuity. He surpassed both men in winning bigger majorities in Congress and the statehouses. And he did it all

TO WORK WE GO

Bush, with his beloved dog Barney, enters the Oval Office the back way

while conducting an increasingly unpopular war, with an economy on tiptoes and a public conflicted about many issues but most of all about him.

The argument over whether his skill won the race and fueled a realignment of American politics or whether he was the lucky winner of a coin-toss election will endure; the lessons Bush draws from his victory are the ones that matter most. The man who in 2000 promised to unite and not divide now sounds as though he is prepared to leave as his second-term legacy the Death of Compromise. "I've got the will of the people at my back," he said at the moment of victory. From here on out, bipartisanship means falling in line: "I'll reach out to everyone who shares our goals." Whatever spirit of cooperation that survives in his second term may have to be found among his opponents; he has made it clear he's not about to change his mind as he takes on Social Security and the tax code.

So unfolds the strange, surprising, high-stakes decade of the Bush presidency. For sharpening the debate until the choices bled, for reframing international reality to match his design, for gambling his fortunes—and ours—on his faith in the power of leadership, George W. Bush is TIME's 2004 Person of the Year.

Refuse to Sit Tight

THE LIVING ROOM OF BUSH'S RANCH IN CRAWFORD, TEXAS, is a place for thinking. There are big windows with long views, a wall of books and on one side a table that is usually freckled with jigsaw pieces. It was a few days after New Year's in 2003. The President had been out clearing cedar, and Laura Bush was lying on a sofa reading, or at least pretending to. That Christmas holiday was a deep breath between the 2002 midterm elections and the walk-up to the war in Iraq. Karl Rove, chief strategist for the Bush re-election campaign, arrived at the house with his faded blue canvas briefcase in hand. He had come to help put together a different kind of puzzle.

On his laptop was a PowerPoint pitch titled POTUS Presentation. It was no secret what the first piece of Bush's re-election strategy would be: to reach out to the base and make sure the Evangelicals, who Rove believed stayed home in 2000, came out this time. But appealing just to one part of one party would never produce 270 electoral votes, so Rove had prepared a series of slides, each with a great big goal in tall letters: BROADEN, PERSUADE, GROW. These were designed to show how Bush could assemble a winning majority by drawing in more typically Democratic voters, like Hispanics, Catholics and suburban moderates, among others.

But before Rove could begin his song and dance, Bush cut in. "You're not the only smart guy that's been thinking about it," he said. "So before we get going, let me tell you what I've been thinking about." Bush had learned something from the midterm elections, in which he had gambled his popularity by swooping into tight races. Although the President's party usually loses ground in midseason, with his help the Republicans had made historic gains. That fueled Bush's faith in what could happen when a President resists the temptation to sit tight and instead is willing to spend political capital. For the 2004 campaign, Bush told Rove, he wanted to spend again to further expand his party's majority in Congress. Bush intended to keep doing risky and not necessarily popular things; to lead a revolution, he would need more troops.

The Democrats are supposed to be the party with the deep grass roots and the ardent volunteers, but in 2000 Bush had managed to draft an army that saw itself as a band of outsiders storming the gates. "It gave people a lot of energy and enthusiasm," he said. "We can't lose that. I want to leave it so that some number of years from now, people look back and say, 'You know, I really wasn't involved much in politics until the Bush-Cheney '04 campaign asked me to get involved.' "

Keep to the Right

WHEN THE RACE BEGAN FOR REAL LAST spring, Bush had the support of 91% of Republicans and 17% of Democrats. This was the biggest gap in the history of the Gallup poll, and it led journalists to write about the Polarizing President and armchair strategists to remind the White House of the First Rule of Politics: once your base gets you nominated, you have to soften the edges and sweet-talk the center to get elected. Yet in his re-election year, far from becoming more accommodating, Bush seemed to do the reverse. In the summer of 2000 he delivered a bridge-building address to the N.A.A.C.P.; in the summer of 2004 he snubbed the organization. Two-thirds of Americans favored extension of the assault-weapons ban; in September he conspicuously let it die. He repeatedly offered swing voters expressly what they told pollsters they did not want: a multiyear commitment in Iraq, a constitutional amendment to ban gay marriage, private Social Security accounts, restricted federal funding of stem-cell research. The most he would do is hint that radioactive Attorney General John Ashcroft wouldn't make it to a second Bush presidency. But even at the height of the Abu Ghraib prison-abuse scandal, Bush would not consider calls to dump Defense Secretary Donald Rumsfeld.

Most voters said they were looking for a change in direction, but Bush was betting that what they wanted more was leadership. Through it all, the one category in which he never fell behind John Kerry in the polls was being a strong leader. In dangerous times, courage is a currency, so while Kerry ran on his combat record, Bush, who didn't have one, suggested that the courage that matters most in a politician is the political kind. "The role of the President is not to follow the path of the latest polls," he told voters. "Whether you agree with me or not, you know where I stand, what I believe and where I'm going to lead. You cannot say that about my opponent." By taking a hard line on divisive issues, he made character—not his record—the issue.

If you go hunting for Bush's margin of victory, you won't find it among Evangelicals, who voted in roughly the same proportion as in the past. You'll find it among groups that traditionally don't vote Republican. Bush improved his standing among blacks, Jews, Hispanics, women, city dwellers, Catholics, seniors and people who don't go to church. His biggest improvement came in the bluest of regions, the corridor from Maryland up through New Jersey and New York to Massachusetts. In Kerry's home state, Bush found close to 200,000 more voters than he did in 2000. He won a majority of the vote in a country that a majority of voters thought was heading in the wrong direction. Since, according to polls, more people consider themselves conservative than liberal, he didn't need to win over a majority of the voters in the middle. He just needed to convince enough to put him over the top.

Run as an Outsider

DURING THE 2000 CAMPAIGN, BUSH NEVER LEFT HOME without a podium. To support the promise to "restore honor and dignity to the White House" and combat the notion that he was a lightweight, his team wanted to make him look presidential whenever possible. But four years later,

TREK
98

SPEED RACER

At a Secret Service training facility, Bush bikes and listens to Van Morrison's *Brown Eyed Girl* on his iPod

MAKING FRIENDS

The President receives the new ambassador from Chad and his family

with the re-election campaign under way, his imagemakers had the opposite worry. There was too much pomp, too many suits. They needed to get him out from behind the lectern and let him be a regular guy. So Bush went from set speeches to town-hall meetings, from suits to shirtsleeves.

Of course, the audiences were carefully screened to admit only high-fiber Bush supporters. But the overall goal of running an outsider campaign came naturally. Bush has always been a punk at heart—the guy who in 1973 used to walk around Harvard during antiwar protests wearing cowboy boots and a bomber jacket, who was an outsider even in his own, high-achieving family. Forty-one newspapers that endorsed Bush back when he ran as a pragmatic reformer revoked their support this time around. But that just made it easier; he was running against the mainstream media, and his campaign was feeding the bloggers and surfing talk radio.

Expanding the party depended on reaching out to outsiders, the literal ones, pioneers of the new American frontiers that ring the old cities and suburbs—places like Colorado's Douglas County, Ohio's Delaware County and Farmwell Hunt in Ashburn, Va., which advertises itself as a place "where family values, engaged residents, nature, fun and safety come together to form a premier community." And then he went even further, to the rural communities that Presidents don't visit very much because of the potential inefficiencies of spending precious time on such sparsely populated locales. Bush put dozens of such communities on his itinerary, and he can still rattle off their names. In "Poplar Bluff, Missouri," he notes, "23,000 people showed up in a town of 16,000 people." He won 97 of the 100 fastest-growing counties in the country—generally by a wide margin.

Turn into the Wind

IF A CENTRAL DRAMA OF THE SLALOMING KERRY CAMPAIGN was his agreeing with the last person he spoke to, the drama of the Bush campaign was his refusing to. "If you know me, I guess that's called stubborn," the President says. A Bush adviser puts it more bluntly: "He likes being hated. It lets him know he's doing the right thing."

People close to Bush have their theories about this. Some think he likes the cries of outrage because they signal that he's making tough calls, which is how he views his job description. "Part of it could be his faith," says an adviser. "Being persecuted is not always a bad thing." Some of it may be learned. He has hated the political echo chamber ever since he watched insiders he viewed as self-preserving and backbiting carve up his father's Administration. When you're a lie-in-wait politician like Bush, who has gained so much from being underestimated, absorbing criticism toughens your skin and eases the wait for the coming reward. "There's no victory for Bush that is sweeter," says an aide, "than the one he was told he couldn't have."

Bush admits to savoring a good fight. He talks about how he relishes the moment when the political world is at his feet as he stands before Congress to deliver the State of the Union. "Sometimes I look through that teleprompter and see reactions," he recalls. "I'm not going to characterize what the reactions are, but nevertheless it causes me to want to lean a little more forward into the prompter, if you know what I mean. Maybe it's the mother in me." As he says that, he practically leans out of his chair, as though his antagonists were there in the room.

The piece of advice Bush ignored most diligently was the call for him to admit mistakes. It was not just the New York *Times* demanding that he apologize for alleging there was a link between Saddam Hussein and al-Qaeda, or Michael Moore saying he should apologize to dead soldiers' families for sending their kids into a war over oil. As Kerry became more aggressive in his criticism of Bush's Iraq policy, other Republicans said the President had to beat back the challenger's charge that Bush was out of touch. "We had to admit that we'd gotten some things wrong," said a senior Republican, "or we were beginning to look like we were living on another planet."

Bush thought people were expecting him to call the whole Iraq invasion a mistake, which he was not about to do. Privately, he did acknowledge there had been blunders, but that didn't mean it made sense to say so publicly. At the second presidential debate, a town-hall meeting of undecided voters, a woman called Linda Grabel asked Bush to name three mistakes he had made while in office. A part of Bush wanted to answer; his father had landed in trouble during a town-hall debate when he fumbled a young woman's question about how the national debt personally affected him. But when you are running a character campaign, Bush felt, you don't wring your hands. So he dodged the question, and Kerry walloped him for doing so.

Then a funny thing happened on the way to the motorcade. Once the cameras were off, Bush went into the audience and tracked Grabel down. "I appreciate your question," he told her, according to an aide. "And I hope you appreciate my answer, because with the political climate we live in, I know it was not your intent to play gotcha with the President of the United States. But this is where it ends up. Let me just assure you, I know that I haven't done everything right."

Keep Your Focus

ONCE RE-ELECTED, BUSH HAD NO TIME TO LOSE. THE TWO years he has before he's perceived as a lame duck will be the most powerful period of his presidency, given his enlarged majority in Congress and the absence of any election distractions. His domestic goals for the second term—from Social Security reform to tax restructuring to deficit reduction—mirror in ambition the foreign policy revolution of his first. In his second term, he will need to make peace with a Congress that sees the world differently from its end of Pennsylvania Avenue. Not just Democrats but fellow Republicans as well carry some bruises from the first term, during which they feel they were treated like junior partners in everything from the fight over tax cuts to the war on terrorism.

In his pursuit of a second term, Bush was just as radical as he was in his conduct of a pre-emptive war. As a politician, he showed the same discipline, secrecy and nerve he demonstrated in his conduct as President. So he emerges with his faith only deepened in the transformational power of clear leadership. Whether or not the election actually yielded a mandate for his policies, he is sure to claim one for his style, because he stuck to it against all odds, much advice and the lessons of history. And on that choice at least, the results are in. ■

HEADING OUT

In the elevator of their residence, the First Lady checks Bush's suit

THE INTERVIEW

"I've Got All the Power I Need"

On a sunny afternoon in Decmeber, President George W. Bush sat down in the Oval Office with White House correspondents Matthew Cooper and John Dickerson and editor at large Nancy Gibbs to talk about Iraq, his second term and how he views his place in history.

TIME: *What kind of turnout are you looking for in the Iraqi elections—50%, 70%?*
BUSH: I would hope as many people as possible.

TIME: *What does it feel like to have no more re-elections?*
BUSH: I've always felt politics would be just a chapter of my life, not my life. And so I don't have any remorse about saying, Oh, gosh, no more campaigns. I say that now. Maybe 10 years from now, when you find me somewhere, I'll be longing for a campaign. I doubt it.

TIME: *Sheriff Bush . . .*
BUSH: Yes, exactly. Some say I've already got it. *[Laughter.]*

TIME: *How was your re-election campaign different from those waged by Ronald Reagan and Bill Clinton?*
BUSH: Mine was different because the circumstances were different. I had to make it very clear that the foreign policy of this Administration would lead to peace. This was a tough four years for the American people. I know it has been. And I think it's very important for somebody running for office to say that, one, I will confront problems and not pass them on but also that by having confronted problems, that the next four years will be hopefully a more peaceful period of time for people.

TIME: *Another thing you did is that you told people what they might not want to hear: "You may not agree with me, but you know where I stand."*
BUSH: Well, I guess that's called stubborn. Wasn't that the word they used at some point in time, stubborn?

Look, I believe that if you believe something, you've got to stand your ground, particularly in the face of criticism. I think the American people are looking at somebody running for office and they want to know what they believe, why they believe it and do they really believe it. And it's particularly important in these kinds of unsettling times.

Take, for example, my wish for the Iraqi elections. I believe they ought to be on January the 30th, and I've said so, point-blank. Otherwise, if it were vague—"Well, we'll see what it looks like at the time"—you can bet people will find a reason not to do the hard work. I believe strongly when I say something, I generally believe it. Not generally believe it—I believe it. Scratch the *generally.*

President Bush speaks with Dickerson, left, Cooper and Gibbs in the Oval Office

CHRISTOPHER MORRIS—VII FOR TIME

TIME: *Another issue you have been out front on is steroids. You talked about it in the State of the Union last year. And, of course, it has become a big deal in the past few weeks.*
BUSH: First of all, baseball should be focused on solving the problem before a lot of fans begin to really fall away from the game. I love baseball, and I understand how important the history of baseball is from one generation to the next.

I was more worried about the example that major leaguers, adults, were setting for youngsters, who basically said, "Juice up, and you'll make more money." I believe adults have a responsibility to set good examples, particularly when you've got a spotlight on you. And baseball now must get its act cleaned up. And they've heard a warning signal from Senator John McCain that said, "Clean it up in a meaningful way, or we will." My hope is that they do. But I will sign legislation if McCain can get it to my desk.

TIME: *Knowing what you know now, do you think more highly or less highly of your predecessors?*
BUSH: Of my predecessors? Very interesting. More highly of them all.

TIME: *All of them?*
BUSH: Well, I would say all of them. I've got a much better appreciation of what they've been through, some more than others.

My appreciation for Lincoln has grown immeasurably. He is a President who was a visionary for the good of the country. I've got his painting right there. And he's there because he had this great vision about a United States of America in incredibly difficult times.

I have sat here and thought about what it would be like to be the President when brother was fighting brother and cousin killing cousin. And the deep anguish his writings reflected about seeing the country torn asunder. And yet he had a clarity of vision the whole time. He clearly saw what needed to happen about keeping this country united.

All the people who serve here serve in different circumstances, but they have the same basic requirement, and that is the capacity to make decisions and know where you want to lead.

TIME: *What about Bill Clinton?*
BUSH: This is a person who embraced the job and loved it. He took on issues; he took them on with enthusiasm and energy. He loved being the President. That's an admirable trait.

TIME: *Some people have said that in making your personnel changes for the second term, you're consolidating power.*
BUSH: I'm consolidating power? I've got all the power I need.

TIME: *Some say the people you trust are your closest friends, and they will give it to you with the bark off. But nobody in your Administration will talk about any instance in which you got it with the bark off. When have you, and have you listened to them?*
BUSH: I can't think of an incident right now, but it happens all the time. Part of my management style is to provoke thought and get people thinking, is to lay something out there. And they'll say, "That's not a good idea, Mr. President" or "You know, I can't believe you said that."

McCain is a guy who—we get along well, we agree a lot, and sometimes we don't agree. A lot of my friends are people that don't understand or agree with some of the decisions I've made and question why I made the decision I made. ■

Paying Homage

After his recent annual physical at the National Naval Medical Center in Bethesda, Maryland, President Bush took the opportunity to visit with injured troops

EN ROUTE

The President sits aboard Marine One before choppering back to the White House

Photographs for TIME by Christopher Morris—VII

"I have to look at people in their eye who have been wounded and say, 'I believe what you're doing is going to make the world a better place.' And if you're faking it, the people will read you like a book."

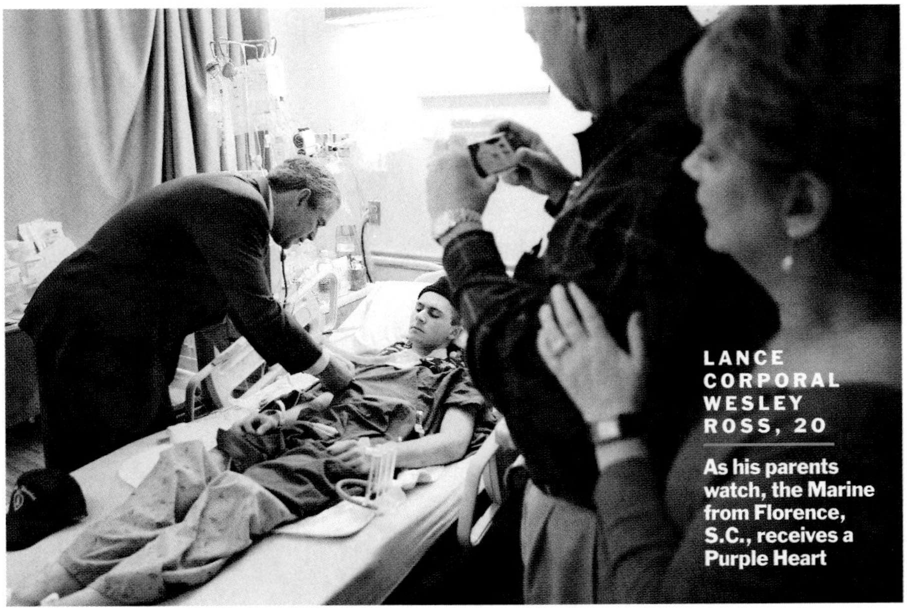

LANCE CORPORAL WESLEY ROSS, 20

As his parents watch, the Marine from Florence, S.C., receives a Purple Heart

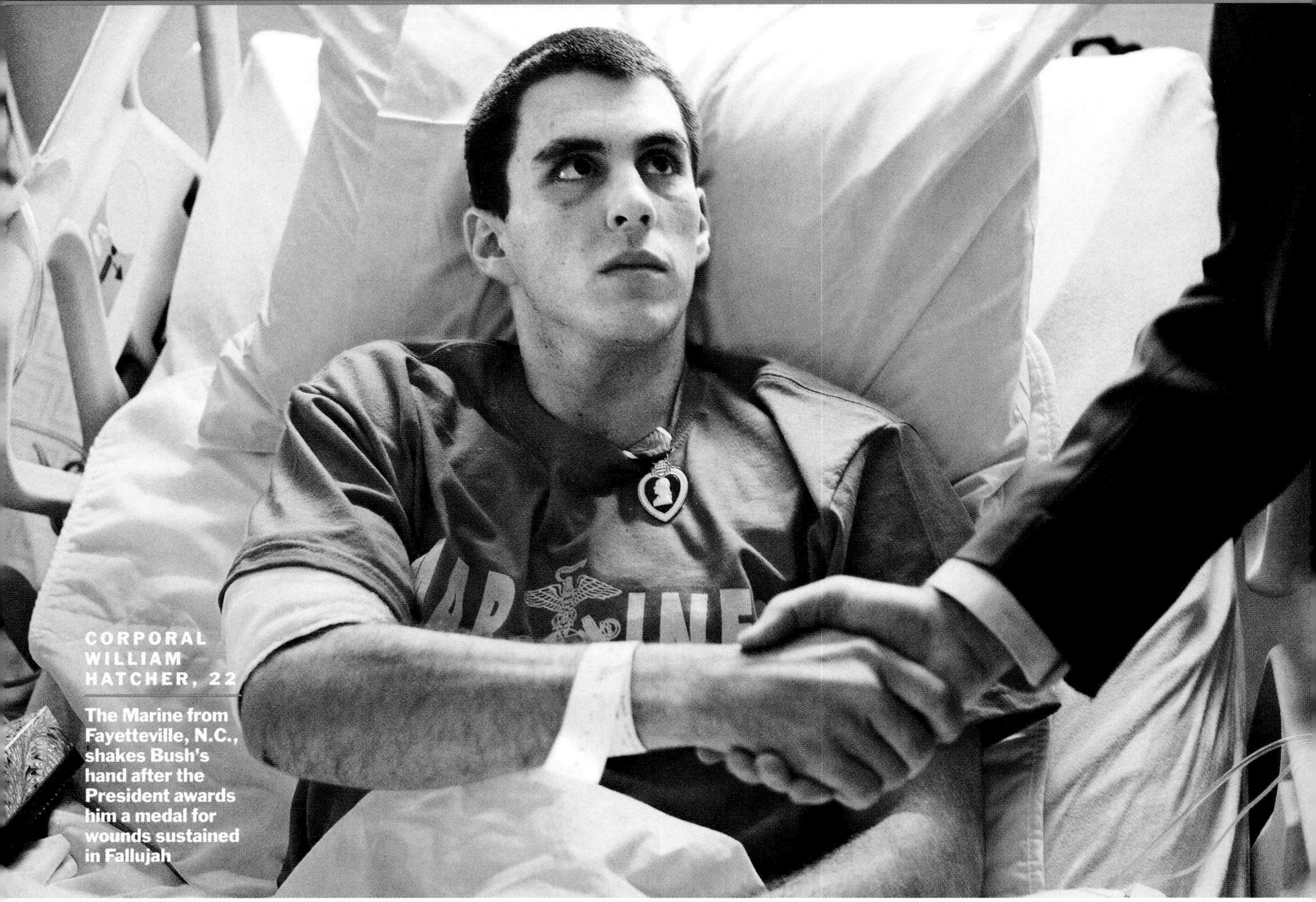

CORPORAL WILLIAM HATCHER, 22

The Marine from Fayetteville, N.C., shakes Bush's hand after the President awards him a medal for wounds sustained in Fallujah

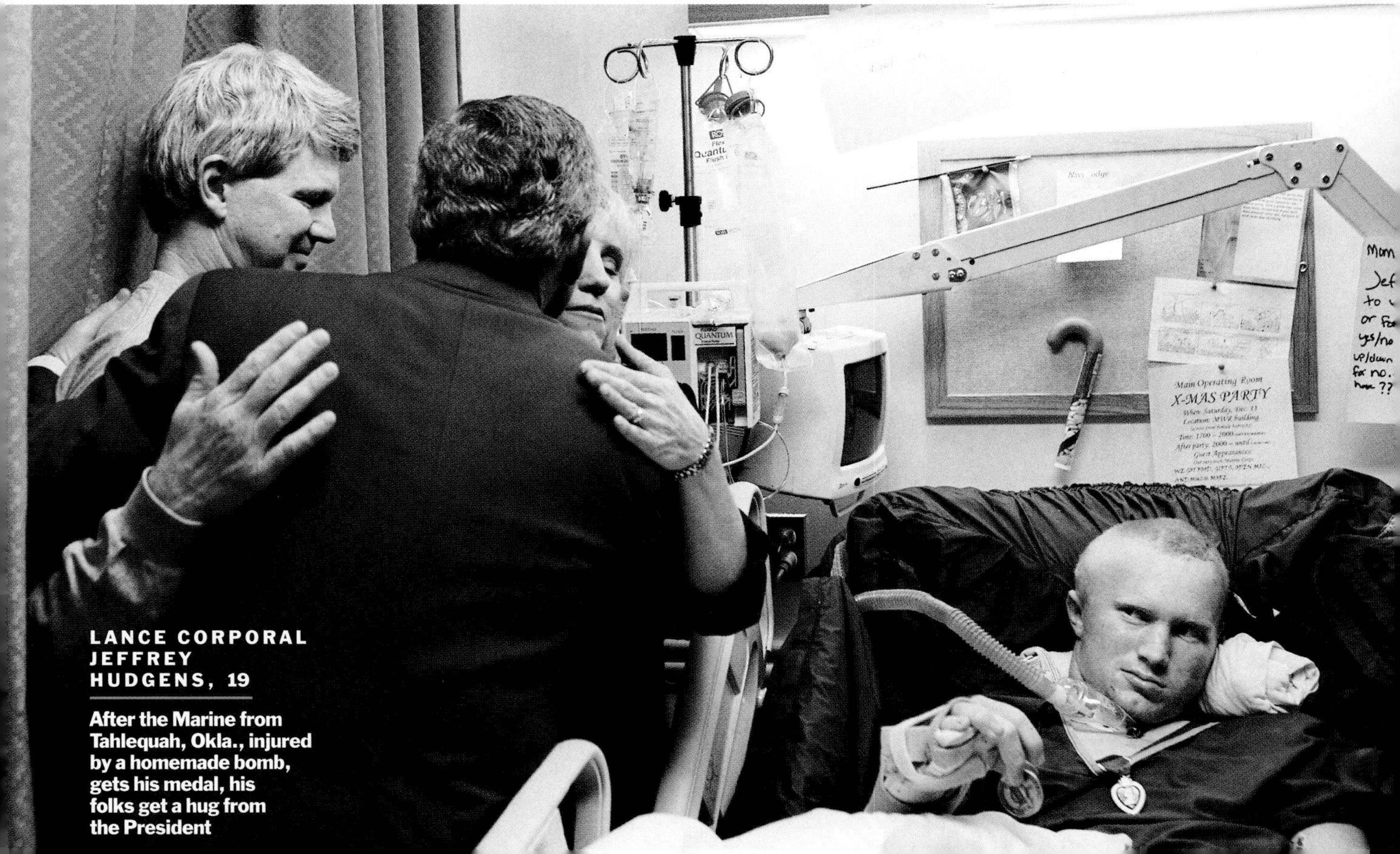
Main Operating Room
X-MAS PARTY

LANCE CORPORAL JEFFREY HUDGENS, 19

After the Marine from Tahlequah, Okla., injured by a homemade bomb, gets his medal, his folks get a hug from the President

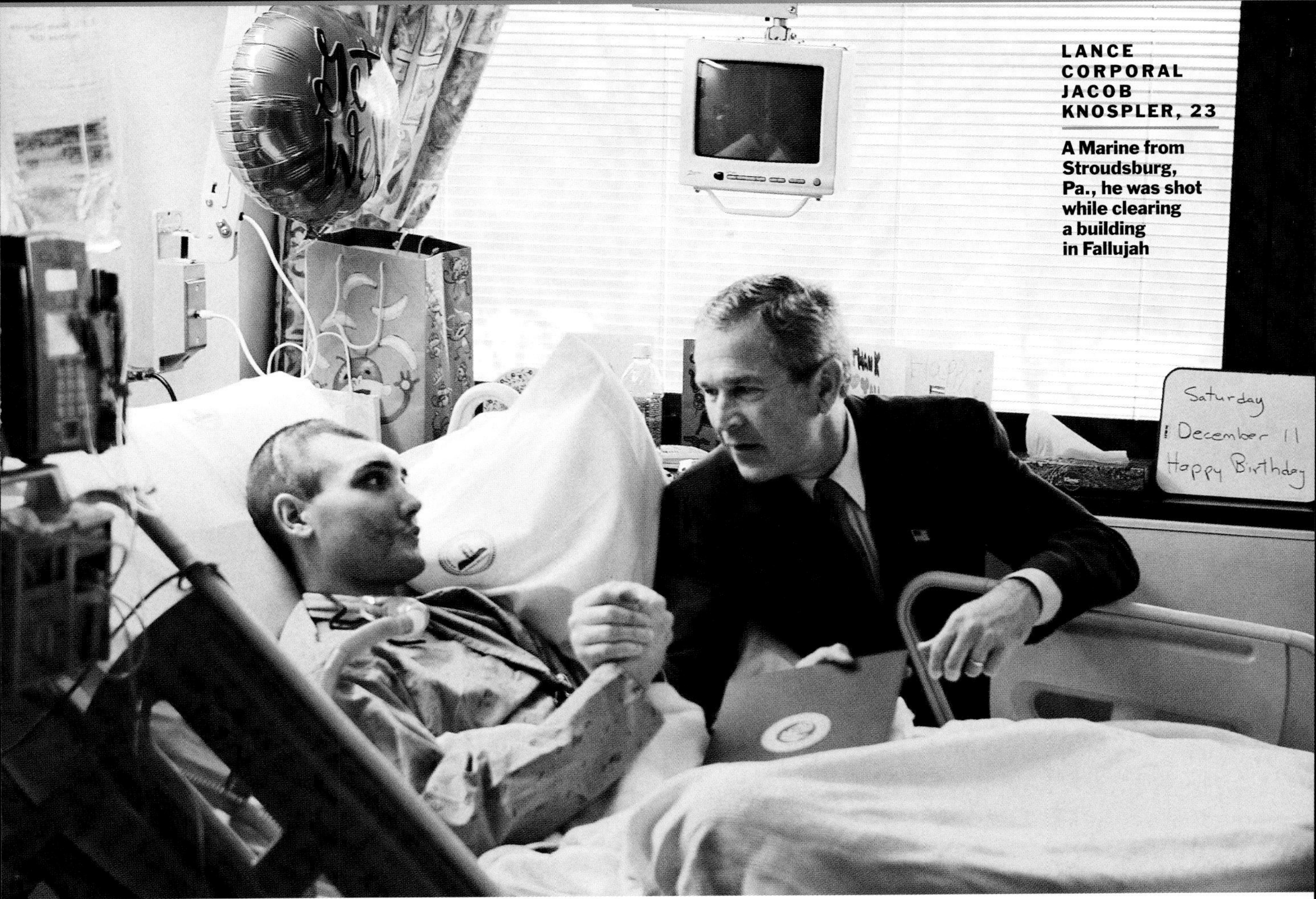
Saturday
December 11
Happy Birthday

LANCE CORPORAL JACOB KNOSPLER, 23

A Marine from Stroudsburg, Pa., he was shot while clearing a building in Fallujah

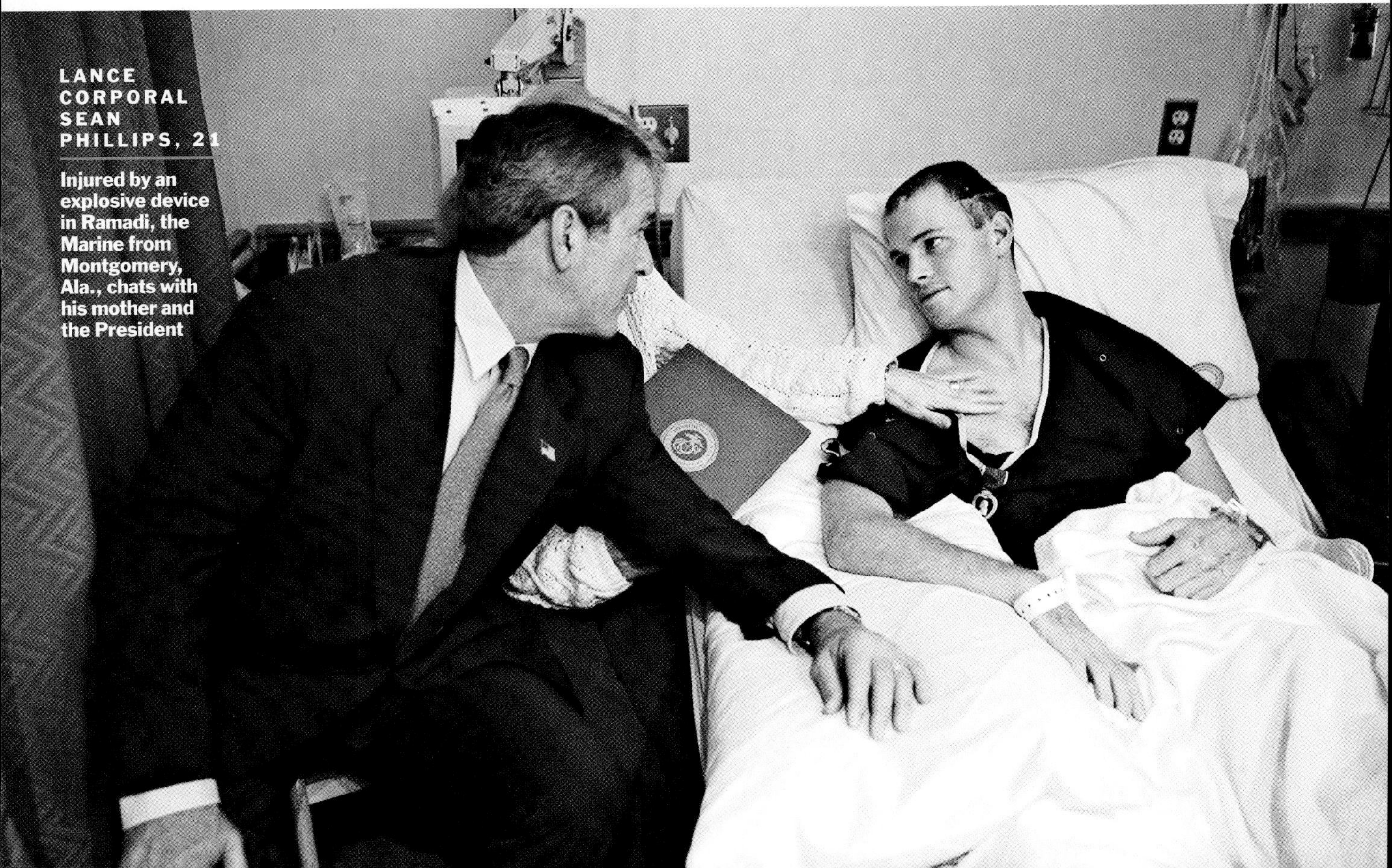

LANCE CORPORAL SEAN PHILLIPS, 21

Injured by an explosive device in Ramadi, the Marine from Montgomery, Ala., chats with his mother and the President

BRENDAN SMIALOWSKI—GETTY IMAGES

A Belated Tribute To Beloved Vets

Culminating a process that took 17 years, the National World War II Memorial was dedicated on Memorial Day weekend on the National Mall in Washington.

Some critics disliked the siting of the memorial, which interrupts the vista from the Washington Monument to the U.S. Capitol; others were underwhelmed by architect Friedrich St. Florian's design (including TIME critic Richard Lacayo, who called it "purest banality"). But when former Senator Bob Dole and actor Tom Hanks, who spearheaded the project, joined President George W. Bush to dedicate it, criticism and caviling took a backseat. As thousands of members of "the Greatest Generation" looked on—many of them openly weeping—there was a strong sense that America's debt to its World War II veterans had at last begun to be formally acknowledged.

A LONG, HARD SLOG

After achieving "catastrophic success" in the 2003 war to topple Saddam Hussein, the U.S. and its allies in Iraq learn a bitter lesson: conquest is far easier than control

BLOODIED: U.S. troops inspect the scene of a September car bombing in Baghdad that left four American soldiers wounded

MAX BECHERER—POLARIS

AMERICA'S FIGHTING MEN AND WOMEN in Iraq, along with their civilian bosses in Washington, began 2004 on a high note, still basking in the afterglow of having captured alive only weeks earlier the most-wanted man in Iraq, fugitive former dictator Saddam Hussein. But they were soon reminded that this war promised to be—as Secretary of Defense Donald Rumsfeld had warned in a memo to his subordinates in October 2003—"a long, hard slog." The year was barely a week old when nine U.S. soldiers were killed after their Black Hawk helicopter was shot down near Fallujah. Days later, an improvised explosive device, one of the homemade bombs that have bedeviled U.S. troops, detonated on a road south of Baghdad, killing three more U.S. servicemen and bringing the total number of American deaths in Iraq to 500.

The first month of the year was no kinder to those directing the war: in January, U.S. Secretary of State Colin Powell, National Security Adviser Condoleezza Rice and British Prime Minister Tony Blair all reluctantly acknowledged that Iraq's vaunted stockpile of weapons of mass destruction—their most compelling rationale for going to war—was nowhere to be found and might not exist. The Bush Administration's embarrassment was compounded before the month's end when David Kay, the American who had been placed in charge of searching occupied Iraq for Saddam's secret weapons, testified before Congress that the intelligence on which the decision to invade had been based was "almost all wrong."

These events were a bracing reveille for 2004, a crucial year in which the U.S. and its partners in Iraq—having easily achieved what President George W. Bush called "catastrophic success" in winning the war—now turned their attention to a far more difficult task: winning the peace.

The battle to bring peace to Iraq would be waged on two fronts, the military and the political. To U.S. and coalition soldiers fell the mission of suppressing an insurgency that would grow in strength, skill and viciousness throughout the year. This struggle to stabilize a country teetering on the brink of lawlessness and chaos would be waged even as diplomats and politicians worked toward the second goal: patching together a sturdy, legitimate government from the disparate mix of religious, ethnic, tribal and political factions that make up Iraq.

By year's end, neither of these missions had been achieved; and, perhaps surprisingly, more progress had been made on the political front than the military one. As 2004 ended, the insurgent forces remained resilient, effective, numerous and deadly. But in the political sphere, Iraq was nominally under the control of a ruling council made up of Iraqis and appeared to be on track to hold a national election on Jan. 30, 2005, the date agreed upon by U.S. and Iraqi leaders for the nation's first, and thus highly symbolic, election following Saddam's fall.

AS ALWAYS, THE MOST DANGEROUS WORK FELL TO THOSE bearing arms, not portfolios—some 138,000 U.S. troops and 22,000 from allied nations. The frequency and violence of the attacks against them had been steadily mounting since President Bush declared the coalition's "mission accomplished" in May 2003. The strikes were carried out by a mixed bag of Saddam loyalists, Shi'ite militants based mostly in southern Iraq and so-called foreign fighters—young Muslims from around the Arab world who came to wage jihad against the U.S. and whose numbers appeared to be growing during the year.

Early in 2004 the worst violence was largely confined to the Sunni triangle north and west of Baghdad, Saddam Hussein's home region and longtime base of support. These attacks were sporadic, seemingly disorganized and often deadlier to Iraqis than to Americans. But the nature of the resistance underwent a sea change two months later, sparked by a scene of horror in Fallujah, only 50 miles west of Baghdad in the hostile triangle. After four U.S. contractors drove into an ambush on March 31, at least three men cut off their convoy of SUVs and opened fire with assault rifles. Three of the U.S. civilians apparently died instantly; another was badly wounded, only to be beaten to death with bricks by a mob that quickly gathered. As the crowd grew, it began burning the cars, reducing the bodies inside to charred, unrecognizable forms. The corpses were beaten, then two were dragged behind a car to a bridge over the Euphrates River, where they were suspended from a girder for all to see. There they hung for six hours; finally, members of the Iraqi security forces showed up to disperse the mob and claim the mutilated bodies.

AS 2004 ENDED, THE INSURGENT FORCES REMAINED RESILIENT, EFFECTIVE, NUMEROUS AND DEADLY

KARIM SAHIB—GETTY IMAGES

FALLUJA SEMITU AMERICA
الفلوجة مقبرة

HORROR: An Iraqi mob celebrates in March in Fallujah as an SUV that carried slain U.S. civilians burns; the bodies were later mutilated. The sign held by an Iraqi boy reads, "FALLUJAH, THE CEMETERY OF THE AMERICANS"

TIMELINE 2004

Jan. 8 Fallujah Nine U.S. soldiers die when their Black Hawk helicopter is shot down

Feb. 1 Arbil 100 are killed and 200 injured in bombings of the main Kurdish political parties

March 2 Karbala Bombs kill more than 180 as some 100,000 religious pilgrims observe a Shi'ite holy day

March 31 Fallujah Four U.S. civilian contractors are ambushed, killed and brutalized

April 7 Fallujah, Ramadi, Najaf, Nasiriya, Basra, Baghdad Uprisings by Shi'ite militants engulf these cities in violence

April 21 Basra Suicide attacks on Iraqi police buildings kill 50, including 20 children

May 5 Karbala U.S. forces assault insurgents loyal to Muqtada al-Sadr

May 24 Najaf U.S. troops fight rebels loyal to Muqtada al-Sadr in a mosque, killing dozens

June 25 Mosul Multiple car bombs kill 62 people, including one U.S. soldier.

July 9 Samarra Insurgents mortar a military base, killing five U.S. soldiers and at least one Iraqi guard

July 14 Baghdad A suicide car bomber kills 11 at the gates of the U.S.-fortified Green Zone

August 7 Najaf U.S.and Iraqi forces battle fighters loyal to Muqtada al-Sadr, killing 300

September 4 Tal 'Afar U.S. and Iraqi troops kill 11 Iraqi militants and wound more than 50

Sept. 9 Tal 'Afar, Samarra, Falluja U.S.-led forces launch new offensives against rebel strongholds

Sept. 18 Kirkuk A suicide bomber kills 19 at an Iraqi National Guard station

Nov. 13 Fallujah U.S. forces re-take the city, killing some 1,000 insurgents

ENEMY TERRITORY
A swath of land that the U.S. patrols but insurgents dominate
NO-GO AREAS
Rebel-held cities that have been off-limits to U.S. troops
FLASHPOINTS
Shi'ite areas under government control but prone to instability
REBEL FRIENDLY HAVENS
Pockets of growing insurgent support
A LAND DIVIDED
Iraq's ethno-religious divide
Kurd
Sunni
Shi'ite
Sunni Turkoman
Sparsely populated areas
Striped areas reflect mixed populations
TURKEY
IRAN
IRAQ
SAUDI ARABIA
KUWAIT
Diyarbakir
Mahabad
Zanjan
Hamadan
Kermanshah
Zakhu
Al 'Amadiyah
Dahuk
Aqrah
Rawanduz
Tal 'Afar
Mosul
Arbil
Kuysanjaq
Tigris River
Kirkuk
As-Sulaymaniyah
Ba'iji
Tikrit
Samarra
Euphrates River
Anah
Khanaqin
Sunni Triangle
Al Hadithah
Mandali
Ramadi
Fallujah
Baghdad
Badrah
Lake Ar-Razzazah
Al Hillah
Al Kut
Karbala
Ad Diwaniyah
Najaf
Nukhayb
Al 'Amarah
As Samawah
Nasiriyah
Suq ash-Shuyukh
Basra
As-Salman
Al Faw
Kuwait City
Persian Gulf

Then, on April 4, he issued a call for his black-clad militiamen to "terrorize your enemy." Thousands took to Baghdad's streets to attack U.S. forces, and soon a string of cities across the formerly pacific Shi'ite heartland was aflame with running gun battles aimed at ending the occupation.

The horrors in Fallujah and the April uprising finally brought the military response that coalition strategists had long held back, fearing it would alienate the population they were trying to win over. The result was the bloodiest week since the start of the war: 46 U.S. soldiers were killed, along with 10 times as many Iraqis. Marines surrounded Fallujah, battling insurgents for control. In Ramadi, up to

Days later, a firebrand Shi'ite cleric with vast political ambitions decided to roll the dice. Muqtada al-Sadr, 30, is the senior cleric in Najaf, site of the Imam Ali shrine, the holiest site in Shi'ite Islam. He had been delivering rabble-rousing anti-American sermons for months while he built up his Mahdi Army (named for the Shi'ite Messiah). But al-Sadr had always stopped short of calling for violence.

UNDER FIRE: U.S. soldiers take cover in August at the cemetery in Najaf, the scene of heavy fighting for days

CAROLYN COLE—LOS ANGELES TIMES

a dozen Marines were killed in intense fighting near the provincial governor's palace, although heavier losses were taken by the rebels. Seven U.S. soldiers were killed in Sadr City, and Baghdad itself erupted as U.S. soldiers battled rebels in the streets.

SUDDENLY, WHAT HAD SEEMED A SCATTERED GUERRILLA RESISTANCE EXPLODED INTO A FULL-FLEDGED, MULTIFRONT WAR

The Americans weren't the only troops seeing action: in Najaf, Spanish soldiers struggled against al-Sadr's militia forces, who had taken control of the city, while Polish and Bulgarian soldiers repelled a series of attacks in Karbala and Italian forces fought to defend Nasiriyah. Amid numerous victories for U.S. and coalition troops, the insurgents scored a few short-lived wins of their own. In one case, American troops had to relieve Ukrainian forces who were under attack in Kut, where rebels seized police stations and government buildings.

Suddenly, what had seemed a scattered guerrilla resistance had exploded into a full-fledged, multifront war. In one sense, this development was almost a relief: a conventional army that tries to fight without a visible, identifiable enemy is at a serious handicap. The essential characteristic of guerrilla warfare—that the enemy is at once everywhere and nowhere—favored the rebels: each time coalition forces engaged the insurgents head on, they scored a clear-cut victory, killing dozens (sometimes hundreds) of enemy fighters and taking physical control of the battlefield. But each time, the value of this victory was undermined when the coalition troops withdrew, and insurgent forces that had fled before them trickled back to their former positions to resume their attacks. Each of these towns and cities became, in effect, Iraq in miniature—proving that conquest is far easier than control.

SO IT WAS THAT NAJAF, WHICH HAD BEEN SUBDUED IN April, had to be retaken in August, after attacks on coalition troops had resumed and al-Sadr, along with hundreds of his heavily armed fighters, had gone to ground in the holy city. As the battle unfolded amid the dusty vastness of the city's Valley of Peace cemetery, adjacent to the golden-domed Imam Ali shrine, U.S. Marines engaged in a tomb-to-tomb fight with black-clad Mahdi

KEY PLAYERS IN THE STRUGGLE TO CONTROL IRAQ

One of the reasons Iraq remains tumultuous is that the country is a loose coalition of ethnic and religious groups, natural rivals who have no tradition of uniting in a common cause. Like Yugoslavia under Tito, Iraq has been held together since the early 1980s by the force of its leader, Saddam Hussein, and his political apparatus, the Baath Party. Under Saddam, minority Sunnis dominated the Shi'ite majority, and ethnic Kurds were strongly discriminated against.

GRAND AYATULLAH ALI SISTANI
The elder statesman of Shi'ite clerics, Sistani is the revered spiritual leader of Iraq's 15 million-strong Shi'ite majority; he holds a strong hand. Concerned that the interim constitution gave short shrift to his followers, he threatened to issue a *fatwa* (religious edict) against it, raising the possibility of civil war.

MUQTADA AL-SADR
The son of a much loved cleric killed in 1999 by Saddam's men, al-Sadr, only 30, has built a following among poor urban Shi'ites by calling on them to resist occupation forces. With his April call to revolt, he leap-frogged from the status of a junior cleric to make himself a serious rival to Ali Sistani.

ABU MUSAB AL-ZARQAWI
The Jordanian-born acolyte of Osama bin Laden's has been waging jihad since he was a teenager, when he trekked to Afghanistan to fight the Soviets. Now 37, he is believed to be al-Qaeda's top operative in Iraq and the mastermind behind numerous kidnappings, suicide bombings and other terrorist deeds.

IYAD ALLAWI
A neurologist by training and a Baathist by background, Allawi left Iraq in the 1970s for exile in London, where Saddam Hussein tried to have him assassinated. Iraq's interim Prime Minister has shown a willingness both to disagree with his American sponsors and to take a hard line with rebels.

GEORGE CASEY
A U.S. general who is new to the Middle East, George Casey is nonetheless a respected figure who brings experience navigating the political and military shoals of Bosnia (where he served as a senior peacekeeping officer in the 1990s) to his new job as commander of all U.S. forces in Iraq.

SADDAM HUSSEIN
The deposed dictator remains defiant in captivity. He has told his jailers next to nothing and insisted on being addressed as "the President of Iraq" during his July courtroom appearance. Saddam interrogated the Iraqi judge and demanded to know under what authority he was holding the hearing.

CLOCKWISE FROM TOP RIGHT: SUNGSU CHO—POLARIS; NIKOLA SOLIC—POOL—AP/WIDE WORLD; KAREN BALLARD—AP/WIDE WORLD; NABIL MOUNZER—EPA; GHAITH ABDUL-AHAD—GETTY IMAGES; EPA

ATROCITIES OF WAR

CIVILIANS BEHEADED

Isn't this starting to read like a mystery novel ...?" 26-year-old Nicholas Berg wrote to friends in America in an e-mail from Iraq. The utility repairman had headed to the war zone hoping to make some money and do some good at the same time. In April, apparently planning to leave Iraq, Berg checked out of his hotel and went missing. A month later, U.S. soldiers found his decapitated body, and a grisly video of his beheading appeared on an Islamic website. On this tape, one of Berg's captors reads a statement about avenging the suffering of Iraqi prisoners at Abu Ghraib, then grabs the screaming young man by the hair and cuts off his head with a long knife. CIA officials believe that knife was wielded by terror kingpin Abu Mousab al-Zarqawi. In September, al-Zarqawi's group kidnapped and beheaded two more U.S. civilians, engineer Eugene Armstrong and construction worker Jack Hensley. Weeks later, militants taped the execution of 12 Nepalese contractors. In all, more than 100 foreign civilians have been abducted since the war's start. Of these several dozen are known to have been executed, a handful have been released, and the fate of many more is unknown.

MURDER: The Berg death video

APTN—AP/WIDE WORLD

NIGHTMARE IN ABU GHRAIB

Under Saddam Hussein, Baghdad's Abu Ghraib Prison was a nest of torture and random murder. That was supposed to have changed when coalition forces took over in 2003 and began filling the jail with insurgents. But when photos taken at the jail by U.S. guards were obtained and broadcast by CBS News in April 2004, a shocked world saw indelible images of U.S. soldiers abusing and humiliating their wards. The impact on U.S. prestige was devastating; an angry President Bush denounced the deeds and vowed justice would be swift. By year's end, a total of 45 Army personnel had been referred for courts-martial in the case; of these, four soldiers had either entered a guilty plea to reduced charges or had been convicted at trial. The highest- ranking soldier charged as of December is Staff Sergeant Ivan L. (Chip) Frederick II, sentenced to eight years in prison in October. Additionally, 12 letters of reprimand have been issued to officers. Brigadier General Janis Karpinski, the overall commander of Abu Ghraib, was formally admonished and removed from her command in April.

TORTURE: A blow to U.S. prestige

fighters. Meanwhile, al-Sadr vowed not to leave his bunker in the shrine "until the last drop of my blood has been spilled." In the end, al-Sadr backed down rather than be slaughtered, while coalition military leaders chose not to throw the knockout punch they had been poised to deliver, fearing that a military victory could become a political defeat by sparking rage among the country's majority Shi'ite population (and perhaps among the wider Muslim world) if the shrine were destroyed.

In September the total number of U.S. troops who had died in Iraq passed 1,000, and similar (if smaller scale) battles were played out at rebel strongholds in Tall 'Afar, Samara and Fallujah. In October, Samara had to be taken again, this time drawing more than 3,000 U.S. troops into a pitched, three-day battle; Ramadi and Fallujah were also retaken. More than any other city in Iraq, Fallujah played out a by now familiar, grim cycle: U.S. victory, a temporary truce and withdrawal, then reoccupation by the rebels, kick-starting another round of the pattern.

In November, Fallujah had to be taken again; as the base of Abu Mousab al-Zarqawi, al-Qaeda's top operative in Iraq, it was the nerve center of violent Sunni resistance. The fall battle here was billed as a climactic clash between roughly 10,000 U.S. soldiers and Marines and about 2,000 newly minted Iraqi troops against the estimated 1,500 to 3,000 armed militants who had turned the city into Iraq's biggest rebel haven. U.S. troops battled armed insurgents not just street to street or even house to house but also room to room at point-blank range. By Nov. 13, the allies controlled the city, now a wasteland. It was impossible to count the number of enemy dead, and the jihadist leadership escaped the city, but the U.S. victory did remove an important staging ground for the insurgents—who quickly asserted their power by striking in a number of other cities, even as the Fallujah offensive was in progress.

AMID THIS SWIRLING CAULDRON OF ANCIENT GRUDGES and diverging agendas, the drive to bring political stability to Iraq made steady (if agonizingly slow) progress in 2004. "If you break it, you bought it," Secretary of State Powell had warned the President about Iraq before the war. Yet in taking on responsibility for a country the size of California with a population of 25 million, the U.S. seemed ill-prepared to maintain order, separate warring factions and rebuild the physical and political infrastructure, all while creating a new democratic government in a nation that had never had one. Critics, who included top U.S. military officers, blamed the problems on the Administration's focus on a quick battlefield victory at the expense of planning for what would follow.

In March, a new democratic constitution was ratified by the Interim Iraqi Governing Council, the U.S.-appointed group of 25 Iraqis leading the country for the seven months between the June handoff of power by U.S. occu-

OFFENSIVE: A U.S. soldier fires a rocket at insurgent positions from a rooftop perch during the battle for Fallujah in November

AT YEAR'S END, THE STRUGGLE TO WIN THE HEARTS AND MINDS OF THE IRAQI PEOPLE WAS YET TO BE DECIDED

pation chief Paul Bremer's Coalition Provisional Authority and before the January '05 election. Two months later, Dr. Iyad Allawi, a former Baath Party member who broke with Saddam Hussein, was named prime minister of the interim government. On June 28, Bremer placed the reins of government in Allawi's hands two days ahead of schedule, in a surprise move designed to avert possible terrorist attacks planned for the day. Another benchmark came in July, when a haggard-looking Saddam Hussein appeared before an Iraqi judge to begin his rendezvous with justice.

Yet each step on the road to legitimacy was halting and hard-earned. By November, the security situation in Iraq had become so precarious that Allawi invoked his authority under the new constitution to declare a 60-day nationwide state of emergency, sealing Iraq's borders and imposing round-the-clock curfews in hot spots like Fallujah and Ramadi. Allied troops could not even guarantee security on the road to the Baghdad airport.

The critical initiative to hand the nation's security over to Iraqis was making slow headway. President Bush said during his re-election campaign that some 145,000 Iraqi troops would be mission-ready by Jan. 1, 2005, but most independent observers called that number far too optimistic. As of Dec. 1, the Brookings Institution's Iraq Index tallied just 7,582 Iraqis fully or partly trained for army operations, plus 38,338 less-élite national guardsmen. These troops proved of little value in action, and U.S. commanders feared they were plagued by corruption and infiltrated by insurgents. "This is—and is going to be—a largely U.S. show all the way," said a U.S. Central Command officer.

As 2004 ended, the most important battle in Iraq—the struggle for the hearts and minds of the Iraqi people—was yet to be decided. Although very few Iraqis regretted the fall of Saddam, fewer still suffered the presence of a foreign occupier gladly. The constant grind of violence, and the shortage of such basic necessities as food and water—often caused when U.S. resources intended to help rebuild the country were diverted to fighting the insurgents—led many Iraqis to question the merits of the U.S. intervention.

The belief in American good faith weathered its most shattering blow when graphic photos of U.S. Army personnel abusing Iraqi prisoners at the Abu Ghraib prison in Baghdad became public. And as stepped-up operations against the insurgents claimed the lives of Iraqi civilians as well as guerrillas (and as rebels killed U.S-friendly civilians to intimidate their neighbors), more former moderates were driven into the arms of leaders who called for driving out the "crusaders."

Ambiguity on the battlefield led to ambivalence about the war on yet another front—the home front. Throughout the year, polls portrayed Americans as divided about the war: a November Gallup poll showed that a slim majority of Americans (51%) felt it was not a mistake to have invaded Iraq, while a slightly larger majority (55%) disapproved of the President's overall handling of the war.

As a new year approached, the verdict on how far the U.S. had come in Iraq—and how far it had yet to go—remained unclear. All eyes were trained on the election scheduled for Jan. 30, 2005, which could prove, for good or ill, to be a tipping point, after which Iraqis might either accept the new government as legitimate or watch their nation descend further into chaos and bloodshed. Yet to ensure a truly national ballot, the U.S. would need to achieve the one thing that had eluded all America's humvees and all America's men: stability. In December an additional 15,000 U.S. troops were rotated into Iraq.

After a year of struggle on two fronts in Iraq, George W. Bush's very large gamble in this nation was still a slippery mixture of success and catastrophe, the ratio of the two seeming to change with each new day's headlines. For now, one of the few certainties about the U.S. presence in Iraq was that Donald Rumsfeld's fears about it had been realized: this mission was a long, hard slog. ■

WHAT ABOUT SADDAM'S WEAPONS?

What a difference two years can make. In the fall of 2002, President Bush declared that Iraq "possesses and produces chemical and biological weapons, [and] it is seeking nuclear weapons." Yet the central conclusion of a report issued in October 2004 by Bush's handpicked investigator, veteran arms inspector Charles Duelfer, was just as clear: most U.S. assumptions about Iraq's weapons had been incorrect. In every category of weapons of mass destruction (WMDs), Iraq seems to have been nowhere near being able to pose a threat to the U.S. or even its neighbors.

The Duelfer report concluded that Iraq probably destroyed all or most of its biological agents in 1991 and '92 and hadn't shown any interest in biowarfare after it destroyed its al-Hakam bioweapons plant in 1996. Although Saddam may have hoped to relaunch a chemical-weapons program someday, there were no "credible indications" that Iraq had produced any such agents after 1991. No such materials were found at a site shown in 2002 satellite photos, contrary to suggestions made by Secretary of State Colin Powell during his prewar presentation to the U.N. in February 2003.

Iraq's nuclear program had also atrophied, the report said, with Saddam making no serious moves to reconstitute it after 1991—though Duelfer believes Saddam hoped to do so someday. It was on the subject of rockets that the Bush Administration seems to have come closest to the mark: Iraq was indeed planning on developing long-range ballistic missiles that could travel 600 miles or more. Yet none of the designs were close to production.

After the 1991 Gulf War, the report suggests, Saddam—fearing his neighbors, especially Iraq—encouraged the world to believe he still had doomsday weapons squirreled away. This elaborate bluff seems to have been a colossal misjudgment that cost Saddam his rule.

KSTP/ABC NEWS—AP/WIDE WORLD

APRIL: A U.S. soldier seeks weapons

HAMMERED!

CHARLEY
AUG. 15

FRANCES
SEPT. 7

Disaster strikes Florida
in alphabetical order,
as the Sunshine State
reels from a quartet
of massive hurricanes

WEST
EAST
10
10

IVAN
SEPT. 16

JEANNE
SEPT. 27

SANS SOUCI
TARP

SEPT. 22 A car hits the beach in Pensacola

SEPT. 18 A surprise landing in Pensacola Beach

WHAT WORDS CAN SUM UP THE FOUR HURRICANES that mauled Florida—as well as other Southeastern states and several Caribbean islands—in the late summer of 2004? A good choice might be the name the 19th century French poet Arthur Rimbaud gave to his tortured 1873 work, *A Season in Hell.* In a period of only six weeks, a quartet of monster storms killed more than 100 people in the U.S. and more than 1,000 in the West Indies, deprived millions more of power and fresh water and caused billions of dollars in damage.

For Floridians, the season in hell began Aug. 13, when Hurricane Charley ripped helter-skelter through the Sunshine State and up the East Coast, earning a bitter nickname, the "Friday the 13th Hurricane." In 2003 meteorologists at Miami's National Hurricane Center were remarkably accurate with their storm-landing forecasts. But with the first hurricane of the 2004 season, that winning streak washed out to sea. After 1 million people were ordered to evacuate the Tampa area, Charley instead slammed into the shoreline 100 miles to the south. The 145-m.p.h. winds twisted aluminum siding as if it were gift ribbon and snapped 100-year-old pine trees. Then, as people raced inland, the storm followed, reminding everyone that on this extremity of land, there is little room to escape. "What we've managed to do is to evacuate a lot of people into the path of a hurricane," said a Tampa official. When Charley at last let up, survivors emerged from their hiding places to a nightmare of destruction—yachts hurled into trees, houses and bridges swept from their pilings and motels and condominiums smashed to splinters.

No sooner had residents of Florida draped tarps over roofs damaged by Charley than Frances came along—and no sooner had they started to clean up after Frances than Ivan loomed. Although devastating, Frances could have been worse. While still at sea, it was a Category 4 storm with winds in excess of 145 m.p.h. But when it made land-

MARC SEROTA—REUTERS—CORBIS

SEPT. 14 Traffic clogs Interstate 10 outside Panama City as Hurricane Ivan approaches Florida's Panhandle

SEPT. 25 Haitians line up for water in Ivan's wake

Sales Office·Park Here
AUG. 14 A trailer park shows Charley's power

SEPT. 16 Ivan knocked out a section of the bridge over Alabama's Escambia Bay, killing the driver of this truck

fall on Sept. 4, just north of Palm Beach, Frances had lost some of its punch, and it was downgraded to a Category 2 hurricane with winds of 115 m.p.h. Moving across Florida toward the Gulf of Mexico, it lost more power and was reclassified as a tropical storm. Its peak winds winds diminished to 65 m.p.h., but it was still strong enough to dump more than 13 in. of rain on the central part of the state, flooding some areas under 4 ft. of water.

Twelve days later, it was Ivan's turn. The storm made landfall in Alabama, but not until after it had devastated Grenada, Jamaica and Haiti—and even then it had plenty of destructive power to spare. Along Mobile Bay, a 16-ft. storm surge, topped by giant waves, overran almost a mile of Alabama coastline, in some places to a depth of 10 ft. In the Florida Panhandle—one section of the Sunshine State spared by the previous blows—tornadoes spun off from Ivan's leading edge and bent streetlights, uprooted trees and ripped the roofs off buildings. Across the South, in Georgia, Tennessee and North Carolina, Ivan's heavy rains turned creeks into rivers and rivers into inland seas.

Batting clean-up in this murderer's row of tropical storms was Hurricane Jeanne. A few minutes before midnight on Sept. 25, Jeanne—following almost the same path taken by Frances three weeks before—landed near Fort Pierce as a Category 3 storm. More than 400 miles wide, Jeanne churned up floods and tossed debris through the air from Miami to Daytona Beach. When Jeanne let up, it had deprived 1.5 million people of electric power and killed more than half a dozen people. As Floridians turned to the massive task of rebuilding, Florida Governor Jeb Bush offered words of cheer: "This is part of the price we pay, I guess, for living in paradise." That's one name for it; Rimbaud had another. ■

LARRY DOWNING—REUTERS—CORBIS

SEPT. 8 Florida Governor Jeb Bush and his brother, the President, hand out supplies after Frances' rampage

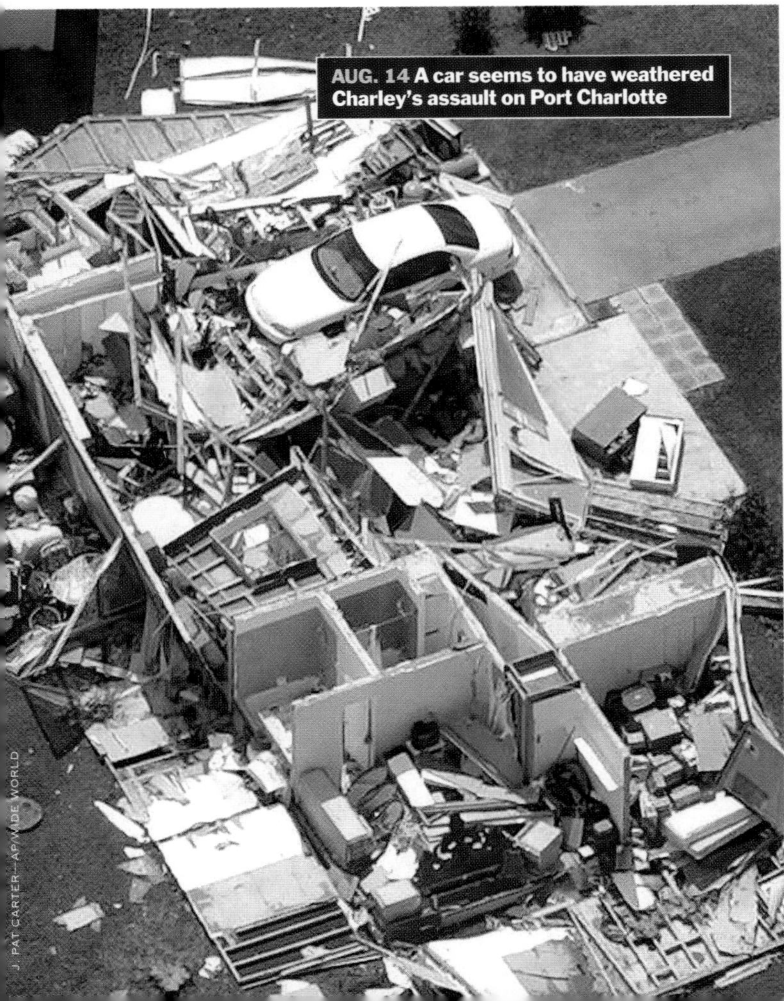

AUG. 14 A car seems to have weathered Charley's assault on Port Charlotte

J. PAT CARTER—AP/WIDE WORLD

LOOTERS
WILL BE
KILLED

AUG. 14 Terry Frey guards his home in Port Charlotte

HAIL TO THE CHIEF

A state funeral caps a week of mourning as ordinary Americans join the powerful and the celebrated to honor Ronald Wilson Reagan

WHEN RONALD REAGAN DIED AT AGE 93, AFTER A long struggle with Alzheimer's disease, Americans and world leaders gathered in the nation's capital to mourn the 40th President. It was the first state funeral for a fallen chief executive since Lyndon Johnson's death in 1973; Richard Nixon's 1994 service was private. More than 100,000 people—some 3,000 an hour—filed through the Rotunda of the U.S. Capitol, where the body lay in state; many others were turned away. The funeral service, an invitation-only affair for 4,000, was held at the National Cathedral and was attended by all four surviving former Presidents—Gerald Ford, Jimmy Carter, George H.W. Bush, Bill Clinton—and their wives.

In the days before the service, while American television ran nonstop coverage of Reagan's life and times, President George W. Bush offered the use of Blair House to former

POMP: Mourners gather at the Capitol Rotunda, above. At top right, the President's coffin is borne through the streets. Right, President George W. Bush escorts Nancy Reagan to her seat amid Washington's power élite at the National Cathedral. Former Senator John Danforth, an Episcopalian priest, presided at the funeral service

First Lady Nancy Reagan, 82, who received many world leaders at the ceremonial residence. Attending the funeral were 36 present and past heads of state, including Tony Blair of Britain, Silvio Berlusconi of Italy and Gerhard Schröder of Germany. Britain's Prince Charles, Afghanistan's Hamid Karzai and the Secretary-General of the United Nations, Kofi Annan, were also present—as was an old adversary who lived to become an admirer, Mikhail Gorbachev.

Though unable to speak owing to a series of minor strokes, Reagan's great ally and friend, former British Prime Minister Margaret Thatcher, declared in a taped message, "His politics had a freshness and optimism that won converts from every class and every nation—and ultimately from the very heart of the evil empire." As President Bush put it, "Ronald Reagan belongs to the ages now, but we preferred it when he belonged to us." ■

Nation Notes

■ **PROFILE**

Clinton's Surprise Detour

Bill Clinton had big plans for 2004: he'd release his autobiography, campaign to aid the Democratic ticket in the election and bask in the opening of his state-of-the-art presidential library in Little Rock, Ark. After pushing himself to complete his memoir, *My Life,* Clinton embarked on a round of bookstore signings and publicity gigs that proved his gift of gab, charisma (and ability to infuriate his numerous foes) were intact. The book drew mixed reviews but sold well; by November some 2.6 million copies were in print.

MARY ALTAFFER—AP/WIDE WORLD

CLINTON: Always looking for a hand out

Clinton's speech to his fellow Democrats at the national convention in July rocked the roof, but the former President's schedule for 2004 was put on hold when he was rushed to a New York City hospital on Sept. 3; days later he underwent a quadruple heart-bypass operation. Clinton, no stranger to junk food, had experienced chest pains and had difficulty breathing. The operation was a success, but the rope-line veteran was sidelined for the most critical segment of the fall campaign.

On Nov. 18 the "Comeback Kid" was back, beaming, on a rainy day as he was joined by Jimmy Carter and George Bushes 41 and 43 to open his library. Widely praised, The modern structure resembles the "bridge to the future" that was a favorite trope of the Man from Hope.

MATT YORK—AP/WIDE WORLD

NABBED: A U.S. border-patrol officer stands guard over undocumented aliens

America's Porous Borders

Despite all the talk of homeland security, sneaking into the U.S. is scandalously easy and on the rise. Millions of illegal aliens poured across the U.S. border in 2004; millions more will do so in 2005. In a single day, more than 4,000 illegal aliens walk across the busiest unlawful gateway into the U.S., the 375-mile border between Arizona and Mexico. In a January speech, President George W. Bush called for a new temporary-worker program that would give three-year renewable work visas to "the millions of undocumented men and women now employed in the United States."

A Right Turn for the Court?

President Bush's re-election was expected to have a strong impact on the future direction of the Supreme Court, and that chance may come soon: William Rehnquist, Chief Justice since 1986, said on Oct. 27 that he was suffering from thyroid cancer and would work from home in the fall term. Bush may be able to fill as many as three vacancies in the next four years: Justices John Paul Stevens, 84, and Sandra Day O'Connor, 74, are thought to be likely to retire.

J. SCOTT APPLEWHITE—AP/WIDE WORLD

THE COURT: Vacancies are expected in the near future

BART AH YOU—AP/WIDE WORLD

SUSPECT: Peterson during the trial

Scott Peterson: Guilty

Every year or two a murder trial transfixes the nation. Throughout 2004 tabloid newspapers and TV shows picked apart the trial of Scott Peterson, 32, charged with killing his pregnant wife, Laci, 27, and their unborn child, who were found dead in Modesto, Calif., in April 2003. On Nov. 12 a jury found Peterson guilty of first-degree murder in the death of his wife; on Dec. 13 he was sentenced to death.

TAMI SILICIO—ZUMA PRESS

■ IMAGE

Homeward-Bound

In a year when Americans divided over issues of all kinds, the photo at left touched off a furor. The Pentagon forbids pictures of the coffins of slain U.S. soldiers, but cargo worker Tami Silicio took a picture of 20 coffins being loaded onto a cargo plane in Kuwait that was obtained and published by the Seattle *Times*. Silicio and her husband David Landry were fired by their employer, military contractor Maytag Aircraft Corp.

DENNIS COOK—AP/WIDE WORLD

GOSS: New boss of U.S. spooks

Restructuring Intelligence

On July 22 the National Commission on Terrorist Attacks released its report on the deadly deeds of 9/11/01. The 567-page report, widely hailed as a bipartisan effort, did not blame either the Bush or Clinton administrations for the attacks but said they should not have come as a surprise. The report called for a single director to coordinate all U.S. intelligence efforts, including those of the CIA and FBI. A bill that would do so passed Congress on Dec. 7, after meeting early opposition from House leaders. CIA Director George Tenet resigned in June, and the President named Florida Congressman Porter Goss to replace him.

CLOCKWISE FROM TOP LEFT: BRIAN BRANCH PRICE—AP/WIDE WORLD; MATT SAYLES—AP/WIDE WORLD; BOB CHILD—AP/WIDE WORLD

STATE OF THE STATEHOUSES

The old American issue of states' rights vs. federal power is simmering again. And there's a twist this time around: Republicans have long championed the power of individual states, but it's Democrats who are pushing such issues as gay marriage, medical marijuana and stem-cell research through America's statehouses, while Republicans advocate federal authority in these areas. Other news from the nation's capitals was tinged with scandal in 2004.

NEW JERSEY On Aug. 12, Governor James McGreevey resigned his post, saying "I am a gay American." McGreevey, twice married and the father of two, acted after Golan Cipel, an Israeli on the Governor's staff, charged him with making sexual advances

CONNECTICUT John Rowland resigned his position on June 21, amid impeachment proceedings and a federal inquiry regarding allegations he had accepted tens of thousands of dollars in cash and gifts from state contractors. He acted after months of fighting to remain in office

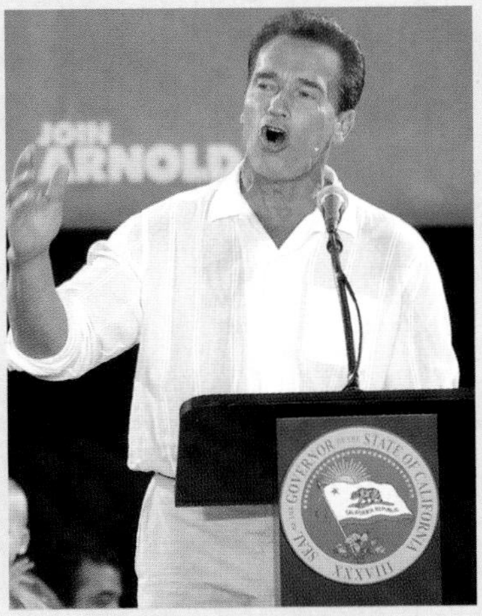

CALIFORNIA Arnold Schwarzenegger rammed through a new budget, spoke at the G.O.P. Convention and announced he'd fund stem-cell research. Fans hope to amend the Constitution to permit the Austrian-born actor to run for President

World

EMILIO MORENATTI—AP/WIDE WORLD

Building a Future, A Brick at a Time

Workers unload bricks from a kiln outside Kabul, where some 50 small concerns like this one fire handmade blocks that are used in rebuilding the capital. Both the physical and social bonds that hold a nation together remain ramshackle in the Central Asian land. For 25 years it has known little but trouble, beginning with the Soviet invasion in December 1979 and continuing through the reign of the Taliban in the 1990s, followed by the toppling of that Islamist regime by U.S. and coalition forces in December 2001. Some 18,000 U.S. troops remain in Afghanistan, which held its first national election in October 2004, as it seeks to forge its first democratic centralized government. Though the election was denounced by some as a U.S. propaganda ploy and was tainted by charges of fraud and faulty ballots, some 8 million Afghans, including more than 3 million women, succeeded in casting their first votes.

GOODBYE: On Oct. 29, an ailing Arafat bids farewell to followers as he goes to Paris for medical treatment

END OF THE JOURNEY

Yasser Arafat dies at 75 with his dream of a Palestinian state unrealized. Will his passing bring a new dawn for peace hopes in the Middle East?

A FEW MONTHS AFTER ISRAELI AND PALESTINIAN LEADers signed the Oslo peace accord in 1993, Yasser Arafat lamented, as a man without a country, that even his final resting place was uncertain. "Can you imagine what it means to be a Palestinian?" he asked TIME. "I don't know where I am to be buried." He had always hoped it would be in a Jerusalem that was the capital of the state of Palestine.

Arafat realized neither wish. After his death at 75 in a Paris hospital, two weeks after he was flown to France suffering from a disease that neither Palestinian nor French officials would reveal, he was interred on Nov. 11 in a temporary grave at the battered West Bank compound in Ramallah, where he spent his final years, imprisoned by Israeli tanks. The closest he came to the Jerusalem holy site that Muslims call the Noble Sanctuary and Jews call the Temple Mount was the handfuls of dirt brought from the shrine to cover his coffin. Palestinians attached handles to his marble tomb, anticipating the day they can move it to the capital of their dreams.

After Arafat, the world wondered, might that dream be closer? Could the death of the unyielding Palestinian leader bring a fresh opportunity to break the stalemate in the Israeli-Palestinian conflict? A multitude of obstacles that have wrecked previous opportunities lie in the way. The chaotic tears and gunfire that accompanied Arafat to his Ramallah grave were emblematic of the conflicted, dangerous void he left behind.

Although the U.S. and Israel considered Arafat an obstacle, he was, for good or ill, the glue that held the pieces of Palestinian political life together. But his one-man rule crippled the development of potential successors and institutions that could provide stability after him. His death left a vacuum that could be filled by hard-line nationalists, warlords and terrorists. The dozen-plus security organizations that Arafat set up have fought one another for dominance. In Gaza, a policy of armed resistance and generous social services has made Hamas the power to be reckoned with, whether or not it participates in elections. Some West Bank cities, cut off from central authority, have degenerated into separate fiefs.

Faced with this hornet's nest, the Bush Administration took a cautious line. Despite the words of British Prime Minister Tony Blair, who called peace in the Middle East the "single most pressing challenge in the world today," President George W. Bush came out of a conclave with Blair only days after Arafat's death offering no tangible sign—such as the naming of a special envoy or the convening of an international conference—to prove the U.S. was ready to back up its talk of measured optimism by taking control of the peace process. And Prime Minister Ariel Sharon indicated Israel would not budge from its policy of shunning contact with the Palestinians until new leaders brought terrorism to a halt. Yet Arafat's successors (four men will take on the titles he alone held) face an uphill struggle just to legitimize their right to rule, much less to back away from Arafat's violent, uncompromising course.

Hours after Arafat's death, Mahmoud Abbas, 69, the moderate former Prime Minister and longtime No. 2 in the Palestine Liberation Organization, stepped into the top slot as chairman. He will share authority with another Old Guard moderate, current Prime Minister Ahmed Qurei, 67, who will continue to run day-to-day government operations. And as Palestinian basic law dictates, Parliament speaker Rauhi Fattuh, 55, a largely powerless functionary, will be caretaker president until elections scheduled for Jan. 9, 2005, can be held.

Optimists say that vote for a new president could hold the key to progress. For more than two years the U.S. and Israel turned their backs on the Palestinians. Now a democratic vote could empower Arafat's heirs with the mandate to make peace. And that could present the Bush Administration with an opportunity to press Sharon into expanding his unilateral withdrawal from Gaza into a negotiated pullback from much of the West Bank.

Everyone eager to change the conflict's dynamic looks to the U.S. to step in with decisive influence. But President Bush is extremely wary of rushing into the fray before the Palestinians secure a new order, a White House official told TIME. Instead, Bush will sit back, talk up elections, offer commitments of aid and support if the Palestinians develop democratic institutions, and see how they do.

That puts the burden squarely on the Palestinians to turn themselves into a moderate partner before the U.S. or Israel will stretch out a hand. Yet the Palestinians may need help to stabilize themselves and take a new direction. Opportunities for peace have been squandered time and again by refusals to take risks. If anything good is to come from Yasser Arafat's death, it will require everyone involved in the region to cut through that knot. ■

THE PARADOXICAL PALESTINIAN

Yasser Arafat died as he had lived—a paradox. Was he a hero? Yes—but only to a small constituency, the Palestinians. Was he a terrorist? Certainly in the early years and arguably again toward the end. A governor? No. He performed miserably as a hands-on leader in the West Bank. A peacemaker? No. He refused to make the compromises that peace demands. A freedom fighter? Yes. He articulated the cause of Palestinian independence, organized and fought for it and, despite sometimes deplorable means—including the attack on Israeli athletes at the 1972 Munich Olympics—won legitimacy for his people's demand for an independent homeland.

AGUSTO MENESES

■ EARLY YEARS Born in Cairo in 1929, Arafat grew up in Jerusalem. In 1948 he waged guerrilla warfare against the new state of Israel. He studied engineering in Cairo in the 1950s and supported Palestinian causes. In 1969 he was named chairman of the Palestine Liberation Organization (P.L.O.), then based in Jordan, above, where his HQ was a bunker in a cave

DIRCK HALSTEAD—TIME LIFE—GETTY IMAGES

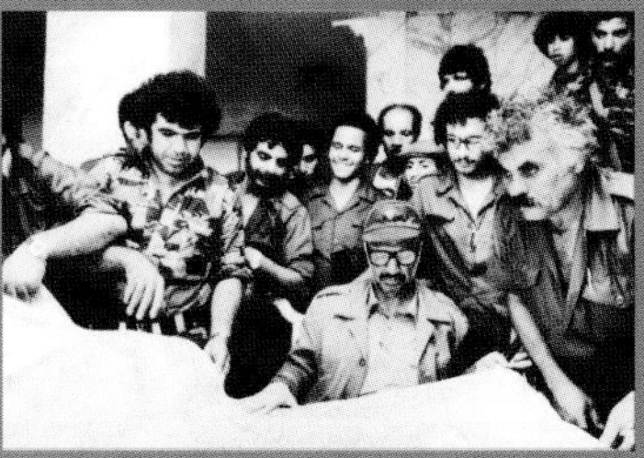

■ EXILE Jordan expelled the P.L.O. in 1970 and Arafat moved operations to Lebanon, where he directed several terrorist acts, including the murder of Israeli athletes at the 1972 Olympics. When Israel invaded Lebanon in 1982, left, Arafat fled to Tunis

■ PROGRESS In 1988 Palestinians in the West Bank and Gaza Strip began a revolt, the *intifadeh*, against Israel. In 1993, after secret talks, Arafat signed the Oslo accord. He joined Bill Clinton and Israeli P.M. Yitzhak Rabin at the White House in 1993, right

CYNTHIA JOHNSON—TIME LIFE—GETTY IMAGES

DAVID GUTTENFELDER—AP/WIDE WORLD

■ FAILURE Arafat returned to Gaza in 1994 and became president of the Palestinian Authority in 1996. After a failed summit at Camp David in 2000, a second *intifadeh* began. Confined to Ramallah for two years, he was buried there in November, left

НТВ

HOSTAGES: Militants in the gym sent this video image to Russian TV stations on the first day of the siege to publicize their deed

SCHOOL UNDER SIEGE

Terrorists hold more than 1,200 students and teachers hostage in a Russian school for three days, and their ordeal electrifies the world

SOMETIMES IT IS THE GIFT OF CHILDREN TO KEEP THEIR parents strong. Elena Kasumova felt her hope dying as she huddled with her son Timur, 9, in the sweltering gymnasium of School No. 1. It was Friday morning, and the hostage nightmare in Beslan, a small town in the Russian republic of North Ossetia, some 1,000 miles south of Moscow, was in its third day. Kasumova, a 37-year-old teacher at the school, and Timur were among the nearly 1,200 hostages packed into the gym. Most of the children had long since stripped down to their underwear; some fainted from thirst, while others drank their own urine. The place was festooned with bombs: explosives hung down from the beams and the basketball hoops, some so low that the taller hostages banged their heads on them as they went to the toilet.

That made the guerrillas very nervous. From the bombs came tangled wires snaking through the tight rows of children, connected to two spring-loaded detonator pedals held down by the feet of two guerrillas. If either man moved, the hostages were told, the room would explode. "Bear this in mind," one of the guerrillas said, referring to the Russian commandos outside. "They are planning a storm. We will defend you to the last bullet, then blow ourselves up. We have nothing to lose. We came here to die."

Kasumova could see that the guerrillas were tense and exhausted. Since the siege had started, she had counted 16 of them—mostly bearded men in their 20s and most of them Chechen, the rest Ingush and Ossetian—though she suspected other fighters were stationed elsewhere in the school compound. What little mercy they had shown earlier in the siege was now gone. They fired their assault rifles to keep the Russian troops at bay. They bellowed orders at the hostages, refused pleas for water and threatened to kill if the hostages didn't keep silent.

At one point, Kasumova looked down and realized that she was still clutching the program from the celebration of the first day of school, when the nightmare began. But when she felt her hope running out, her little boy rescued her. Timur massaged her feet and kissed her, and he told her stories about all the water and juice they would drink when it was finally over. "He was so good to me," Kasumova says. Like the other children of Beslan, Timur became a soldier that day.

The explosion came at just after 1 p.m. One of those dangling bombs had apparently detonated. "A wave of burning hot air hit me and knocked me down," Kasumova says. "I saw two severed legs lying next to me." The gym was full of smoke and screams, but she saw children climbing out of a window. She and Timur clambered through the opening and ran. "The guerrillas opened fire on us, and I saw one child go down, and then another," she says.

Russian special forces returned the rebel fire, joined by armed locals who, a general said, "got in the way." Russian soldiers grabbed Kasumova and Timur and hustled them off to safety. Behind them, there were more explosions, the roof of the gymnasium collapsed, and then there was pandemonium. Half-naked children, some burned or wounded, streamed out of the school as bullets whizzed around them and helicopters clattered overhead.

The security cordon around the buildings broke down, with locals whisking the injured to safety in their arms, in scruffy little Soviet-era Zhiguli cars and in at least one Mercedes well before ambulances showed up. Police said some terrorists escaped wearing sports gear; gunfire spread to other parts of the city as the afternoon drew on, suggesting a manhunt. In the mayhem, one shocked and disheveled young woman who made it to safety moaned, "They are killing us all!"

By the time it was over, at least 350 lay dead—more than half of them children—and some 700 were wounded. Twenty-six terrorists were also dead. The carnage was the most ghastly episode in a terror spree that began in July 2004, leading up to a presidential election in Chechnya that was widely criticized as rigged by Moscow. The vote was made necessary when the Kremlin's hand-picked incumbent, Akhmad Kadyrov, was blown up in May at a rally in Grozny's Dynamo Stadium.

SYSOEV GRIGORY—PHOTAS AGENCY—GETTY IMAGES

MOURNING: Relatives weep on the day after the siege ended

S. DAL—REUTERS—LANDOV

FREE! A volunteer carries an injured boy to safety as the siege is lifted

Within one week in July, two bus stops were bombed in the city of Voronezh, 300 miles south of Moscow, killing three. On Aug. 24, an explosion ripped through a Moscow bus stop, injuring four. Three hours later, two female suicide bombers detonated explosives on two passenger planes they had boarded at Moscow's most modern airport, downing the planes and killing 90. On Aug. 31, a woman blew herself up outside a busy Moscow metro station, killing eight others.

But all that was mere prelude to the school siege, which Russians would come to call their 9/11. In the wake of the event, President Vladimir Putin went on television and pledged to strengthen his security services and mobilize the nation against the "total, cruel, full-scale war" being waged on Russia by "international terrorism." Paraphrasing Joseph Stalin, he said, "We have shown weakness. The weak ones get beaten."

Putin blamed the crisis on the "direct intervention of international terrorism." Chechen rebel leader Shamil Basayev, who claimed "credit" for Beslan, said there were two Arabs among the group of 33 hostage-takers. The Chechen conflict doesn't fit easily into the struggle many Americans call the "war on terror." Most Chechens do not share al-Qaeda's religious fundamentalism, and they don't seek a return of the caliphate. What they want is their own state, something Putin has vowed never to give them. Still, Chechen rebels and foreign Islamic terrorists do have links that have grown stronger as the war for independence has dragged on. If Russia is to be spared a second 9/11, Putin must address the problem of Chechnya. ■

TERRORISM'S FRONT LINES

Afghans go to the polls, but deadly strikes in Spain and Egypt and the re-emergence of Osama bin Laden remind the world that terrorism is everyone's problem

AFGHANISTAN

Despite two postponements, numerous allegations of ballot fraud and a rash of bombings intended to scare voters away from the polls, 8 million Afghans stepped forward in October and democratically elected a leader for the first time in the nation's history. Adding to the sense of a miracle in the making was the fact that more than 3 million of those votes were cast by women, who, under the Taliban regime, could not hold jobs, attend school or appear in public without a male relative. By the time of winner Hamid Karzai's December swearing-in—which was attended by U.S. Vice President Dick Cheney and Secretary of Defense Donald Rumsfeld—Afghans had adopted a progressive constitution, welcomed home more than 3 million refugees driven abroad by decades of nonstop war, and coaxed a long-moribund economy into showing signs of life. Yet Afghanistan still has a long way to go: the Taliban remain dangerous, warlords control vast stretches of the country, and the opium trade is thriving. It may be some time before this former flash point can be declared a win in the war on terrorism.

AL-QAEDA

AL-JAZEERA

Four days before the U.S. presidential election, Osama bin Laden surfaced on videotape for the first time in more than a year. It was not quite the October surprise that some Democrats had feared—bin Laden doing a perp walk in an orange jumpsuit—but it rattled U.S. voters just the same. On the tape, the al-Qaeda leader admitted for the first time that he was the architect of the 9/11 attacks and warned Americans that "there are still reasons to repeat what happened." Dressed in traditional white robes, a turban and a golden cloak, bin Laden also decried the U.S. campaign in Iraq and heaped criticism, both personal and political, on President Bush. The tape was a grim reminder that bin Laden remained at large, three years after 9/11.

EMILIO MORENATTI—AP/WIDE WORLD

YONATHAN WEITZMAN—WORLD PICTURE NEWS

EGYPT

Taba's Hilton Hotel is located just yards from Egypt's border with Israel on the Sinai peninsula. On Oct. 7, the last day of the Jewish holiday of Sukkot, it was packed with vacationing Israelis. That evening a car bomb exploded in front of the 10-story building, collapsing its front. Simultaneously, two more bombs rocked other Sinai tourist sites. The attacks killed 34 people—including Israelis, Egyptians, Italians and Russians—and wounded more than 100. Although suspicion fell initially on al-Qaeda, Egyptian security officials now believe the bombings were the work of Palestinian militants.

PABLO TORRES GUERRERO—EL PAIS—REUTERS

SPAIN

On March 11, three days before Spain's general election, 10 bombs detonated in and around Madrid train stations, killing more than 200 people. The Spanish government—too quick to blame Basque separatists for the attack—was toppled when it became clear that al-Qaeda was deeply involved. In a victory for terrorists, new Prime Minister José Luis Rodríguez Zapatero quickly withdrew Spanish soldiers from Iraq.

BLASTOFF: Pakistan tests a Ghauri missile, which can carry nuclear warheads 900 miles

NUCLEAR DREAMS

South Korea and Pakistan can't be trusted, but Libya can. Welcome to the puzzles and paradoxes of proliferation

HOPES FOR LIMITING THE SPREAD OF NUCLEAR weapons around the world were stymied in 2004 by unexpected letdowns from two U.S. allies; advanced by pleasant surprises from two erstwhile adversaries; and clouded by predictably bizarre behavior from the leader of a rogue nation that rejoices in its own isolation.

Pakistan, an ally in U.S. efforts to contain Islamist terrorism in Asia, revealed in January that one of its leading atomic scientists, Abdul Qadeer Khan, had been trafficking in nuclear secrets for years—apparently peddling information to Iran, Iraq, Libya and North Korea. Khan, who resides in an opulent Islamabad mansion, is revered as a national hero and the "father of the Islamic bomb." But multiple investigations by Pakistani and American authorities point to a second, less heralded role for Khan: as one of the godfathers of nuclear proliferation, a dangerous salesman who helped bring the Bomb within closer reach of other powers eager to join the world's exclusive nuclear club.

Among the questions about Khan's activities that remain unanswered (and that no one involved seems eager to address) is whether Khan and his colleagues operated on their own or at the behest of the Pakistani government. President Pervez Musharraf, pressed by Washington, sacked Khan as head of nuclear-weapons development in early 2001. The President insisted that his four-year-old government has never dabbled in nuclear trade, whatever past regimes might have done.

Ironically, the first smoking-gun evidence that Khan's network was selling nuclear expertise came as part of a welcome surprise from a longtime U.S. foe in the Middle East. In the closing days of 2003, Libya's mercurial dictator, Muammar Gaddafi, abruptly renounced his nuclear ambitions and exposed Khan's ties to Libya's abortive nuclear program in the process.

In stark contrast, a close U.S. friend, South Korea, startled Washington (and the world) in September when Seoul reluctantly admitted that its scientists had been caught enriching uranium and refining plutonium—the very activities that a coalition of six nations has been trying to get North Korea to halt. South Korea forswore its nuclear weapons program in 1975 and has since been under an inspection regime monitored by the Vienna-based International Atomic Energy Agency (IAEA). In February 2004 the government signed a protocol giving the IAEA the right to more information and to inspect sites anywhere in the country. Seoul was given six months to make a full declaration of its nuclear research, after which the IAEA would begin asking uncomfortable questions. Although South Korean researchers do not appear to have produced enough enriched uranium to build a weapon, the revelation couldn't have come at a more awkward time; it raised fears that countries like North Korea and Iran could object that they had been unfairly vilified for developing their own nuclear programs.

Later that month, a similar scare emerged from

RADIANT: Iranian M.P.s inspect the nuclear plant at Isfahan

EPA—LANDOV

north of the DMZ. For all the bragging it has done about its nuclear program, North Korea has never, to anyone's knowledge, tested a nuclear bomb. (It is thought to have at least two, if not more, nuclear devices.) So the world was alarmed on Sept. 9, when satellite photos showed what looked like an explosion and a mushroom-shaped cloud over a remote area in the northern part of the country. Pyongyang denied it had exploded a nuclear device and even escorted a group of foreign ambassadors to the area, where they saw thousands of workers toiling mostly by hand to build a dam. Although former residents of the area say it doesn't have a river worth a dam, the region is known to house a missile base and a munitions plant.

Western intelligence analysts eventually discounted the possibility of a nuclear explosion but also argued that an accidental explosion of rocket propellant (possibly from a missile launch gone awry) could have caused the mushroom cloud. Another possibility: Pyongyang blew up something to keep the world guessing about its nuclear intentions, a tactic the regime has used in the past.

As autumn progressed, the focus of proliferation concerns shifted to Iran. In late September, just days after the IAEA adopted a resolution demanding that Iran suspend all uranium-enrichment activities, a defiant Tehran announced that it had begun converting some 37 tons of uranium oxide (yellowcake) into UF6 gas—the feed material for enriched uranium. President Mohammed Khatami even hinted that if its hand were forced, Iran might withdraw from the Nuclear Nonproliferation Treaty. Meanwhile, Israel agreed to buy 500 so-called bunker-buster bombs from the U.S., which Israeli security sources said could be used against an underground nuclear facility. In response, Tehran fulminated it would react "most severely" to any Israeli strikes. By mid-November, however, tensions subsided with an announcement by France, Britain and Germany that they had reached a formal understanding with Iran, which would guarantee economic and technological aid to Iran in exchange for the freezing of its uranium enrichment and reprocessing programs. Tehran, however, has made promises before—and broken them.

Good news seldom offers more than a temporary respite from concerns about nuclear material falling into hostile hands. Less than a week after the progress in Iran was announced, senior U.S. security officials revealed to TIME that a key al-Qaeda operative captured in Pakistan had offered an alarming account of the group's potential plans to target the U.S. with weapons of mass destruction. Sharif al-Masri, an Egyptian who was captured in late August near Pakistan's border with Iran and Afghanistan, has told his interrogators of al-Qaeda's interest in smuggling nuclear materials to Mexico; operatives could then carry the matter into the U.S. and put it to disastrous use.

Small wonder that George W. Bush and John Kerry, who agreed on few issues in the 2004 election, found common ground in the first debate, both stating that the greatest threat in today's world is the spread of nuclear know-how. Proliferation makes for strange bedfellows. ■

KIM JONG IL: Does North Korea's boss, center, have something to hide?

KOREA NEWS AGENCY—AP/WIDE WORLD

■ PAKISTAN'S NUCLEAR PEDDLER

Some 30 years ago, Pakistani scientist Abdul Qadeer Khan allegedly stole blueprints for enriching uranium from the top-secret Dutch lab where he worked. For decades, his team labored to produce enough of the fuel to make A-bombs. In 1998, he watched proudly as Pakistan detonated its first nuclear device; he became a national hero.

Khan on TV

MIAN KHURSHEED—REUTERS

In 2001 Khan was sacked by Pakistani President Pervez Musharraf at U.S. urging. By then Khan had amassed a personal fortune that funded a lavish lifestyle. Many, including U.S. intelligence analysts, believe he acquired those riches peddling his nuclear expertise; in 2004 some of those charges were proved. Yet both U.S. and Pakistani officials remain leery of squeezing Khan, who is a Pakistani icon, too tightly. Arresting him could trigger dangerous protest among Islamist extremists and senior military officers who distrust Musharraf's White House connection. Instead, he is kept comfortable and watched closely, while officials in Washington hope that his nuclear giveaway is history.

DARK DAYS IN DARFUR

Genocide stalks Sudan, where 50,000 are dead, thousands more will die, and more than 1 million people have lost their homes

THE WORLD WATCHED AT A DISTANCE, DITHERING, while calamity ravaged Sudan. For two decades, a civil war has raged in the nation's south, claiming more than 2 million lives. But in 2004 new heartache was heaped onto the people of Africa's largest country, as the farming region of Darfur was afflicted by starvation, disease, widespread violence and a refugee problem that ranks among the world's worst.

These afflictions were man-made and deliberate. Their roots lie in the long-standing conflict between Sudan's two major racial groups, black Africans and ethnic Arabs. Both are Muslim, but Sudan's government is dominated by Arabs, whereas the country's black population has long felt the sting of discrimination. The tension finally boiled over in a February 2003 uprising in which blacks in Darfur (and other areas of western Sudan) rebelled against the government in Khartoum.

Since then, government-sponsored Arab militiamen known as Janjaweed (roughly: "evil horsemen") have conducted a campaign to drive Darfur's black African civilians from the land. It has been a grim success: more than 1.4 million Sudanese blacks have been routed from their homes, while another 160,000 have fled into neighboring Chad. Along the way, more than 70,000 people have died, and tens of thousands more have been tortured, mutilated and starved. Some 10,000 Darfurian women have been raped—many gang-raped. The sexual assaults have a double intent: to make what the Janjaweed say will be lighter-skinned babies and to ensure that the non-Arabs will be too degraded to return to their homes. Nearly everyone left alive in Darfur is now at risk of the diseases that prey on refugee populations, including cholera and dysentery.

Declaring that Darfur is the worst humanitarian disaster in the world today, the United Nations threatened Khartoum with an end-of-August deadline to halt the Janjaweed. But the deadline was toothless, and the international body took no action when it passed.

Testifying before the U.S. Congress in September, Secretary of State Colin Powell declared, "We concluded—I concluded—that genocide has been committed in Darfur, and that the government of Sudan and the Janjaweed bear responsibility, and that genocide may still be occurring." But professions of outrage have done nothing to stop the killing. Immediately after labeling the Janjaweed's slaughter genocide, Powell told lawmakers, "No new action is dictated by this determination"—despite the fact that the international Genocide Convention, signed by the U.S. and 134 other countries, obligates signatories to "prevent and to punish" genocide where it is occurring.

Already stretched thin in Afghanistan and Iraq and wary of intervening in another Muslim state, the Bush Administration ruled out sending troops to Sudan. Instead, it threw its support behind a proposal to deploy several thousand African observers to the region, not to halt the violence but to monitor it.

By early November, peace talks in Nigeria between Darfur's rebels and the Sudanese government had made some progress: the government had agreed to stop the military overflights of the Darfur region, which had terrorized the population, and both sides said they would allow international aid workers into the refugee camps. Apart from that, however, neither side promised it would halt the fighting and no one could foresee an end to Darfur's misery. ■

ADRIFT: As refugees from Sudan stream into neighboring Chad, two women are overtaken by a desert sandstorm

World Notes

PROFILE

Gaddafi's Extreme Makeover

Yes, the smiling chap below is Libyan strongman Muammar Gaddafi, former sponsor of terrorists, purchaser of nuclear secrets and bitter nemesis of President Ronald Reagan, who dispatched U.S. warplanes to bomb his compound in Tripoli in 1986. In the past two years Gaddafi has changed his tune. He began compensating the victims of Pan Am Flight 103, which blew apart over Scotland in 1988, while denying state responsibility for the deed. Late in 2003, Gaddafi said he would back off from his secret efforts to build unconventional weapons (they

THIERRY CHARLIER—AP/WIDE WORLD

GADDAFI: Is the desperado's reform real?

turned out to be surprisingly far advanced). At the same time, Gaddafi fingered Pakistani scientist Abdul Qadeer Khan as a merchant of nuclear secrets.

Gaddafi's initiatives were hailed by his erstwhile foes. British Prime Minister Tony Blair traveled to Libya and met with Gaddafi in March, a month later the Libyan addressed a meeting of the European Union, and the U.S. restored diplomatic relations with Libya in June. But Gaddafi's charm offensive took a hit that same month, when charges surfaced that Libya had plotted to kill Saudi Arabia's Crown Prince Abdullah in 2003. Gaddafi opposed the U.S. war in Iraq but is eagerly courting American energy executives, who see great potential in his oil-rich land.

GURINDER OSAN—AP/WIDE WORLD

INDIA: Parents mourn a child drowned by a tidal wave

Disaster Swamps Asia

Tsunamis—giant walls of water bred by the fourth-largest earthquake in a century—crashed onto shoreliness across broad swaths of Southeast Asia on Dec. 26, killing more than 120,000 people in one of history's greatest natural disasters. The earthquake, which registered 9.0 on the Richter scale, struck six miles deep at the junction of two tectonic plates off the island of Sumatra, sending giant waves hurtling across the region. The death count soared in the days following the quake and was expected to go higher, while millions were left homeless. The quake struck exactly one year to the day after a giant tremor killed 31,000 in the city of Bam in Iran.

Sharon's Surprise Plan

They were words few Israelis ever expected to hear from Ariel

MENAHEM KAHANA—POOL—AP/WIDE WORLD

SHARON: A stunning about-face

Sharon: that he could imagine a time when "there will be no Jews in Gaza." Israel's hard-line Prime Minister made the statement in February 2004, broaching the idea of evacuating all 7,500 residents from the 17 Israeli settlements in the Gaza Strip. After months of turmoil, in October Sharon won the Knesset's approval for the plan, which was opposed by many Israelis. The pullouts in Gaza were set to begin in June 2005.

Aristide Flees Haiti

Early on the morning of Feb. 29, President Jean-Bertrand Aristide boarded a plane and left Haiti, after

PABLO ANELI—AP/WIDE WORLD

HIS DAY: Rebel chief Guy Philippe

a week of steadily increasing signals from Washington that he must go. Aristide, 50, the former priest once revered as the hope of Haiti's poor but now widely reviled as a corrupt and incompetent tyrant, blamed the U.S. for his overthrow. After he fled, rebel leader Guy Philippe entered Port-au-Prince after it was looted one last time by Aristide's heavily armed thugs, the *chimères* (Creole for "mythical monsters").

IVAN SEKRETAREV—AP/WIDE WORLD

IMAGE

Revolt in Ukraine

Ukraine reeled after Prime Minister Viktor Yanukovych, backed by outgoing President Leonid Kuchma and Vladimir Putin's Kremlin, was named winner of a Nov. 21 runoff election over reformer Viktor Yushchenko. Protesters called the vote corrupt and blocked central Kiev for days; on Dec. 3 Ukraine's high court called for a new vote on Dec. 26. Yushchenko, who had been poisoned by dioxin during the first campaign, easily won the second election.

JANE MINGAY—AP/WIDE WORLD

BLAIR: The Teflon Prime Minister?

The Nine Lives of Tony Blair

Talk about an escape artist: after Britain's Prime Minister, Tony Blair, survived two scares that could have brought down his government in a single week early in 2004, a Tory opponent called him "a mixture of Harry Houdini and a greased piglet ... barely human in his elusiveness." On Jan. 27, Blair, 51, squeezed through a five-vote victory (despite his party's 161-vote majority in the House of Commons) to clear a path for a bill to charge college students more to attend university. The very next day, Blair and the rest of his government were cleared in a government inquiry into the death of weapons-expert David Kelly, who killed himself in 2003 after being named as a source for a BBC report that Blair's Labour government had "sexed up" the case for war against Iraq.

Blair clung to his post despite polls showing his countrymen widely disapproved of his support for the war. When the P.M. visited Washington after the November election, a journalist asked President George W. Bush if he regarded Blair as his "poodle." Blair's joking counsel to his ally: "Don't answer yes to that question."

A NEW LEADER IN INDIA, AND NEW HOPE IN KASHMIR

ANJUM NAVEED—AP/WIDE WORLD

MUSHARRAF: Time to talk peace?

AJIT KUMAT—AP/WIDE WORLD

SINGH: A new direction for India

Pakistan and India, whose quarrel over the disputed territory of Kashmir has threatened to start a nuclear war, turned down the heat in 2004. Indians were stunned after the Congress Party won a May election, when its leader Sonia Gandhi handed power to Manmohan Singh, 71, the first Sikh to lead India. Continuing a thaw that began in 2003, Sikh said he would pursue peace in Kashmir; in September he met with Pakistan's President Pervez Musharraf in New York City amid hopes for a lasting peace deal.

Business

NASDAQ

Wall Street Ogles Google's Moguls

Where are the snow jobs of yesteryear? Those feeling a twinge of nostalgia for the heady days of the Internet bubble—when snotty twenty-somethings became instant millionaires by launching initial public offerings for businesses that often proved to be little more than digital smoke and mirrors—got the fix they needed in August. That's when Larry Page, 31, co-founder of Google, the dominant search engine on the World Wide Web, signed his name for posterity as he and partner Sergey Brin, 31, (not pictured here) took their company public on the NASDAQ market. The big difference between this offering and the clunkers of the '90s: Google isn't vaporware. Its site registers some 200 million hits a day, making it a magnet for advertisers. Investors made very rich men of Page and Brin, who started the site in 1998 in their Stanford University dorm room. By November, Google shares, which debuted at $85 apiece, were trading for $195. *Ca-ching!*

NASDAQ VIA GETTY IMAGES

CONNECTED: College student Amanda Smith surfs the Web on the banks of the Spokane River

CHRISTOPHER ANDERSON

NO STRINGS ATTACHED

Spokane, Washington, is one of the first cities in America to offer free wireless access, turning its downtown into a wi-fi hot spot

SPOKANE, WASH., IS ONE OF THOSE SLEEPY CITIES that's bursting with small-town pride—its residents will be glad to inform you, for example, that it's the smallest city ever to be host of a World's Fair—but there's a lot more going on here than meets the eye. Spokane is on the frontier of urban wireless technology, a live-in laboratory where city-employed nerds are crash-testing the wireless technotopia of the future. All of downtown Spokane is a massive wi-fi hot spot, a whole neighborhood enveloped in an invisible field of high-volume Internet access that covers 100 city blocks. Just as some coffeehouses offer wireless Internet access, downtown Spokane is now a wireless zone for Internet surfers.

Spokane is by no means the only project of its kind. It's easy to imagine that by the end of the decade most U.S. cities will exist beneath an invisible dome of wi-fi: "city clouds," in the jargon of the industry. Cook County, Ill., is planning a massive 940-sq.-mi. cloud that would light up all of Chicago. Philadelphia announced a humongous hot zone of its own in September 2004. Los Angeles and New York City are soliciting bids from wireless contractors. Wi-fi is just too cheap and too useful not to have.

Wireless technology is taking off in the U.S. As of mid-2004, there were some 21,000 wi-fi hot spots, both station-

CHRISTOPHER ANDERSON

REAL ESTATE AGENT: Stopping by a mural in downtown Spokane, Doug Hurd signs on to the HotZone to show the latest listings to customers who are also online

ary and mobile around the nation. That figure is projected to quadruple in the next three years, even as the size of many hot spots may sharply expand. There are now some 500,000 users of hot spots in the U.S.; that number is expected to reach more than 5 million by 2007.

How did Spokane get out in front of the pack? Vivato, the high-tech start-up that supplies the technology to light up downtown Spokane, began with a Hewlett-Packard engineer named Skip Crilly, who lived in the hills outside Spokane and couldn't get anybody to run a high-speed line to his house. Like any good engineer, he thought outside the box: maybe he could get the speed without the wiring. The standard wireless Internet technology, wi-fi, was cheap and fast, but it worked only at a range of about 300 ft. What if he could boost that range?

In 1999, Crilly, working with another HP engineer named Bob Conley, figured out a way to run a regular wi-fi signal through a phased-array antenna, a powerful piece of hardware that's used mostly by the military. Suddenly, they had a wi-fi hot spot a couple of miles wide. The world had never seen that before. If a regular wi-fi transmitter was a candle, this thing was a baseball-stadium spotlight. They called it, for some geeky reason or another, Little Joe.

All they had to do was figure out what to do with it. Hewlett-Packard wasn't interested in the project, so Crilly and Conley went out and started their own company. They raised some $65 million in venture capital, most of which they burned through pretty quickly. They sold a few hundred Little Joes, but not nearly as many as they needed to sell. Don Stalter came onboard as CEO in October 2003. A fast-talking veteran of the high-tech scene, he specializes in taking over companies that have lost their way. Stalter's job: to figure out what Little Joe was good for and who would pay good money for it.

The answer came from an unexpected direction. Every year Spokane plays host to Hoopfest, the world's largest three-on-three basketball tournament—another source of local pride. Hoopfest involves some 6,000 three-person teams from all over the world playing 25,000 games around the city. Scoring and scheduling are a nightmare of confused people scurrying about, carrying little slips of paper with numbers on them—exactly the kind of problem technology is supposed to eliminate. So somebody had the bright idea of sticking one of Vivato's prototype wi-fi transmitters on top of Spokane city hall and flooding a few blocks of downtown with wi-fi, thus allowing all the scoring to be done online.

The setup was about as ugly a piece of jerry-built hackery as you're ever likely to see—the workers ended up bolting one of Vivato's phased-array antennas onto an extra Hoopfest backboard—but it worked perfectly. Downtown Spokane was suddenly blessed with wireless goodness, and the tournament went off without a hitch, all those pesky little slips of paper having been replaced by sleek, wireless PDAs. And then everyone promptly forgot about the whole thing.

Well, almost everyone. It was the city's computer gnomes who first noticed that people were still using that Vivato antenna. Because the city never turned it off, it was still up there, pumping out free wireless Internet, and people were logging on. "All the time we're watching, there were always 10 to 15 people on the network," said Garvin Brakel, director of management information services for the city of Spokane. "It was unadvertised, unknown, but people were finding it regardless."

That started those computer gnomes thinking. City employees—police, fire fighters, meter cops and others—tend to roam around a lot. They need information, but they can't be bogged down with wires and cables. Maybe a huge zone of wireless Internet access could be part of the city's infrastructure ... Meanwhile, a local commercial ISP called 180 Networks had been studying ways that urban wi-fi could attract more people to Spokane's downtown area, which was in need of a little revitalizing. As Starbucks has learned, people tend to hang out more if there's free Internet access to be had. They check their e-mail. They linger. And while they're lingering, they spend mon-

CHRISTOPHER ANDERSON

POLICE OFFICER: After a traffic stop involving a suspicious driver, Elise Robertson downloads mug shots to the wireless onboard computer in her squad car. The guts of the PC are in her glove compartment; the touch-screen monitor is close at hand

ey. Light bulbs lit up: soon, city geeks, the Vivato geeks, the 180 Networks geeks and a local business group called the Downtown Spokane Partnership got together and created the Spokane HotZone.

But it's not just the Starbucks crowd that's benefiting from the HotZone. Police officers use it to run suspects' plates and download arrest warrants, criminal records and affidavits to their squad car. Fire fighters can download the floor plans of burning buildings while they're on the way to the scene. Soon, a traffic warden who writes you a ticket in Spokane will also be able to run your plates to see whether your car is properly registered. And when your time runs out, the fancy wi-fi-enabled parking meters will be smart enough to page a meter cop, so you will get all the parking tickets you deserve. Instant information is a two-edged sword: it can empower you, but it can also invade your privacy. A balance will have to be achieved.

We tend to think of data as a liquid; we talk about how it flows through conduits—wires and cables—or gathers in pools in hard drives. But wi-fi converts data into a vapor that seeps into places it has never been before. Farewell, sleepy old Spokane; hello, hazy new HotZone! ■

Invisible Link

Whether you two are watching TV or listening to U2 on your music system, wires aren't required

SONY

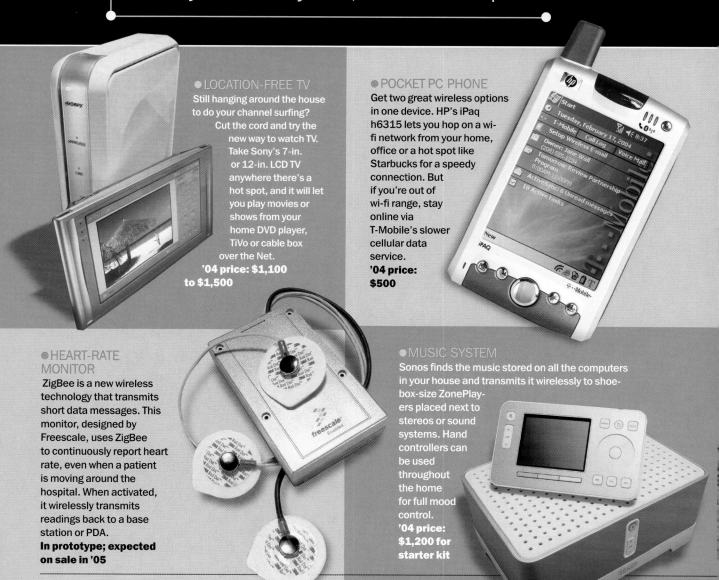

LOCATION-FREE TV

Still hanging around the house to do your channel surfing? Cut the cord and try the new way to watch TV. Take Sony's 7-in. or 12-in. LCD TV anywhere there's a hot spot, and it will let you play movies or shows from your home DVD player, TiVo or cable box over the Net.

'04 price: $1,100 to $1,500

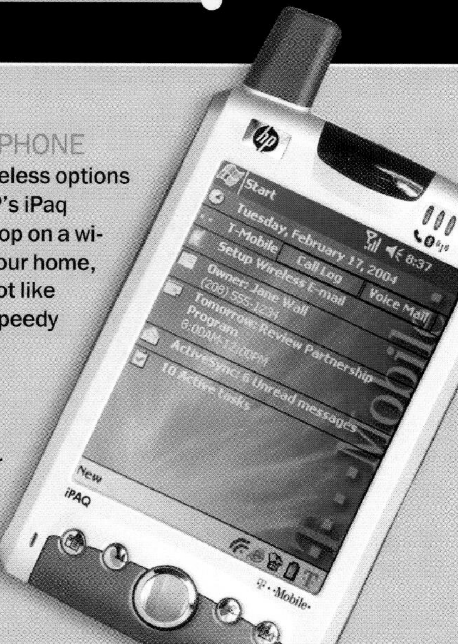
hp
Start
Tuesday, February 17, 2004
T-Mobile
Call Log
Voice Mail
Setup Wireless E-mail
Owner: Jane Wall
(208) 555-1234
Tomorrow: Review Partnership Program
8:00AM-12:00PM
ActiveSync: 6 Unread messages
10 Active tasks
New
iPAQ
T-Mobile

POCKET PC PHONE

Get two great wireless options in one device. HP's iPaq h6315 lets you hop on a wi-fi network from your home, office or a hot spot like Starbucks for a speedy connection. But if you're out of wi-fi range, stay online via T-Mobile's slower cellular data service.

'04 price: $500

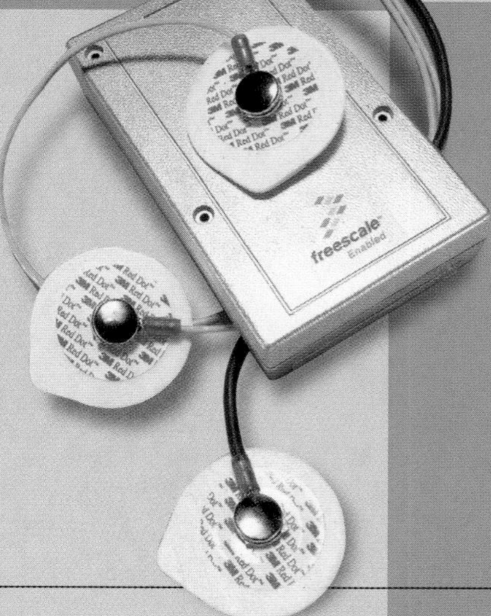
freescale
Enabled

HEART-RATE MONITOR

ZigBee is a new wireless technology that transmits short data messages. This monitor, designed by Freescale, uses ZigBee to continuously report heart rate, even when a patient is moving around the hospital. When activated, it wirelessly transmits readings back to a base station or PDA.

In prototype; expected on sale in '05

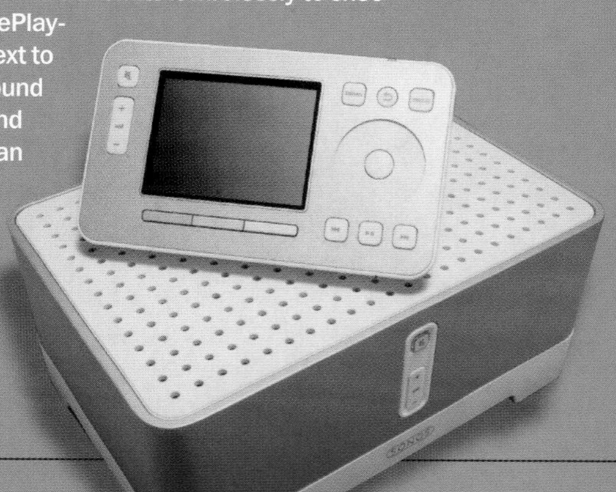

MUSIC SYSTEM

Sonos finds the music stored on all the computers in your house and transmits it wirelessly to shoebox-size ZonePlayers placed next to stereos or sound systems. Hand controllers can be used throughout the home for full mood control.

'04 price: $1,200 for starter kit

Levi's
LEVI STRAUSS & CO.

GONER: Levi Strauss & Co. closed its plant in San Antonio, Texas, in 2004. All Levi's products are now made overseas

ERIC GAY—AP/WIDE WORLD

Why U.S. Jobs Are Heading Abroad

Love it or hate it, outsourcing—unlike the jobs it destroys—is here to stay

OUTSOURCING IS A BLAND YET OMINOUS PIECE OF BUSIness jargon that touched a deep nerve in Americans in election year 2004. To some, the buzzword is shorthand for a harmful process that is moving every call center, programming job and Wall Street back-office task from the U.S. to India. To others it represents one of those healthy economic transformations that disrupts a few but serves the many, as when Henry Ford's cheap cars made buggy whips obsolete.

Outsourcing refers to the practice of turning over noncritical parts of a business to a specialist company. At first corporations outsourced ancillary functions, like running the cafeteria. Then they started moving the practice up to corporate-service functions: Why pay high-priced American workers to operate a call center if all you needed to run one was information technology (IT) and employees who spoke English?

Hello, India. Silicon Valley, which for years had been importing highly educated Indian code writers, realized it was a lot cheaper to export the work to the same folks back home in Bangalore. So did Wall Street, which employs a back-office army of accountants, analysts and bankers. Next on the list: medical technicians to read your X rays, accountants to prepare your taxes, even business journalists to interpret companies' financial statements.

Why is outsourcing exploding? For one thing, U.S. companies are gun-shy about committing to full-time workers and their attendant fringe benefits. Another factor: there's money to be made in facilitating outsourcing, as the two young U.S. and British entrepreneurs who founded OfficeTiger in 1998 discovered. They moved to India, set up a team of accountants and desktop-publishing experts and began persuading investment banks in New York City to outsource the preparation of financial documents and client presentations halfway around the world. Six years later, OfficeTiger plans to increase the number of its employees in India from 1,500 to 2,500.

One small consolation: at some point in the future, the trend that is pulling jobs out of America will catch up with India. Somewhere a lower-wage alternative will develop—say, in Central Asia or Thailand—and Indian politicians and workers will be clamoring about foreigners taking their jobs. It's not pretty wherever it happens, but in 2004, that was the way the business world turned. ■

START YOUR ENGINES

Chrysler races to the head of the Detroit pack with a bling-bling update of an endangered species, the sedan

BRIDGET A. BARRETT

CHRYSLER 300 Designer Ralph Gilles poses with his pride and joy in Detroit. Born in New York City to a Haitian immigrant family, Gilles, 34, was raised in Montreal and began drawing cars at age 8; 23 years later he was appointed one of Chrysler's seven studio chiefs. His car's muscular engine, oversized front grill and stylish interior detailing made it a runaway success; it is Chrysler's best-selling new model since the Jeep Grand Cherokee in the early 1990s

DAIMLERCHRYSLER

JEEP RESCUE With a folding front windshield and a retractable back window, a sliding glass sunroof in front and a folding canvas roof in back, Chrysler's versatile new concept Jeep can be stripped down to run almost totally "open"

How do you jump-start an ailing carmaker? Since German auto giant Daimler merged with Chrysler in 1998, the company has struggled as it tried to drive the venerable U.S. brand upmarket with a series of premium cars and a new emphasis on design. In 2004 Chrysler finally found the sweet spot in the market with a model that made an unexpected splash in an era of SUVs and pickup trucks: a sedan.

The new 300 series was the hottest iron out of Chrysler in a generation, and by July it had helped drive the brand's sales up 17% over 2003. Beefy, brash, styled like a gangstermobile, the 300 sedan resonated with urban hipsters and popped up in music videos and car-makeover magazines tricked out with big wheels, lowered suspensions and interiors with mini-bars and reclining seats. Owners include Shaq and Snoop Dogg: 'nuf said? The top-end 300C features Chrysler's powerful, popular 340-h.p. Hemi engine—a revival of the legendary V-8s that Chrysler built in the 1950s and '60s—the most car muscle you can buy in the $35,000 price range.

The Chrysler 300 is in the vanguard of a trend that Detroit sought to package as "the year of the sedan." Another contender: Ford's new 500 sedan. Its plain-vanilla style, aimed squarely at the middle-of-the-road buyer, didn't make as many heads swivel as Chrysler's 300s. But Ford scored a big hit with its madeover Mustangs; buyers loved their vintage look, and dealers sold them as fast as they could get them. Chevrolet also updated a classic, releasing a newly designed Corvette, only the fifth makeover in the classic American sports car's history. As Detroit rediscovers retro's appeal, look for more cars that look forward for performance and in the rear-view mirror for design. ■

FORD GT

FORD

FORD GT In a labor of love, top Ford designer J Mays virtually replicated Ford's great race car of the late 1960s. This 550-h.p., V-8-powered scream machine comes at a price that might shock thrifty Henry Ford: $142,000

DAIMLERCHRYSLER

DODGE SLINGSHOT This nifty two-seater concept car will be inexpensive and fuel-efficient; it's far from overpowered, with only a three-cylinder rear-mounted engine. But it certainly looks great

DAIMLERCHRYSLER

MERCEDES MCLAREN SLR Let's get straight to the specs: 0 to 60 m.p.h. in 3.8 seconds; revolutionary carbon-fiber body; 617-h.p. V-8 engine; gull-wing doors. Base price: $400,000

Business Notes

PROFILE

An Ungraceful Exit at Disney

Michael Eisner weathered a tough 2004; his name seldom appeared in print without the accompanying tag: "the embattled Walt Disney Co. chairman and CEO." At the annual shareholder meeting in March, Eisner was staggered by what seemed a career-ending smackdown: a 43% vote of no confidence. But the docile Disney board kept him on, lopping off his chairman title and tapping director George Mitchell to replace him in that role.

In September Eisner turned himself into a very lame duck, declaring he would leave the company but not until 2006. That ignited speculation as to his successor; critics have long bemoaned his failure to groom an heir. After the accidental death of colleague Frank Wells in 1994, Eisner feuded and split with animation boss Jeffrey Katzenberg, who left to join DreamWorks. Later that year Eisner hired Hollywood *Uber*-agent Michael Ovitz as his second-in-command, only to fire him 14 months later, sending him off with a golden handshake totaling $140 million.

In November Eisner testified in a Delaware case filed by Disney investors charging that he had overpaid his fired hand, Ovitz. Only then did Disney find a silver lining in a cloudy year—a surge in the company's fiscal fourth-quarter profits. Still, for Eisner—that's all, folks.

NICK UT—AP/WIDE WORLD

OUTGOING: One of these ducks is lame

UNITED

UNITED AIRLINES—AP/WIDE WORLD

UNITED: America's No. 2 carrier frantically cut costs in an attempt to stay aloft

Fewer Wings, More Prayers

The airline industry continues to encounter turbulence as the giant airlines of yesteryear fight to survive competition from newer, nimbler rivals like Southwest and JetBlue. Chicago-based United Airlines was in the worst spot: it has been operating in bankruptcy since late 2002, and in June federal officials refused its request for major loans. In October United trimmed its fleet of jets and its U.S. destinations. In November it said it would slash jobs and seek federal approval to terminate its pension plans.

A Crude Awakening

Consumers ached and Wall Street quaked as global oil prices rose sharply throughout 2004, with U.S. prices driven up 60% over 2003 by the highest demand in 25 years. The price spikes began in the spring, as costs soared to more than $2 a gallon. In November the U.S. Energy Department said heating oil bills could rise 28% over the winter.

Unleaded Plus
237 9/10
Performance Plus
2.59 9/10
High Performance
2.65 9/10
OPEN 24 HOURS

DAMIAN DOVARGANES—AP/WIDE WORLD

OUCH! Prices jumped at the pump

BIG

KEVORK DJANSEZIAN—AP/WIDE WORLD

BIG DEAL: A retail David buys Goliath

Kmart Swallows Sears

Topping off a remarkable comeback for a company that had sought bankruptcy protection as recently as 2002, retail giant Kmart Holding Corp. announced in November it would acquire one of the most historic names in American business, 118-year-old Sears, Roebuck & Co. The $11 billion deal was engineered by Kmart chairman Edward Lampert, who is also the single largest shareholder in Sears; the board of the new company, Sears Holdings Corp., will be dominated by Kmart executives. The new entity will be the nation's third largest retailer, after Wal-Mart and Home Depot.

DREAMWORKS

IMAGE

Big Fish to Fry

Surprised to see an animated-fish story on a Business page? Don't be: there's gold in them thar gills. When DreamWorks released *A Shark's Tale* in October, the film netted $49 million in its first weekend. The studio's spring release, *Shrek 2,* brought in a mind-boggling $873 million at the worldwide box office, topping rival Pixar's 2003 hit, *Finding Nemo,* as the top-grossing animated film of all time. DreamWorks' two big 2004 hits gave the company the leverage it needed to spin off its animation unit, headed by Disney refugee Jeffrey Katzenberg; it went public in November, valued at $4.1 billion.

PAUL SAKUMA—AP/WIDE WORLD

ELLISON: In search of PeopleSoft

Database Soap Opera

In a long-running takeover drama, software giant Oracle Computer Co. struggled through 2004 to acquire smaller competitor PeopleSoft. In September a federal judge shut down a Justice Department attempt to stop the takeover; a week later, PeopleSoft's board fired CEO Craig Conway. New boss David Duffield, the firm's returning founder, proved just as resistant to Oracle's brash chief, Larry Ellison. The two giants finally struck a deal on Dec. 13, with Oracle buying PeopleSoft at $26.50 per share—a sum of $10.3 billion.

SCANDAL SCORECARD, 2004 EDITION

The mills of the gods grind slowly, the adage goes, and justice has only begun to be visited upon some of the corporate malefactors whose misdeeds came to light in recent years. The one person below who occupied a jail cell in 2004—media star Martha Stewart—is a piker compared with the others; her conviction for lying to federal agents about a personal stock transaction is a far less serious infraction than the ones with which the other three are charged.

MICHAEL RIGAS Cable company Adelphia's first family went on trial; father John and brother Tim were convicted. Michael's case ended in a mistrial, but he may be tried again

MARTHA STEWART The Omnimedia CEO was convicted of lying to federal agents; she began serving a five-month sentence in a West Virginia penitentiary in October

BERNIE EBBERS The ex-CEO of Worldcom was indicted on March 2 for conspiring to commit securities fraud; former colleague Scott Sullivan will testify against him

KENNETH LAY The former chairman and CEO of energy giant Enron was indicted in July; he is charged with 11 counts of conspiracy, securities fraud and making false statements

CLOCKWISE FROM TOP LEFT: LOUIS LANZANO—AP/WIDE WORLD; BEBETO MATTHEWS—AP/WIDE WORLD; MICHAEL STRAVATO—AP/WIDE WORLD; MASAHIKO YAMAMOTO—AP/WIDE WORLD

Society

BRENDAN SMIALOWSKI—GETTY IMAGES

Honoring the First Americans

Maurice Cato prays to Mother Earth and Grandfather Sky on the National Mall in Washington as the dome of the U.S. Capitol looms in the distance. Cato, an Appalachian Cherokee from West Virginia, joined some 25,000 fellow Native Americans to celebrate the opening of the Smithsonian Institution's National Museum of the American Indian at a six-day festival on the Mall. With more than 600 tribes from around the hemisphere represented, the sounds of drums and chanting filled the air, while Navajo in moccasins mingled with Sioux in T shirts and jeans. One participant felt right at home under the Capitol dome: Senator Ben Nighthorse Campbell of Colorado went directly from the Mall to a Senate hearing, dressed in the full ceremonial robes of a chieftain of the Northern Cheyenne.

FACING THE SUNRISE

The nation's capital welcomes a beautiful new museum where Native Americans are invited to tell their version of their story

THE ENTRANCE OF THE SMITHSONIAN INSTITUTION'S new National Museum of the American Indian faces east, toward the rising sun, in the manner of many Indian dwellings. It also faces the nearby dome of the U.S. Capitol, headquarters of the Great White Fathers who repeatedly authorized the theft of Indian lands but who also provided about $120 million of the museum's $219 million price tag. (The remainder came from private funding, a third of it contributed by Indian tribes.) The grand new edifice is fully intended to spark a new appreciation for the cultures of America's first peoples. For the showplace's director, curators and staff are largely Native Americans, and its conception involved years of consultation with tribal groups all over the western hemisphere. The goal is to allow the the tribes to tell their story as they see it themselves, not as outsiders have preferred to tell it.

It is quite a setting in which to tell a tale. The flexes and curves of the museum's honey-colored limestone walls evoke wind-sheared Western mesas. In keeping with the themes of nature that are threaded all through the display areas, the building is landscaped with 150 species of trees and shrubs in a design guided by Donna House, a Navajo ethnobotanist. There's also a lily pond, plantings of corn, beans, squash and tobacco and massive Canadian boul-

SERENE: The 250,000-sq.-ft. museum and its landscaped grounds occupy four-plus acres on the National Mall. At top right are sculptures representing the Seneca Nation; below, Musqueam Elder Larry Grant blesses *The Beaver and the Mink*, a sculpture in red cedar by British Columbia artist Susan Point

PABLO MARTINEZ MONSIVAIS—AP/WIDE WORLD

ders. The building bears the stamp of Douglas Cardinal, architect of the lyrical swells of the Canadian Museum of Civilization near Ottawa. Cardinal, a Blackfoot, won the commission to design the building in 1993 but was dismissed five years later in a dispute over deadlines. Even so, the new museum is a superior addition to the National Mall.

When visitors step inside—and some 4 million a year are expected—they will be in for a surprise. This is not a museum devoted to artifacts from the past, although it has plenty of them. It's not much devoted to historical summary at all. Instead, the curators tell the story of the Indians in three thematic sections. "Our Universes" is about different forms of tribal knowledge, cosmologies and creation myths. "Our Peoples" deals with events that Native Americans see as crucial to their histories. "Our Lives" offers scenes and artwork from modern life, in which running shoes have replaced moccasins, in a world where some Indians live on reservations, some live in rain forests and quite a few live in Chicago. This tale, after all, begins some 10,000 years before Europeans arrived in the Americas. "There was a tremendous 'before,'" says museum director W. Richard West Jr., a Southern Cheyenne. "There will be a tremendous 'after.'" This welcome new museum is well positioned to capture the view in both directions. ■

THE TIES THAT DIVIDE

After a few U.S. cities begin conducting gay marriages, voters in 11 states overwhelmingly approve bans on the controversial unions

DECADES FROM NOW, 2004 MAY BE RECALLED AS A YEAR in which the cause of gay marriage advanced farther and faster—and was pushed back more decisively—than passionate advocates on either side of the issue had previously thought possible. The pendulum of events began to swing in the spring, when Massachusetts and Oregon became the first states to allow same-sex couples to wed, and a number of American cities played host to scores of gay marriages. But eight months later, in November, the extent of the opposition to gay marriage was fully registered, when voters in 11 states (including Oregon) passed ballot initiatives banning the practice. Moreover, President George W. Bush's strong support of a proposed amendment to the U.S. Constitution that would define marriage strictly as a union between and a man and a woman was widely viewed as one of the most significant factors in his re-election.

Appropriately enough, the long simmering issue of gays' right to marry vaulted to the top of the national agenda just before Valentine's Day, when San Francisco's Democratic mayor, Gavin Newsom, decided to act on a position he had taken during his 2003 campaign, in favor of same-sex marriages. Driven in part by his anger over Mr. Bush's 2004 State of the Union address, in which the President vowed to preserve the sanctity of traditional marriage, Newsom studied the 2003 Massachusetts Supreme Court decision that said gay couples could marry, the U.S. Supreme Court's 2003 decision that struck down Texas' anti-sodomy law, and the California constitution. That document's equal-protection clause gave him the rationale he needed: he decided that Proposition 22—the successful 2000 ballot measure in California that defined marriage as taking place only between a man and a woman—was discriminatory and therefore unconstitutional.

Knowing that gay activists were planning to come to San Francisco's city hall as part of an annual protest event called Freedom to Marry, Newsom ordered city officials to to begin granting marriage licenses to gay couples. During the long Presidents' Day weekend, Newsom even officiated at some weddings, including those of his chief of staff and his policy director. In all, some some 4,000 gay couples were wed. On the city hall steps, newlywed couples were saluted by a mariachi band and a tap-dance troupe, while cookies, cake and roses were passed around.

Some observers weren't celebrating; the San Francisco weddings were widely denounced. President Bush declared himself "troubled," while California Governor Arnold Schwarzenegger issued stern warnings that Newsom must heed the California law banning same-sex marriage. Still, within days, a few cities began to follow San Francisco's lead, with semilegal gay marriages spreading to places that had never been known as gay capitals. In New Mexico's Sandoval County, 67 gay couples were granted marriage licenses before the state attorney general ordered the county clerk to stop granting them. In tiny New Paltz, N.Y., Jason West, the Green Party mayor, presided over the weddings of two dozen gay couples.

In March, the pendulum began to swing back. The California Supreme Court granted the request of state attorney general Bill Lockyer to temporarily enjoin San Francisco from issuing marriage licenses to same-sex couples. The court heard arguments from both sides in May. On Aug. 12, the justices unanimously ruled that Newsom had overstepped his legal authority. In a separate, 5-to-2 vote, they

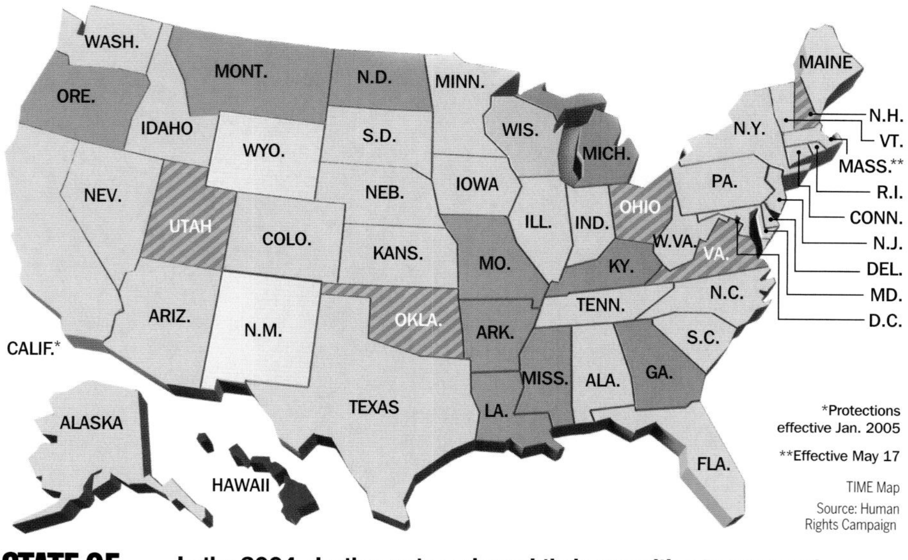
WASH.
ORE.
IDAHO
MONT.
N.D.
MINN.
WYO.
S.D.
WIS.
MICH.
N.Y.
MAINE
N.H.
VT.
MASS.**
R.I.
CONN.
N.J.
DEL.
MD.
D.C.
NEV.
UTAH
COLO.
NEB.
IOWA
ILL.
IND.
OHIO
PA.
W.VA.
VA.
KANS.
MO.
KY.
N.C.
TENN.
S.C.
ARIZ.
N.M.
OKLA.
ARK.
CALIF.*
MISS.
ALA.
GA.
TEXAS
LA.
ALASKA
HAWAII
FLA.

*Protections effective Jan. 2005

**Effective May 17

TIME Map

Source: Human Rights Campaign

STATE OF THE UNIONS **In the 2004 election, voters showed their opposition to gay marriage across the union, in some cases passing constitutional amendments to reinforce laws already banning the practice**

Thirteen states passed ballot referenda adopting constitutional amendments banning gay marriage

Five states adopted statutory bans against gay marriage and/or civil unions, including three that also passed constitutional amendments banning them: Ohio, Oklahoma and Utah

Hawaii voters amended its constitution to effectively ban gay marriage, authorizing the state legislature to define marriage as strictly heterosexual

BAN DIVORCE
ANNOY.COM
TRUST

RAMIN RAHIMIAN—SIPA PRESS

also declared that all the same-sex marriages that had been performed in San Francisco were void.

That slowed the movement's momentum, and in November Americans stopped it dead at the polls. Among the 11 states that banned gay marriage in the election, only three did so with less than 60% of the vote, and four Southern states did so with more than three-quarters of the vote. They joined six states that had previously passed constitutional measures banning same-sex marriage.

Yet the election returns also registered Americans' ambiguity on the subject. Voters in three states (Massachusetts, Vermont and Connecticut) came out decisively against proposed bans on gay marriage. In Oregon, the same voters who passed a ban on gay marriage also sent an openly gay judge to the state supreme court.

That was small consolation to proponents of gay marriage. While the amendments in Mississippi, Montana and Oregon dealt only with marriage, the measures in the other eight states also banned civil unions. This was a considerable victory for conservatives, for polls have consistently shown that a majority of the U.S. public, while harboring serious reservations about same-sex marriage, is in favor of civil unions. One who counts himself among their number, interestingly enough, is George W. Bush, who declared in the last 10 days before the election that he favored same-sex civil unions in states that chose to allow them. ■

SPLIT: Antimarriage protesters pray near San Francisco's city hall in February. Days later, below, marriage proponents rally in the Maryland statehouse in Annapolis

LET MY MOMS MARRY

MATT HOUSTON—AP/WIDE WORLD

THE BOTTOM LINE: Too many Americans are just too hefty

BATTLE OF THE BULGE

Americans are losing the struggle against obesity, and the results are disastrous. Now alarmed nutrition advocates are demanding action

HERE'S WEIGHTY NEWS: AMERICANS ARE JUST TOO FAT, and we suspect you're not surprised to hear it. If the endless parade of articles, TV specials and low-carb diet books were not proof enough, a quick look around the mall, the beach or the crowd at any baseball game will leave no room for doubt: our individual weight problems have become a national crisis.

Even so, the actual numbers are shocking. Fully two-thirds of U.S. adults are officially overweight, and about half of those have graduated to full-blown obesity. The rates for African Americans and Latinos are even higher. Among kids between 6 and 19 years old, 15%, or 1 in 6, are overweight. And things haven't been moving in a promising direction. Just two decades ago, the number of overweight adults was well under 50%, while the rate for kids was only one-third what it is today. From 1996 to 2001, 2 million teenagers and young adults joined the ranks of the clinically obese. People are clearly worried. A TIME/-ABC News poll released in May 2004 showed that 58% of Americans would like to lose weight, nearly twice the percentage who felt that way in 1951.

It wouldn't be such a big deal if the problem were simply aesthetic. But excess poundage takes a terrible toll on the human body, significantly increasing the risk of heart disease, high blood pressure, stroke, diabetes, infertility, gall-bladder disease, osteoarthritis and many forms of cancer. The total medical tab for illnesses related to obesity is $117 billion a year—and climbing—according to the Surgeon General, and the *Journal of the American Medical Association* reported in March 2004 that poor diet and physical inactivity could soon overtake tobacco as the leading cause of preventable death in the U.S.

So why is it happening? The obvious answer is that we eat too much high-calorie food and don't burn it off with enough exercise. If only we could change those habits, some people might argue, the problem would go away. But clearly it isn't that easy. Americans pour scores of billions of dollars every year into weight-loss products and health-club memberships and liposuction and gastric-bypass operations—100,000 of the last in 2003 alone. Yet the nation's collective waistline just keeps growing.

Some people believe the war on obesity can be won. For a handful of researchers and clinicians, the fight to control obesity has become a crusade to change the way Americans live. The nation's landscape, they argue, is littered with junk food masquerading as health food; candy and candylike cereals featuring kids' favorite cartoon characters and toylike packaging; schools that shamelessly hawk soft drinks and snack foods; and multimillion-dollar advertising campaigns to promote such unwholesome products as beneficial.

For decades, these scientists say, the country has seen obesity as a personal problem to be solved by each overweight individual waging a lonely war to trim pounds on the diet du jour. But the personal-responsibility approach has been a big, fat flop. And while biology and personal habits play an undeniable role in the obesity rate, there's much evidence that environmental factors help promote it. Nutrition experts are exploring new ways to counteract them and start slimming down our fat-friendly society.

It starts with the schools. Nothing infuriates the obesity warriors more than the nutrition offerings in public schools, which promote a diet of soft drinks and high-calorie lunches and snacks while ignoring the teaching of basic nutrition and the benefits of an active lifestyle.

Yet kids are not the only ones who can benefit from regular workouts. While most people blame themselves for their sloth, obesity experts say the environment plays a role here too. The goal is to re-engineer American life to promote healthful activity. Experts on obesity want more federal dollars spent to build paths for bikers and pedestrians. And they have even grander ideas for federal action. Obesity, they point out, is on the verge of supplanting smoking as the nation's No. 1 preventable cause of disease and death. So many of their suggestions for federal intervention come directly from the antismoking playbook. Among them: a tax on junk foods; a ban on fast-food and junk-food advertising to tots; a national nutrition campaign advising us all to eat less.

Could any of this happen? In the days when the Marlboro Man was riding high on the airwaves, no one thought you could ban cigarette ads. There's no reason to think an anti-obesity campaign uniting the efforts of U.S. schools, communities and federal and local governments can't succeed—as long as everyone involved acknowledges that the problem is real and that solving it will be a long haul. Marlboro's cowpoke rode into the sunset a long time ago; would you be sorry to see the Hamburglar join him? ■

DR. ATKINS' NEW DIET REVOLUTION
THE SOUTH BEACH DIET
PROTEIN POWER
THE SCHWARZBEIN PRINCIPLE
Fat Flush Plan
NEANDERTHIN

BILL KALIS

HOW LOW CARBS ADD UP TO HIGH PROFITS

How to measure America's ongoing obsession with low-carbohydrate diets? Try these numbers on for size: some 586 distinct new low-carb foods and beverages hit the grocery shelves in the first quarter of 2004, up from 633 in all of 2003 and 339 in 2002, bringing the total over just two years to 1,558 new entries. Low-carb-related sales from such consumables as Michelob Ultra beer and books like *Dr. Atkins' New Diet Revolution* are expected to hit $30 billion in 2004, according to *LowCarbiz,* a trade publication that owes its existence to burgeoning carbophobia.

OBESITY WARRIORS

Advocates of good nutrition are raising their voices to demand a concerted national effort to promote better food choices and a more active lifestyle for all Americans. The effort, they argue, should begin in the schools, to ensure that healthy eating habits are absorbed in youth. School officials across the country are increasingly coming around to this point of view. Los Angeles, San Francisco, Philadelphia, Chicago, New York City and many smaller districts have taken steps to ban the sale of soft drinks in schools. The next step, nutrition advocates say, is to get potato chips, candy and other junk food out of our schools—and more physical education back back into them.

ROSS BIRD

MARION NESTLE

The N.Y.U. nutrition scientist promotes public-service ads to fight the hidden costs of poor nutrition. "If you're a family that has kids with Type 2 diabetes," she says, "your life is not going to be pretty. Nobody has a clue how much this overweight business is going to cost us"

JONATHAN SAUNDERS

KELLY BROWNELL

The Yale psychologist and nutrition advocate favors a national tax on junk food. "We could raise $1.5 billion from a penny-a-can tax on soft drinks," he argues. "With $1.5 billion, we could create a 'nutrition Superfund' to clean up the toxic environment ... and promote healthy eating"

JASON GROW

DAVID LUDWIG

The Harvard pediatrician declares, "We as a society have really abdicated responsibility for teaching kids how to eat right and how to have an active lifestyle." The typical adolescent, he says, gets a whopping 10% to 15% of his or her daily calories from soft drinks

Society Notes

PROFILE

Planting the Seeds of Peace

Kenya's Wangari Maathai is practiced in the art of pioneering. After receiving a master's degree in biology in the U.S., she returned home and in 1971 was awarded a doctorate by the University of Nairobi, making her the first woman in East Africa to earn a Ph.D. She later became the first female professor at that university. Now, at age 64, her career as an advocate for the environment has earned her an even greater distinction: in October she was named the first African woman ever to win the Nobel Peace Prize, and the first person to win it under a broadened definition of peace activism that includes environmentalism.

KAREL PRINSLOO—AP/WIDE WORLD

MAATHAI: A Nobel first for a veteran pioneer

Maathai became involved in environmental and women's rights issues in the 1970s. In 1977 she founded the Green Belt Movement, an organization comprised mainly of women, which has planted millions of trees to fight deforestation and replenish the supply of firewood for cooking. A political activist, Maathai was knocked unconscious by police in 1992 as they broke up a hunger strike by women protesting the holding of political prisoners by President Daniel arap Moi. She has also sown controversy, suggesting that AIDS is a biological weapon that the West planted in Africa to wipe out the black races. "When we plant new trees, we plant the seeds of peace," she declared upon hearing of her award.

ROLL A BALL

LYNSEY ADDARIO—CORBIS FOR TIME

HAVING A BALL: Head scarves were de rigueur on a Muslim day at Six Flags

Not Just a Day in the Park

The amusement park was sniffed for bombs, and security was beefed up at the gate; Sept. 17 was Great Muslim Adventure Day at Six Flags New Jersey. The event wasn't a new idea; the first, in 2000, drew 8,000 customers. Three days after the second, co-organizer Tariq Amanullah died at the World Trade Center. That didn't stop anti-Muslim fanatics who called for boycotts, but the day passed without incident.

A Place for Women Clergy?

The percentage of female seminary students in the U.S. has exploded in the past 35 years, from 4.7% in 1972 to 31% (or roughly 10,470 women) in 2003. Yet women make up only about 11% of the nation's clergy; very few are pastors of mainline Protestant churches. Conservative denominations do not ordain women. But even in more liberal churches, a study found, female clergy tend to be relegated to specialized ministries—and earned on average 9% less than identically trained men in the same positions.

JOHN CHIASSON

EXCEPTION: Vashti McKenzie of Memphis is a rare female bishop

DEAN COX—AP/WIDE WORLD

WOW! The new *Queen Mary 2*

A Queen's Splashy Debut

The grand old Cunard ocean liner *Queen Mary* reigned for 31 years, crossing the Atlantic 1,001 times, three of them carrying Winston Churchill. During World War II, she gave up her old rich crowd to carry servicemen and their families, becoming a great symbol of British pride. But that was then; today the old dowager is a floating hotel at a dock in Long Beach, Calif. So it was big news when cruise behemoth

MGM GRAND
LUXOR

ADAM JONES—GETTY IMAGES

IMAGE

Rat Pack Redux

It's back! Las Vegas is booming again with a profitable mix of sin, skin and sensation. Vegas had an identity crisis in the '90s, as its big draw, legal gambling, spread across the U.S. So the desert oasis tried to become a family-friendly amusement town. No dice. Now it's back, thriving on a beefed-up menu of scantily-clad show girls; lavish new casinos and hotels; and the hottest trend of 2004, high-stakes poker.

Carnival Corp., which bought Cunard in 1998, launched the *Queen Mary 2* at Southampton in January 2004 (with a little help from fellow royal Queen Elizabeth II).

Taller than Notre Dame Cathedral and designed to cruise the North Atlantic at a zippy 30 m.p.h., the 151,400 gross-ton ship cost $800 million and will tower over every port where it docks. Its 2,600 passengers, served by almost half as many crew members, will ante up at least $1,499 and as much as $25,000 to make the six-day Atlantic crossing. Among the ship's highlights: the largest dance floor afloat, the only planetarium at sea and a luxurious 20,000-sq.-ft. spa. But Mr. Churchill might not feel at home: the ship's library is open for only an hour a day.

SWIMMING POOLS WITH THE MIDAS TOUCH

Upscale Americans whose McMansions lack luster are thinking outside the box—the home box. Suburban status wars are going al fresco as the well-to-do load up their pools and patios with a new generation of outsize outdoor gear. Gone are those concrete rectangles we once plowed into our backyard and surrounded with plastic patio furniture; today's homeowners are installing pools with underwater speakers and fake lagoons that emit something the pool industry calls Faux Fog. One hot tub boasts a 42-in. pop-up plasma TV and 49 jets to massage your back (it's already cleaned out your wallet). Small wonder the average cost of a new pool has leaped past $30,000.

Sadly, a palatial pool isn't a good investment. Real estate experts say even the splashiest of them boost an average home's value less than 10%. But that's Faux Fog to most homeowners who construct waterfalls and poolside theaters; they're speculating on their dreams, not their equity.

INFINITY The sleekest new pools are designed to look like they go on forever, blending into the horizon. Their so-called vanishing edges create an optical illusion, as if the water is levitating

LUXURY One new trend in pools is the tropical-lagoon look. Far left, outdoor chefs should enjoy this KitchenAid unit, which includes a giant rotisserie grill, a $1,700 ice-cream maker and a fridge

CLOCKWISE FROM LEFT: KITCHENAID; NATIONAL ...

2004

BACK TO

FROZEN IN MID-flight by a digital camera as they cross the finish line in the 100-m dash, Olympic sprinters assume stylized forms that recall the graceful athletes painted on Grecian urns. The image is an apt symbol of the 2004 Summer Games, which brought the Olympics back to their ancient birthplace. The Games were a success in many ways, but never more so than when they married the present to the past, as when cyclists and marathoners raced through the streets of Athens with the glorious Parthenon looming above them, a reminder of the early Greeks' seminal role in Western culture.

HO—AFP—GETTY IMAGES

THE FUTURE

BY A NOSE: Justin Gatlin of the U.S.A. takes first place in the 100-m dash with a time of 9.85 sec. Second was Francis Obikwelu of Portugal, at 9.86 sec.

THROUGH THE PAST,

FOR AFICIONADOS OF GOOFY PAGEANTRY, FEW EVENTS ARE more rewarding than the biennial opening ceremonies of the Olympic Games, spectacles in which good intentions and bad taste often merge to create a profoundly silly show. Not this time. The creators of the Athens spectacular introduced two unexpected qualities, gravitas and beauty. Highlights included ethereal human "statues" gliding in slow motion above the arena floor; ancient phalanxes bristling with spears; and an aerial Eros, god of love. The low moments: a song from Icelandic sylph Björk, whose costume unfurled endlessly while she lip-synched to a tape, and the usual hapless tyke assigned to represent "the Youth of the World." The arena itself, designed by Spanish-born architect Santiago Calatrava, was an undulating fantasy that came to life when the lofty spire that held the cauldron for the Olympic flame bent down to be lit by the torchbearer. Above all—gods be praised!—Yanni was nowhere to be seen.

LAURENT REBOURS—AP/WIDE WORLD

LIGHTLY

IAN WALDIE—GETTY IMAGES

MICHAEL STEELE—GETTY IMAGES

Panasonic

S KIENZLE—AP/WIDE WORLD

2004 GIDDY GOLDEN GLEE

GARRETT W. ELLWOOD—NBAE 2004 VIA GETTY IMAGES

Lisa Leslie, U.S.A. ▲

The star center of the Los Angeles Sparks of the WNBA celebrates after the talent-rich U.S. team beat a tough Australia squad to take the gold medal. The two teams dominate the international game

Abby Wambach, Julie Foudy, U.S.A. ▼

The torch is passed in U.S. women's soccer as Wambach, 24, ge a hug from "Rowdy Foudy," 33. The U.S. women beat Brazil 2-1 the final to reclaim the gold medal they lost to Norway in 2000

DANIEL BEREHULAK—GETTY IMAGES FOR FINA

Ian Thorpe, Australia ▲

Down Under's charismatic "Thorpedo," a poster boy from the 2000 Games in Sydney, showed he still had the right stuff as he successfully defended his gold medal in the 200-m freestyle race

Gal Fridman, Israel ▼

The windsurfer became a national hero after winning the first gol medal in Israel's history. Fridman, who placed third at Atlanta in '96, had destiny on his side: his first name means *wave* in Hebrev

MENAHEM KAHANA—AFP—GETTY IMAGES

All hail the champs! And who said nice guys have to finish last?

Michael Phelps, U.S.A. ▲

oined by Peter Vanderkaay, left, and Ryan Lochte, right, Phelps who easily lived up to the hype that preceded the Games) cheers after the American men won gold in the 4 x 200-m freestyle relay

Mariel Zagunis, U.S.A. ▲

Zagunis, 19, took first place in the women's individual sabre competition. She is the first American to win a fencing medal since 1984, and the first to win fencing gold in 100 years

Rulon Gardner, U.S.A. ▲

Yes, Garnder is glum, not gleeful, as he leaves his shoes in the ring, symbolically ending his career. But in coming back from njuries to place third, Gardner won our hearts—if not the gold

Hicham El Guerrouj, Morocco ▼

Ending an incredible string of bad luck—he fell in Atlanta in '96 and ran poorly in Sydney in 2000—the world record holder exults after winning the 1,500-m race. The fan favorite won the 5,000 m as well

MOROCCO
ATHENS 2004
2469
KENYA
2348
9

MICHAEL STEELE—GETTY IMAGES

Kerri Walsh, Misty May, U.S.A. ▼

A hit at the Sydney Games in 2000, beach volleyball is the party animal of Olympic sports, featuring amped-up music and scantily clad dancers (and athletes). Walsh and May beat Brazil for the gold

ADAM BUTLER—AP/WIDE WORLD

2004

GOOD VIBRATIONS

PIERRE-PHILIPPE MARCOU—AFP—GETTY IMAGES

Peerless Piersol

Cementing his rep as the world's best backstroker, Aaron Piersol won gold in the 100-m event and seemed to have won a second in the 200 m, until a single judge disqualified him for an illegal kick. After a rhubarb, Piersol was declared the winner

USA
ATHENS 2004
3271
USA
3359
USA
3230

Uncle Sam Sweeps

Seemingly alone on the track, three U.S. men outrun the field to collect all three medals in the 400-m race, an event Americans have long dominated. Jeremy Wariner, 20, a protégé of legendary U.S. runner Michael Johnson's, won the gold medal; Otis Harris, at left, won the silver medal; and Derrick Brew, right, placed third. It was the first U.S. sweep in the event since 1984

USA
6

NICK LAHAM—GETTY IMAGES

Diamonds and Gold

Spirits—and braids—flying, American women celebrate their 5-1 victory over Australia to win the gold medal in softball. Their triumph was the capper to a commanding showing by U.S. women in team sports at the Games, where Americans swept the gold in softball, soccer and basketball. In stark contrast, the U.S. men placed third in basketball, did not win a medal in soccer and failed to quality for the Games in the national pastime, baseball

Bending Over Backward

Carly Patterson shows off the smooth moves that won the silver medal in the balance beam event. Her gold in the all-around competition was America's first since Mary Lou Retton's win in 1984

Dark horses, mighty leaps and clean sweeps

2801
ATHENS 2004

Greece's Golden Girl

Talk about Olympic glory: in a single burst of speed, Fani Halkia, previously a mere mortal, won immortality in her native land. In the early stages of the women's 400-m hurdle event, Halkia was in the middle of the pack. But as she rounded the final curve of the great stadium, the deafening roar of the hometown crowd seemed to propel her past the other runners; she won going away

13
11

NICK LAHAM—GETTY IMAGES

Iraq's Underdogs

Iraq's soccer team, a ragtag squad of which little was expected, brought some welcome smiles to Iraqi faces as it won five games to finish fourth at Athens. Above, Hawar Mulla Mohammed is pumped after netting the first goal as Iraq beat Costa Rica, 2-0

USA

The Real Dream Team

Forget the U.S. men (and we wish we could). The U.S. women, featuring a gangly gaggle of gals from the WNBA, including (from left) a joyous Dawn Staley, Lisa Leslie and Tamika Catchings, easily netted a gold medal

HENRIK MONTGOMERY—AFP/GETTY IMAGES

USA

Fastest Men on Earth

In a terrific finish to the flashiest track event of the Games, the men's 100-m sprint, American Justin Gatlin, closest to the camera, strains to get ahead of Portugal's Francis Obikwelu, middle. Keeping pace in the rear of the picture is Maurice Green of the U.S., the gold-medal winner in 2000. Gatlin pulled ahead at the finish line to win the race, as documented in the opening picture of this chapter

BAD VIBRATIONS

EZRA SHAW—GETTY IMAGES

Golden Gloom

After U.S. gymnast Paul Hamm won the all-around men's gold despite one bad landing, South Korea's Yang Tae Young officially protested the judging. Hamm will keep the gold, but his triumph remains controversial

USA

Down and Out

Twelve years after the legendary U.S. "Dream Team" pulled off the improbable trick of charming its opponents while routing them by an average 43.8 points, America fielded a Nightmare Team that opened the Olympics by dropping its first game to Puerto Rico by 19 points. The team went 5-3 in the Games, finishing third. The good news: in defeat, Allen Iverson, above, and his teammates behaved with impressive grace

ATHENS 2004
ATHENS 2004
ATHENS 2004
ATHENS 2004

Canadian Catastrophe

Canadians, famously partial to sports conducted on ice, suffered through the Athens Games, as their athletes endured a string of bad luck. One example: Perdita Felicien, right, was favored to win the women's 100-m hurdles, but she stumbled early on, eliminating herself—as well as Russia's Irina Shevchenko, center. When will Canada excel at the Summer Games? Perhaps when hell freezes over

Foul-ups, mix-ups, errant bull's-eyes and bobbled batons

A Sad Games for Sydney's Star

Marion Jones was one of the jolly swagmen of the Sydney Games, returning from the land of *Waltzing Matilda* with five gold medals in her tucker bag. But Jones has been battered by bad news of late: an ugly divorce from husband C.J. Hunter was followed by official inquiries into her alleged use of performance-enhancing drugs. Athens was a horror show for Jones, 28. She finished a meek fifth in the long jump—and an hour later, running the second leg of the 4 x 100-m relay, she twice fumbled the baton-pass to Lauryn Williams, fouling out. "I exceeded my wildest dreams," said Jones, "but in a negative sense"

ATHENS
234

Marathon Madness

In a revolting episode, an Irish publicity hound (we won't name him) attacks the leader in the men's marathon, Vanderlei Lima of Brazil, at the 23-mile mark. The gallant Lima won bronze

ANSCH

DONALD MIRALLE—GETTY IMAGES

Ready ... Fire ... Aim

Matthew Emmons of the U.S.A. was in first place in the men's 50-m rifle three-position finals when he fired his last shot at the wrong target. He finished eighth—despite hitting the bull's-eye

2004 PARTING SHOTS

WAS IT ONLY FOUR YEARS AGO THAT A WORLD RACING toward the millennium held a global orgy of good times in Sydney, where the condom machines in the athletes' village famously couldn't be refilled fast enough? Athens '04 was more restrained, a morning-after Games shadowed by concerns about terrorism and ushered in by a scandal in which the two top athletes of the host nation were suspended from their team after refusing to take drug tests. Yet other than a few judging blunders and steroid stupidities, the Games were blessedly placid, yielding wonderful memories and images—we've collected a few of our favorites here. For once, the athletes were the story: when Morocco's Hicham El Guerrouj, perhaps the greatest middle-distance runner ever, finally hauled in the 1,500-m gold medal that had eluded him in '96 and '00, his fellow runners hugged him, laughing, as he danced joyously to the *Zorba the Greek* theme. Farewell, Athens—Hello, Beijing!

DANIEL BEREHULAK—GETTY IMAGES

CHN

ATHENS 2004

JOE KLAMAR—AFP—GETTY IMAGES

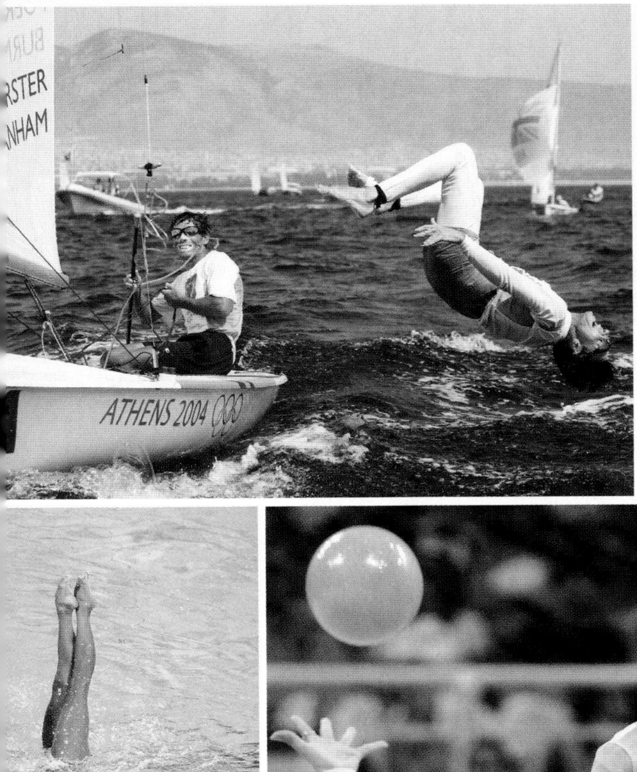
RSTER
NHAM
ATHENS 2004

NS 2004
ATHENS 2004
NS 2004
ATHE

BEN RADFORD—GETTY IMAGES

KAZUHIRO NOGI—AFP—GETTY IMAGES

ATHENS 2004
116

DONALD MIRALLE—GETTY IMAGES

43

STEVE LISS FOR TIME

A Curse Reversed: Sox Nix Babe's Hex

Ah, New England—where, as several generations of schoolkids have been taught, the leaves fall every year, and so do the Red Sox. New England, where doom-afflicted Bostonians ascribed decades of failure to (cue organ tones) the Curse of the Bambino. For the Red Sox hadn't won a World Series since 1918, the year Boston's best player, Babe Ruth, was sold to the hated New York Yankees. But this year the Red Sox triumphed, putting an end to the most celebrated losing streak in American sports history. And they did it in memorable fashion, losing three games in a row to the Yankees in the American League Championship Series, only to come from behind in the ninth inning of the fourth game to hang on. The Sox then swept three from the Yanks, taking the final game in the House That You-Know-Who Built and sparking this exuberant embrace between catcher Jason Varitek and pitcher Alen Embree. The St. Louis Cardinals, a team rich in sluggers, simply folded in the World Series; the Sox won it in four straight games. At this rate, look for the Bosox to return to the Series in 2090.

GOLF GETS A NEW BOSS

After five years as golf's top gun, Tiger Woods proves he's human, and sweet-swinging Vijay Singh becomes the Dean of the Divots

WHAT A SEASON! THE WORLD'S NO. 1 GOLFER WAS just about unbeatable in 2004: he won nine tournaments—including one major championship, the PGA—and raked in $10,905,166 in winnings, an all-time record. And if you think that player was Tiger Woods, well, check your scorecard. Golf's top player of late has been the big Fijian with the wide grin, Vijay Singh, 41, who overtook Tiger, 28, atop the PGA rankings at the Deutsche Bank Championship in September. Once he got rolling, Singh hoped to win 10 tournaments for the year, but his nine trophies still put him in élite company: only Byron Nelson, who won 18 times in 1945; Ben Hogan, who won 13 events in 1946 and 10 events in 1948; and Sam Snead, who won 11 tournaments in 1950, have had higher victory totals for a season. By season's end, Singh's fellow pros were calling him Vijay Bling.

The passing of golf's Years of the Tiger may be good for the game, for it will allow some other terrific players to win a trophy or two. That was certainly the feeling at the year's first major, the Masters Tournament in Georgia, where longtime fan favorite Phil Mickelson, 34, finally snagged his first major trophy. The left-hander, universally known as Lefty, was 0 for 42 in the majors; he was also universally known as the best player never to win a major. But he won the Masters in style, sinking an 18-ft. putt on the last green to avoid a playoff with another crowd pleaser, Ernie Els.

Alas for Lefty! Buoyed by worshipping crowds, he made a great run at the next major, the U.S. Open at Shinnecock Hills on Long Island, N.Y. But Mickelson fell to his old nemesis, getting the putting "yips" under pressure; he double-bogeyed the 17th hole on the last round, and it was South Africa's Retief Goosen, another solid player, who held aloft his second U.S. Open trophy in four years.

When the world's top pros crossed the pond in July to play in the British Open at Royal Troon in Scotland, the game's new, wide-open feel was highlighted when U.S. journeyman Todd Hamilton, 38, walked away with the claret jug. The next month Singh put an exclamation point on his new dominance by outshooting Justin Leonard and Chris DiMarco in a three-hole playoff to win the PGA title at the new Whistling Straits course in Wisconsin.

The king is dead; long live the king. But don't shed too many tears for Tiger. In 2004 his career earnings topped $40 million; in October he wed his longtime girlfriend, Swedish blond Elin Nordegrin, 24, at a snazzy Barbados resort. As Arnold (not Palmer) would say, "I'll be back." ■

ELISE AMENDOLA—AP/WIDE WORLD

PHIL MICKELSON

Finally! Crowd favorite Mickelson shot a blazing 31 on Augusta National's back nine—the best finish since Jack Nicklaus in 1986—to win the green jacket

CHARLES KRUPA—AP/WIDE WORLD

RETIEF GOOSEN

The U.S. Open is considered golf's toughest test. Goosen, 35, proved he's one of today's best players by becoming only the 22nd person to win it twice

STUART FRANKLIN—GETTY IMAGES

TODD HAMILTON

Todd Who? Hamilton prevailed over both Mickelson and Els on the back nine, and for the second year in a row, the British Open title went to a little-known player

Cleveland
GOLF
FORSTMANN
LITTLE & Co

TIGER WOODS

Why does Tiger look perplexed? After holding down the No. 1 ranking for 264 weeks, Woods couldn't find the groove in 2004; he spent the season revamping his swing. But Tiger showed the same grace in defeat as he always has in victory

VIJAY SINGH

Why is Vijay smiling at the PGA? After threatening to overtake Tiger for the past few years, Singh went on a rampage in 2004. The onetime club pro on Borneo got hot after changing his putter in July, and he just kept winning. John Daly is the man in the middle

ERNIE ELS

The Big Easy, 35, had a rough year; he almost won the Masters and missed a 15-footer on the final hole of the British Open that would have forced a playoff

ANDREW REDINGTON—GETTY IMAGES

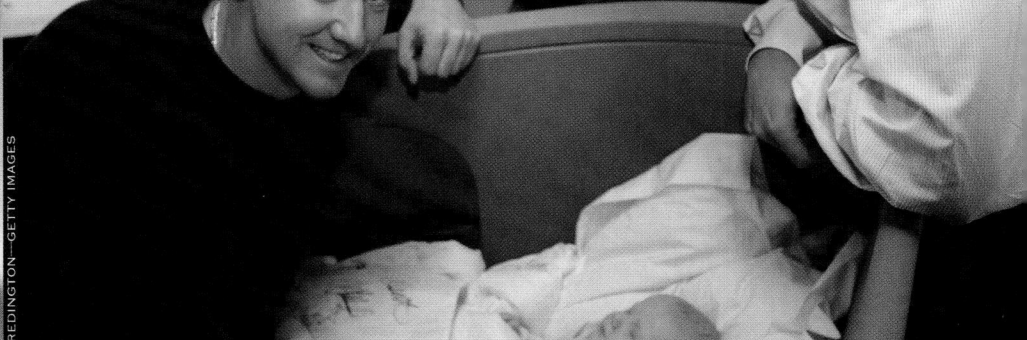

IAN POULTER, PAUL CASEY, SERGIO GARCIA

Talk about precious cargo! The three triumphant European golfers share the Ryder Cup with Poulter's son Luke during their flight back to the Continent on Sept. 20, after whipping a top-notch American team in the biennial event. The U.S. squad collapsed at Bloomfield Hills in Michigan, and the Europeans won the Cup by the largest margin in its 77-year history

TOUR DE LANCE

He did it again! Lance Armstrong becomes the first to win cycling's greatest test in six consecutive years

1999

UN **He looks fresh-faced, but Lance, then age 28, was coming back from his bout with testicular cancer when he won his first Tour. One piece of luck: he managed to avoid a huge pileup that eliminated many of the favorites in the race**

STEFANO RELLANDINI—REUTERS—LANDOV

2000

DEUX **Lance toasts his millennium victory, in which he first established his future winning strategy, taking a big lead over his opponents in the tough climbs of the Pyrenees**

ERIC GAILLARD—REUTERS—LANDOV

2001

TROIS **Challenged by competitor Jan Ullrich, Armstrong passed the German on the grueling ascent of the Alpe d'Huez, then won the psychological duel by flashing a withering glance back at the German**

WOLFGANG RATTAY—REUTERS—LANDOV

How ironic: at a time when Franco-American relations are at their lowest ebb in decades, one of the most familiar images of today's France is a grinning Texan in a yellow jersey, posing against one of the most familiar images of yesteryear's France, the Arc du Triomphe. Yet the juxtaposition is also perfectly fitting, for when it comes to triumphant arcs, the course of Lance Armstrong's career is hard to beat.

He has always been a man in a hurry, rushing through life-altering crises and changes. He beat cancer at age 26 and won his first Tour two years later. He got married, had three kids and was rich and famous by age 30. He wrote a best-selling book. He starred in commercials. He was named Sports Illustrated's Sportsman of the Year. He even got American guys to watch cycling on TV.

By the summer of 2004, Armstrong, at 32, was divorced and living with rock star Sheryl Crow. But he wasn't fulfilled, because he still had a job to do. He was one of five men who were each five-time winners of the Tour de France, cycling's Grail. And Armstrong has never been much for sharing records. No problem: three weeks and 2,100 miles from the Tour's 2004 starting line, after a typically dominating performance, Lance got the job done. He rode into Paris as the first and only person to win the Tour six times in a row.

Armstrong has lived a full life in the years since disease threatened to shorten his. What's next? Certainly he wants to spend more time with his kids, who live with their mother. And he may change what he does for a living. But not how he does it. That will include fighting cancer through his foundation. Given this man's insane commitment to winning, cancer had better watch out. ■

CREDIT
LYONNAIS

SIX: **After hanging back a bit in the early contests, Armstrong geared up to win three consecutive stages and cruised to victory with a comfortable six-minute margin**

2004

GERO BRELOER—DPA—LANDOV

2002

QUATRE **Refuting allegations that he uses performance-enhancing drugs, Armstrong passed a string of drug tests and won the race easily**

PASCAL RONDEAU—POOL—REUTERS—LANDOV

2003

CINQ **In his toughest test, Lance rode out a crumbling marriage, stomach flu and a serious tumble to eke out a 61-sec. victory over Jan Ullrich**

VICTORY!

In a great year for sport, enduring records fall, family histories are embellished and underdogs triumph —except for a beloved racehorse

MARINERS
MARINERS

AL BEHRMAN—AP/WIDE WORLD

Ichiro Suzuki

As baseball records go, few were more venerable than George Sisler's mark of 257 hits in a single season. Ted Williams, Joe DiMaggio and Pete Rose are among the great batsmen who couldn't hit 258—but in 2004 Ichiro Suzuki of the Seattle Mariners finally toppled Sisler's 84-year-old record. Some noted that the fine Japanese hitter passed Sisler in his 160th game; Sisler played only 154 in 1920

Smarty Jones

The last horse to win racing's Triple Crown—the Kentucky Derby, the Preakness and the Belmont Stakes—was Affirmed in 1978. Things looked to change in 2004, when Smarty Jones won the first two legs of the crown, only to lose at Belmont. The chestnut colt, a non-thoroughbred, had captured the hearts of racing fans and given the sport its biggest jolt in years. But he faded at the end, and Birdstone won. Smarty is the sixth horse in eight years to win the first two races and lose the third

PISTONS

Bud
KING OF BEER

ALAN DIAZ—AP/WIDE WORLD

15

TED S. WARREN—AP/WIDE WORLD

Detroit Pistons

David knocked off Goliath in the NBA finals, as the blue-collar Detroit Pistons easily toppled the lordly Los Angeles Lakers dynasty 4-1, denying the Lakers a fourth title in five years. Led by Chauncey Billups, above, the Pistons played as a cohesive, alert unit—in stark contrast to the Lakers, whose offense, led by center Shaquille O'Neal and shooting guard Kobe Bryant, was showy but selfish

Dale Earnhardt Jr.

In February 2004, six years to the day after Dale Earnhardt Sr. won his only victory at NASCAR's biggest event of the year—and three years to the week after the great driver died on the last turn of the last lap of the race—Dale Earnhardt Jr. won his first Daytona 500. And Junior did it in style, dueling Tony Stewart for 30 laps, then passing him on Lap 181 of 200 to triumph in the Great American Race

Seattle Storm

Sparked by the hot shooting of veteran backcourt player Betty Lennox and anchored by awesome Aussie Lauren Jackson at center (No. 15, above), Seattle's scrappy Storm beat the Connecticut Sun two games out of three to win the WNBA crown in October. Though still struggling, the women's pro league is much more exciting now that the reign of the Los Angeles Sparks is past, and other teams are improving. Lennox was named series MVP

700
SBC PARK
25
399

Barry Bonds

The San Francisco Giants slugger passed two milestones in 2004. In April he smacked his 661st career home run, moving him past his godfather, Willie Mays, to take over third place on the list of all-time home-run hitters, behind Babe Ruth and Hank Aaron. Mays, who was in the stands, passed a symbolic torch to Bonds after the game. Five months later, Bonds, now 40 (and still under scrutiny for allegations of steroid abuse, which he firmly denies), stroked his 700th homer. Oh, yeah, he was also named National League MVP. Watch your back, Babe

Sport Notes

■ **PROFILE**

A Superstar's Tough Times

Kobe Bryant, now 26, has been a center of attention since he waltzed into the NBA out of high school at 18. He wore his fame like an itchy turtleneck, never quite comfortable in it yet loath to lose the cloak of stardom. Teammates described him as an aloof, immature brat. Bryant's big problem used to be his rivalry with his L.A. Lakers teammate, the personable giant Shaquille O'Neal—until Bryant was charged with sexual assault in Colorado in 2003.

The story: Bryant, set to undergo a knee operation, checked into a resort near Vail on June 30, 2003. The front-desk clerk, 19, showed him around the place and later visited him in his room. The two kissed by mutual agreement, then they had sex: forced, she said; consensual, he said. Bryant was arrested in July 2003, and his legal plight dogged him the entire season.

TONY GUTIERRZ—AP WIDE WORLD

REPRIEVE: Bryant with attorney

Slowly, though, the case against Bryant collected dents from a series of court foul-ups and from his big-league defense team, which overpowered the locals. In September 2004, as jury selection began, the charges were dropped, and Bryant released a carefully crafted apology. Meanwhile, the Lakers lost the NBA title to the Detroit Pistons, and Coach Phil Jackson and Shaq both decamped. But Kobe's woes aren't over: he still may face a civil suit.

JACK SMITH—AP/WIDE WORLD

PLAY BALL! A sell-out crowd cheers opening day at San Diego's Petco Park

Batter Up in Better Parks

Baseball enjoyed a banner year in 2004: some 73 million people, a new record, took themselves out to the ball game. And the players obliged with a sparkling season that ended on a high note, as the Boston Red Sox were finally crowned World Series champs.

One reason for the game's renaissance: the ongoing debut of nifty new stadiums that match old-time flavor with modern amenities, a trend that began with the debut of the Baltimore Orioles' Camden Yards field in 1992. This season brought two welcome new fields. Citizens Bank Park in Philadelphia features a skyline view beyond center field; a promenade where Geno's and Tony Luke's offer their famous cheesesteaks; and the Phanatic Kid's Corner, where kids can dress their own miniversion of the Phillies mascot.

With a sandbox behind the outfield wall, San Diego's Petco Park, above, is also kid friendly. Trolley rides to the waterfront park and the old brick warehouse in left field are among its other charms. One surprise: the San Diego Chicken, the team's mascot, was retired. Who says there's no progress in the game?

MICHAEL BRYANT—AP/WIDE WORLD

PROGRESS: The old and the new in Philadelphia

Schilling: Willing, Thrilling

Red Sox pitcher Curt Schilling was already a shoo-in for the Hall of Fame; now he's a shoe-in. The veteran right-hander, 38, burnished his legend when he pitched Game 2 of the League Championship Series against the Yankees and Game 2 of the World Series against the Cards despite a dislocated tendon in his ankle. While TV cameras showed his bloody foot, Schilling showed his guts, entering baseball's pantheon. Post-Series surgery went well.

BOSTON

CHARLES KRUPA—AP/WIDE WORLD (2)

GUTSY: Boston's Curt played hurt

ERIK AEDER—BILLABONGXXL.COM

■ IMAGE

Cowabanga!

Don't try this at home. That's Pete Cabrinha, 42, a veteran surfer from Hawaii, riding a wave measured at 70 ft. in January 2004. It was the highest wave ever surfed and recorded. Extreme surfing is growing in popularity as daredevils on boards have learned they can catch up to the big waves, which can reach speeds above 40 m.p.h., by hitching rides on jet skis. Extreme surfing's next big goal: riding a 100-ft. wave.

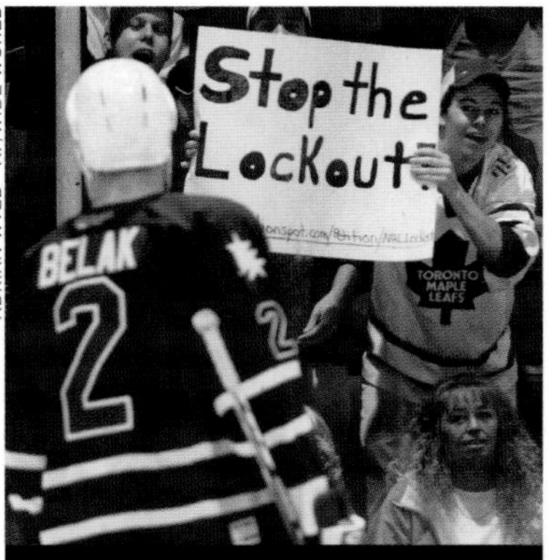
Stop the
Lockout
BELAK
2
TORONTO
MAPLE
LEAFS

ADRIAN WYLD—AP/WIDE WORLD

NO LUCK: Hockey's season is on ice

Penalty Box for the NHL

Hockey, the fabulous invalid of professional sports, hit a new low in 2004. In an angry wage dispute, the owners locked out the players and the season never began. A hat trick of woes—overexpansion, high player salaries and a "defense-first" strategy on the ice—helped the National Hockey League lose $273 million in the 2003-04 season, when the average regular-season game scored lower ratings on ABC than bowling, billiards or poker. Both sides predicted the lockout would last well into 2005.

Wimbledon sans Williams

Maria Sharapova, 17, is a blond Russian-born tennis prodigy with a modeling contract who has had to expend much valuable energy denying that she's the new Anna Kournikova, an adjectivally similar countrywoman who won courtside hearts but no court titles. "Anna isn't in the picture anymore," Sharapova declared before play began in the British classic at Wimbledon. "It's Maria time now."

True and true. With Kournikova absent and fighting retirement, the far less flamboyant, far more focused Sharapova trounced Serena Williams, 6-1, 6-4, to become Wimbledon's third youngest women's champion ever, the first Russian ever to win a Wimbledon title—and the first non-Williams champion in five years.

THE CHAMPIONSHIPS
WIMBLEDON
mph

DAVE CAULKIN—AP/WIDE WORLD

THE "ANTI-ANNA": Sharpshooting Sharapova showed up Kournikova

Science

A Space First for a Double-Decker Duo

Looking a bit like a benign shark, the twin-tailed craft *White Knight* cradles the stubby-winged, star-spangled rocket plane *SpaceShipOne* beneath its fuselage as it prepares to carry the smaller ship some 46,000 ft. aloft. At that height, *SpaceShipOne* is released and fires its rocket engine to climb beyond Earth's atmosphere into space. Both craft were created by visionary aeronautical designer Burt Rutan. A test flight in late June was far from smooth: after its release, *SpaceShipOne* began pitching and rolling wildly, until a backup trim-control system kicked in. But on Oct. 4 the rocket plane completed the second of two successful flights into space in five days, becoming the first private craft to do so. The two flights earned the team headed by Rutan and funded by Microsoft billionaire Paul Allen the $10 million Ansari X Prize, which is underwritten by a group of enthusiasts who hope to launch a new era of private enterprise in space.

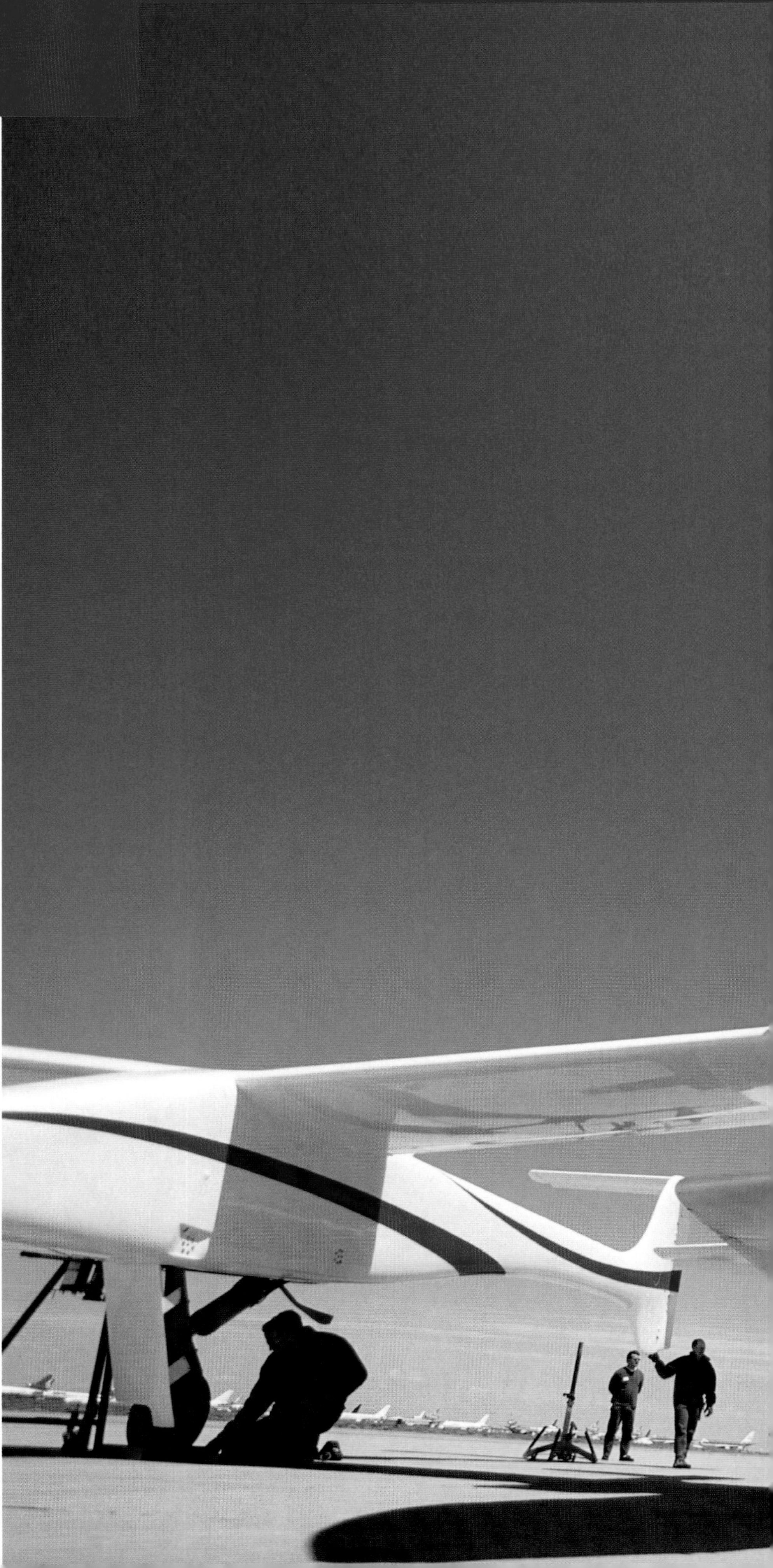

JIM SUGAR—CORBIS

The Red Rings of Saturn, the Blueberries of Mars

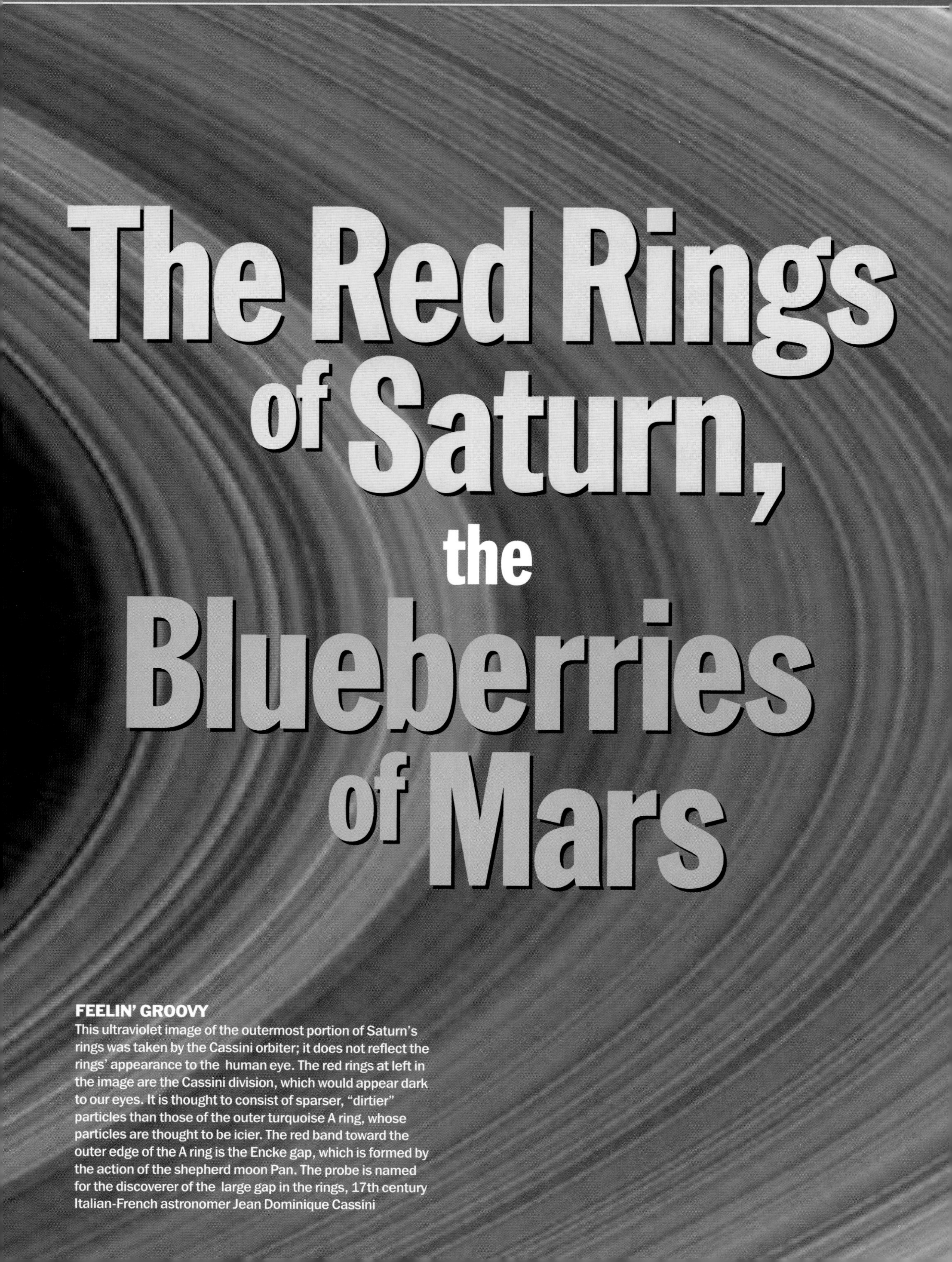

FEELIN' GROOVY

This ultraviolet image of the outermost portion of Saturn's rings was taken by the Cassini orbiter; it does not reflect the rings' appearance to the human eye. The red rings at left in the image are the Cassini division, which would appear dark to our eyes. It is thought to consist of sparser, "dirtier" particles than those of the outer turquoise A ring, whose particles are thought to be icier. The red band toward the outer edge of the A ring is the Encke gap, which is formed by the action of the shepherd moon Pan. The probe is named for the discoverer of the large gap in the rings, 17th century Italian-French astronomer Jean Dominique Cassini

NASA—JPL—UNIVERSITY OF COLORADO

MOST OF US MAY REMEMBER 2004 FOR THE WAR IN IRAQ, the presidential election and the Olympic Games. But history will also record it as a milestone year in the exploration of space. The most exciting discoveries were provided by NASA missions to our neighbors in the solar system, Saturn and Mars.

In June, after a journey of seven years and 2.2 billion miles, the two-part Cassini-Huygens probe settled into orbit around Saturn and began beaming back to Earth fascinating visions of the planet's fabled rings and mysterious moons.

Closer to our home planet, a pair of NASA rovers scuttled across the surface of Mars, transmitting new information about the planet's geology and geography. Among the finds: tiny spheroids, dubbed blueberries, which indicate that water was almost certainly present on the surface of Mars at one time. The news led scientists to suspect that life in some form may also have been present on the Red Planet in the past, though they also said it's much too early to confirm this theory.

Sky gazers have other reasons to call 2004 a landmark year. A private rocket plane, SpaceShipOne, successfully made two flights into the stratosphere, indicating that the days of spaceflight for civilians may be at hand. The planet Venus crossed the surface of the sun, in a rendezvous it had last kept in 1882. The year's biggest letdown was the Genesis mission, which aimed to snare solar particles and return them to Earth; it ended with a crack-up in the desert. But there's no cause to be, um, saturnine about a single failure: it only made the year's milestones in exploration that much sweeter. ■

Lord of the Rings

Ushering in a close encounter with Saturn that will last four years, the Cassini-Huygens probe settles into orbit around the giant planet

FOR A SPACECRAFT THAT HAD SPENT NEARLY SEVEN YEARS in flight and journeyed more than 2.2 billion miles to get where it was going, the Cassini-Huygens Saturn probe did a funny thing when it closed in on the ringed planet on June 30: it hid.

Traveling at a breakneck 54,000 m.p.h.—four times its cruising speed—the ship was no longer flying toward the planet but falling toward it, on a high-speed trajectory that could send it skimming past Saturn and back out into space. If the ship was going to enter a stable orbit, it would have to fire its little braking rocket for 96 min., until it reached the right speed and position to dart upward through a gap in Saturn's rings and begin circling the giant world. But when it comes to the dense rivers of ice and rubble that form the planet's rings, the word gap is an imprecise term. Even a seemingly clear opening can be swarming with dust and particles. A collision with a bit of cosmic buckshot no bigger than a marble could destroy the ship.

Making matters worse, the 930 million miles separating Saturn and Earth mean that even moving at the speed of light, radio instructions take 84 min. to travel there and another 84 to come back. Thus the ship would be operating entirely alone during its high-wire maneuver, all of its commands preloaded into its computer. As it approached the gap, Cassini-Huygens carried out, as preinstructed, one final step to protect itself: it turned around and pointed its large, dish-shaped antenna forward—a makeshift shield to protect the fragile hardware behind.

"Engine turn-on," announced the propulsion engineer at NASA's Jet Propulsion Laboratory in Pasadena, Calif., at 7:36 p.m. (P.T.), when the signal came down that the ship's fire had been lit. For the next hour and a half, the room was largely quiet. It was not until 9:12 that the same engineer spoke the words that meant the engine firing was over and the spacecraft had survived.

"We have burn complete," he said.

At that, the mission controllers, who in recent years have whipsawed between the devastation of the shuttle disaster and the celebration of the Mars landings, once again had reason to cheer, whoop and slap one another on the back. The Cassini-Huygens mission had begun an extended tour of the glittering Saturnian system with its sev-

A LOOK AT THE RINGS . . .

Made of ice and rock, the rings may be just tens of millions of years old—far younger than Saturn, which was formed 4.5 billion years ago. On a planetary scale they are paper thin, perhaps half a mile thick

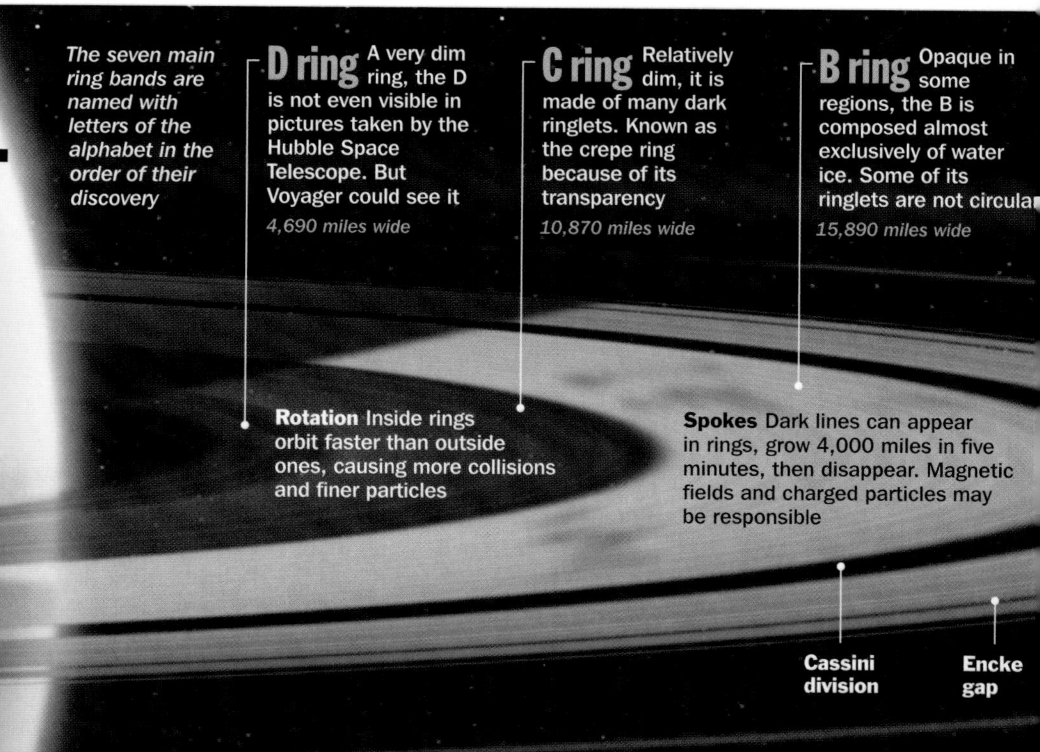

The seven main ring bands are named with letters of the alphabet in the order of their discovery
D ring A very dim ring, the D is not even visible in pictures taken by the Hubble Space Telescope. But Voyager could see it
4,690 miles wide
C ring Relatively dim, it is made of many dark ringlets. Known as the crepe ring because of its transparency
10,870 miles wide
B ring Opaque in some regions, the B is composed almost exclusively of water ice. Some of its ringlets are not circular
15,890 miles wide
Rotation Inside rings orbit faster than outside ones, causing more collisions and finer particles
Spokes Dark lines can appear in rings, grow 4,000 miles in five minutes, then disappear. Magnetic fields and charged particles may be responsible
Cassini division
Encke gap

Note: Ring colors simulated; moons not to scale. Source: JPL
Text by Jeffrey Kluger. Graphic by Lon Tweeten

en rings, 31 moons and untold cosmic secrets. By any measure, it is the most sophisticated planetary probe NASA has ever flown. About the size of a small bus, the Cassini orbiter is more than 22 ft. tall and weighs more than 6 tons when fueled. The engineering marvel is packed with a dozen scientific instruments and powered by a miniature nuclear generator. Carried on its side like a high-tech papoose is the European Space Agency's Huygens lander, a 9-ft., 700-lb. wok-shaped probe that early in 2005 will plunge through the atmosphere of Saturn's moon Titan, aiming for the most remote landing any human-made machine has ever achieved on another celestial body.

The payoff—for space scientists and curious civilians—could be staggering. Three other planets in the solar system—Jupiter, Uranus and Neptune—have rings, but they are faint and thready things, nothing like the magnificently complex cosmic jewelry that decorates Saturn. Seven of the other nine planets have moons, but none that perform the gravitational dances among themselves and within the rings that Saturn's do. And no planet has a moon anything like Titan, a world with much of the preorganic chemistry that Earth had 4.5 billion years ago—offering scientists a one-of-a-kind window into our vanished past.

The Saturnian system is, in a very real sense, the solar system writ small. And while other spacecraft have caught glimpses of it before—Pioneer 11 in 1979, Voyagers 1 and 2 in 1980 and 1981—they were mere flybys, quick hits by ships snapping a few pictures before whizzing off into deeper space. Cassini-Huygens—named after 17th century astronomers Jean Dominique Cassini and Christian Huygens—is there to stay.

RENDEZVOUS WITH TITAN

Saturn's largest moon, Titan, is a veritable world unto itself. One of the largest moons in the solar system—larger than Mercury or Pluto—Titan would be a perfectly good planet if it were orbiting the sun under its own steam. When Cassini-Huygens made its first successful pass by the moon at the end of October, scientists were thrilled—and puzzled—by what they saw. The moon's surface consists of bright, rugged regions adjacent to large, flat dark areas that may be lakes of liquid methane and ethane. Cracks or fissures appear to run across some sections of the moon, though no valleys or mountains appear in these first images, which only surveyed some 1% of the moon's surface. In the next four years, Cassini will make 45 passes of the moon, and it is set to launch the Huygens probe toward Titan on Dec. 24, 2004. The probe, built by the European Space Agency, should enter Titan's atmosphere on Jan. 14, 2005. No one is certain how long it will survive amid temperatures of –290°F, amid Titan's mighty lakes of liquid methane.

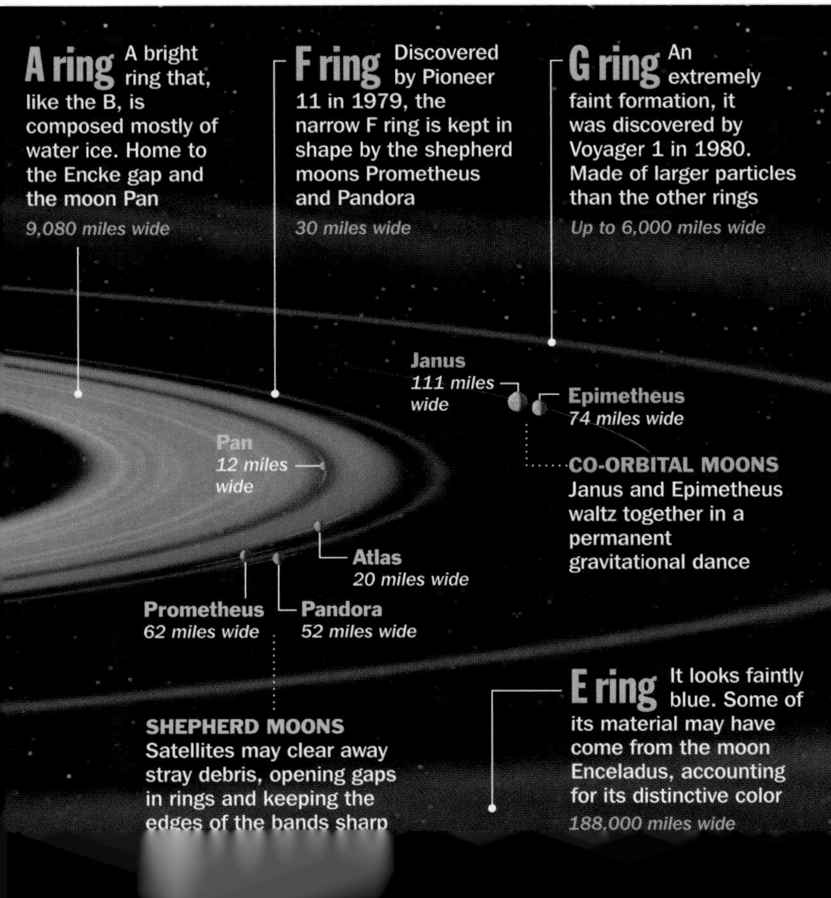
A ring A bright ring that, like the B, is composed mostly of water ice. Home to the Encke gap and the moon Pan
9,080 miles wide
F ring Discovered by Pioneer 11 in 1979, the narrow F ring is kept in shape by the shepherd moons Prometheus and Pandora
30 miles wide
G ring An extremely faint formation, it was discovered by Voyager 1 in 1980. Made of larger particles than the other rings
Up to 6,000 miles wide
Janus
111 miles wide
Epimetheus
74 miles wide
Pan
12 miles wide
CO-ORBITAL MOONS
Janus and Epimetheus waltz together in a permanent gravitational dance
Atlas
20 miles wide
Prometheus
62 miles wide
Pandora
52 miles wide
SHEPHERD MOONS
Satellites may clear away stray debris, opening gaps in rings and keeping the edges of the bands sharp
E ring It looks faintly blue. Some of its material may have come from the moon Enceladus, accounting for its distinctive color
188,000 miles wide

. . . AND HOW THEY CAME TO BE

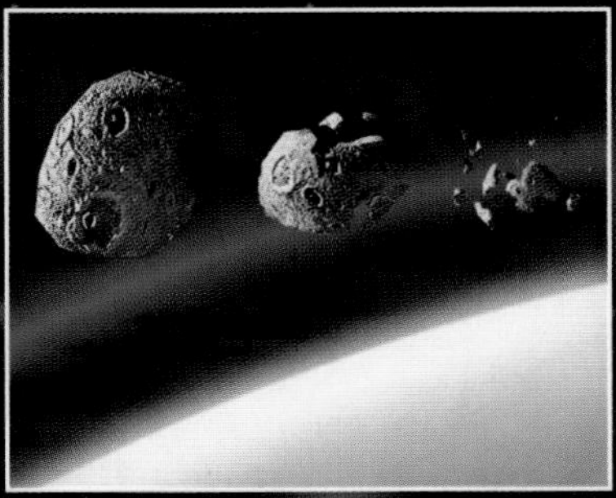

GRAVITATIONAL TURBULENCE When moons move within a region defined by the Roche limit, planetary gravity may rip them apart but not pull them out of orbit. They then disperse into a ring

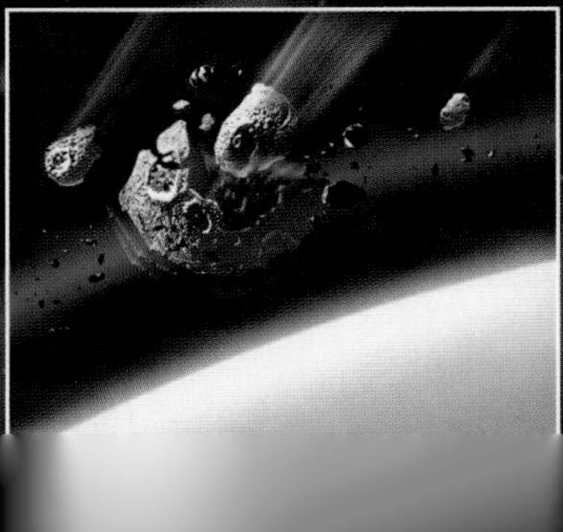

METEOR IMPACTS A hard collision with a rogue rock can shatter a moon, as shown by the near fatal scar on the moon Tethys. More collisions can reduce the heavy rubble to fine debris

FLY ME TO THE MOONS

Over the next four years, Cassini will explore nine of Saturn's 31 known moons. The planet-like Titan will receive the most attention, with at least 45 visits, plus a landing by the Huygens probe in January.

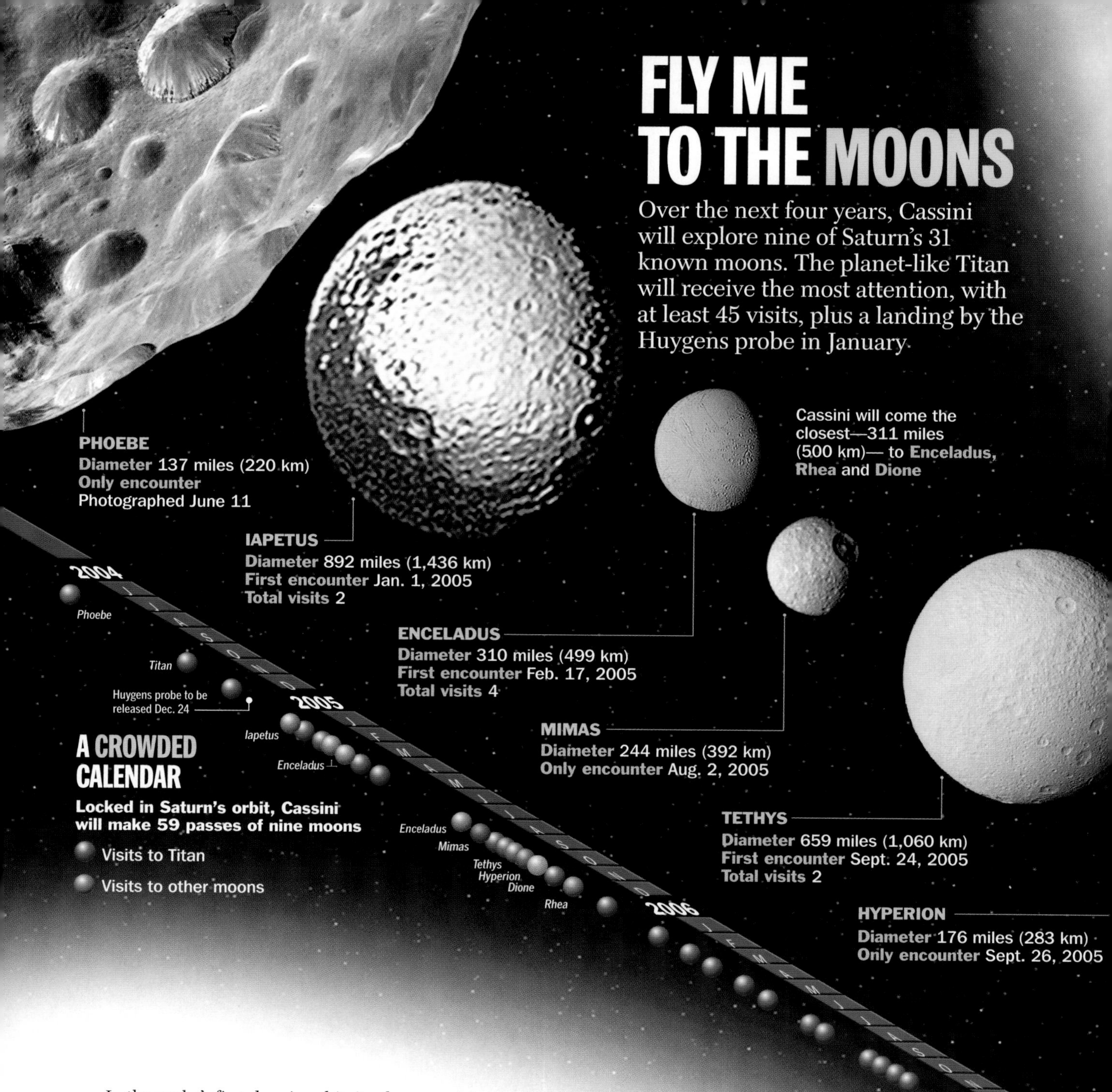

Cassini will come the closest—311 miles (500 km)— to Enceladus, Rhea and Dione
PHOEBE
Diameter 137 miles (220 km)
Only encounter
Photographed June 11
IAPETUS
Diameter 892 miles (1,436 km)
First encounter Jan. 1, 2005
Total visits 2
ENCELADUS
Diameter 310 miles (499 km)
First encounter Feb. 17, 2005
Total visits 4
MIMAS
Diameter 244 miles (392 km)
Only encounter Aug. 2, 2005
TETHYS
Diameter 659 miles (1,060 km)
First encounter Sept. 24, 2005
Total visits 2
HYPERION
Diameter 176 miles (283 km)
Only encounter Sept. 26, 2005
A CROWDED CALENDAR
Locked in Saturn's orbit, Cassini will make 59 passes of nine moons
Visits to Titan
Visits to other moons
2004
Phoebe
Titan
Huygens probe to be released Dec. 24
2005
Iapetus
Enceladus
Enceladus
Mimas
Tethys
Hyperion
Dione
Rhea
2006
2007

In the probe's first days in orbit, its close-up pictures of the giant planet's rings stole the show. Within minutes of Cassini's arrival, the ship's camera had fired off 61 shots of the rings, and by 10 o'clock the next morning, wide-eyed Cassini scientists were showing them off to the press. The scientists were stunned by the complexity and dynamism of the rings' internal structures. Planetary scientists had known since Voyager that the seven broad bands that make up the ring system are not undifferentiated masses of material but rather are made up of hundreds of individual strands, like the grooves in a record album. The strands consist of billions of bits of rubble and ice, some of them crystals smaller than a grain of sand, some of them boulders bigger than a house.

As the pictures from Cassini reveal, the interaction of this orbiting material can create bizarre effects. The edge of one ring shows elegant scalloping, presumably caused by the gravitational wake of a moon cruising alongside it. As the moon sails by at predictable intervals, the random collisions of ring particles become more rhythmic, forming tidy peaks and troughs. Other images show that the moving moons cause equally graceful formations within the rings by tugging on particles and causing them to pile up and thin out, pile up and thin out, rippling outward in what ring scientists call a density wave. Another kind of wave known as a bending wave is caused by a moon that orbits at an angle inclined to the ring plane, warping or corrugating the ring's edge.

Although no one is sure how the rings formed, some of the material is almost certainly the remains of small pulverized moons that were destroyed either by a cataclysmic meteor hit or when they wandered too close to a gravitational danger zone known as the Roche limit: the altitude above a planet at which the difference in gravity between the end of an object closest to the planet and the end farthest from the planet is great enough to pull the object apart while not pulling the remains out of orbit. Instead, the rubble disperses around the planet. Photographs of the debris could help confirm this phenomenon and could even turn up smaller, still undiscovered moons hiding within the rings.

Scientists already know of some moonlets that orbit inside the rings, sweeping areas clean of debris and accounting for at least two conspicuous gaps. Other tiny moons move along the outer rim of rings; these so-called shepherding moons groom the edges of the rings and keep them sharp—or, as we now know, scalloped.

In December 2005, if all goes according to plan, the Huygens probe will separate from Cassini and make its descent to Titan. Cassini will continue to circle Saturn for four more years, completing 76 orbits of the planet. In addition to surveying the rings, the probe will study nine of Saturn's moons in detail: Phoebe, Titan, Iapetus, Enceladus, Mimas, Tethys, Hyperion, Dione and Rhea.

Cassini will also return a wealth of data about conditions on the surface of the planet, which is made up mostly of hydrogen and helium and has a volume 764 times as great as Earth's. That much gas concentrated in one place ought to be dynamic, and Saturn is. The weather forecast: winds of more than 1,100 m.p.h. are expected at the equator—the strongest gusts on any planet in the solar system—and showers of helium rain (well, we think it's helium) may fall out of the clouds. Planning a visit? Bundle up: temperatures at the cloud tops are a frigid −218°F. ■

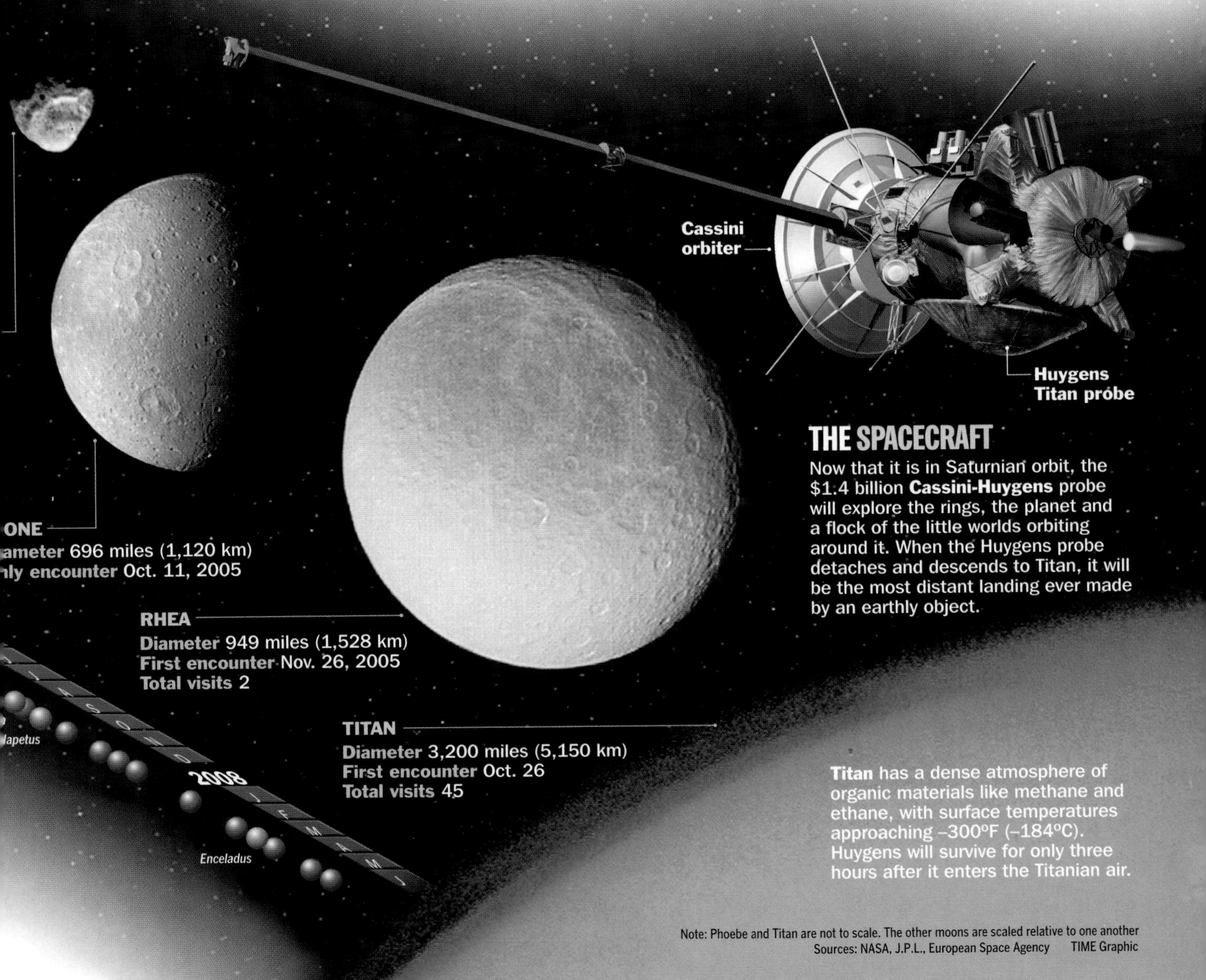
Cassini orbiter
Huygens Titan probe
THE SPACECRAFT
Now that it is in Saturnian orbit, the $1.4 billion Cassini-Huygens probe will explore the rings, the planet and a flock of the little worlds orbiting around it. When the Huygens probe detaches and descends to Titan, it will be the most distant landing ever made by an earthly object.
ONE
ameter 696 miles (1,120 km)
nly encounter Oct. 11, 2005
RHEA
Diameter 949 miles (1,528 km)
First encounter Nov. 26, 2005
Total visits 2
TITAN
Diameter 3,200 miles (5,150 km)
First encounter Oct. 26
Total visits 45
Iapetus
2008
Enceladus
Titan has a dense atmosphere of organic materials like methane and ethane, with surface temperatures approaching −300°F (−184°C). Huygens will survive for only three hours after it enters the Titanian air.

Note: Phoebe and Titan are not to scale. The other moons are scaled relative to one another
Sources: NASA, J.P.L., European Space Agency TIME Graphic

A Liquid Past for Mars

Two NASA rovers land on the Red Planet, begin to poke around—and find strong indications that Mars was once a watery world

FOR MANY NASA SCIENTISTS, THE NEW YEAR ARRIVED A bit late in 2004. Their calendar fired up on Jan. 3, when a team of scientists burst into a courtyard of the Jet Propulsion Laboratory in Pasadena, Calif., cheering and high-fiving over the successful landing of the Spirit rover at Gusev Crater on the surface of Mars. NASA had been in need of redemption since the explosion of the shuttle *Columbia* in February 2003, and in the week after Rover's landing, the beleaguered space agency's website registered 1.45 billion hits. And more good news was in store. Only two weeks after Spirit settled on Mars, its sister rover, Opportunity, bounced to a successful landfall on the other side of the planet, at an area called Meridiani Planum. When, on Jan. 15, President George W. Bush called for a new focus on planetary exploration, including a manned mission to Mars, it seemed as if a new era in NASA's history was about to begin.

The President's vision may have been election-year pie-in-the-sky. But NASA's two rovers on Mars were the real thing: a successful scientific mission that produced fascinating new data on a daily basis. By March, the rover Opportunity had returned new findings on a question that had long intrigued space scientists: Was there ever water on the surface of the Red Planet?

Giovanni Schiaparelli would have told you there was. The Italian astronomer had peered through his telescope one evening in 1877 and discovered what he took to be the Red Planet's famous canals. As it turned out, the canals were an optical illusion, but as more powerful telescopes and, later, spacecraft zoomed in for closer looks, there was no shortage of clues suggesting that Mars was once awash in water. Photographs shot from orbit show vast plains that resemble ancient sea floors, steep gorges that would dwarf the Grand Canyon and sinuous surface scars that look an awful lot like dry riverbeds.

Yet despite all the signs pointing to Mars' watery past, until Opportunity poked its instruments into the Martian rocks, nobody was sure how real that water was. Some of the surface formations that look water carved could have been formed by volcanism and wind. As recently as 2002, University of Colorado researchers published a persuasive paper suggesting that any water on Mars was car-

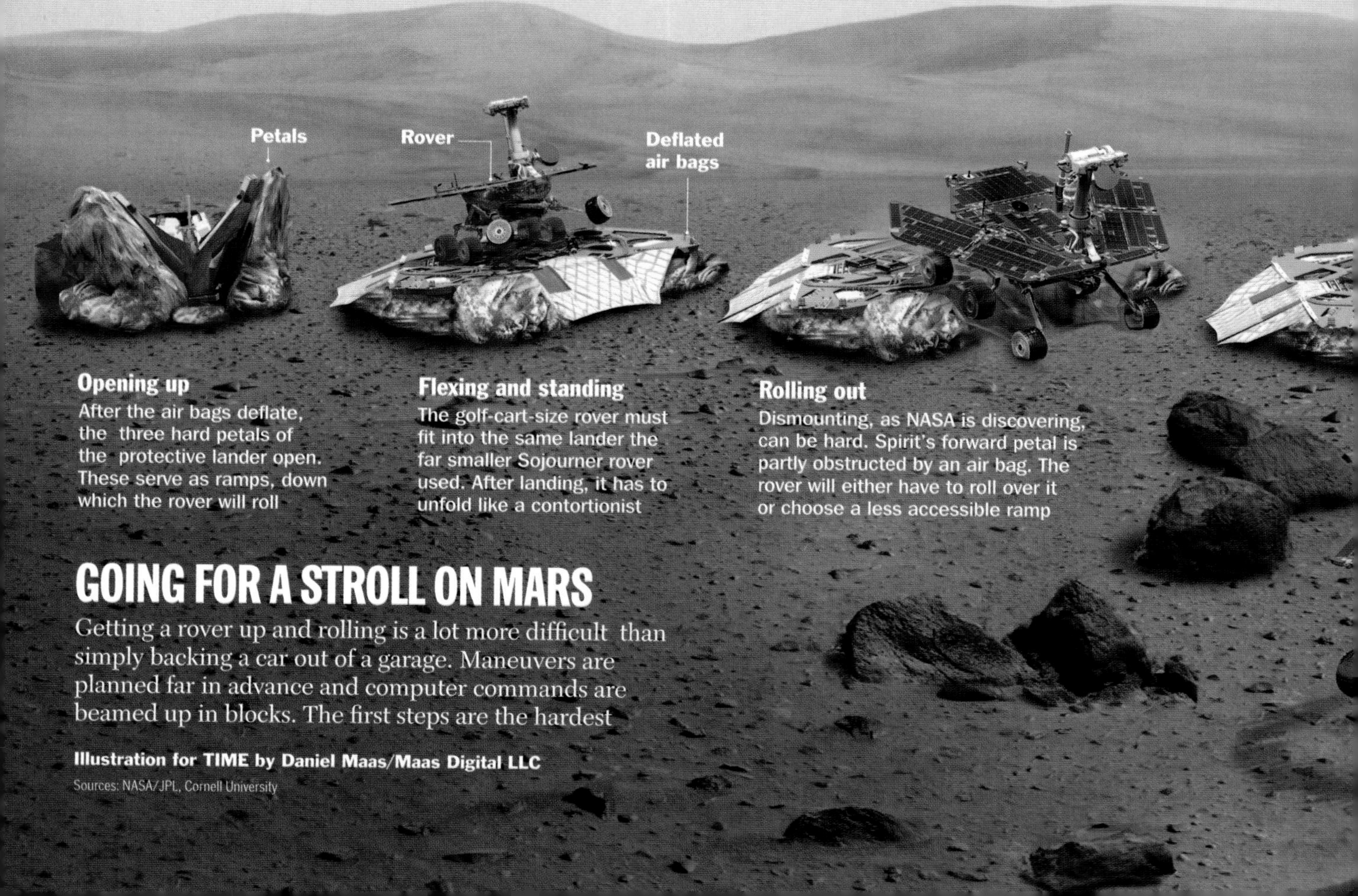
Petals
Rover
Deflated air bags
Opening up
After the air bags deflate, the three hard petals of the protective lander open. These serve as ramps, down which the rover will roll
Flexing and standing
The golf-cart-size rover must fit into the same lander the far smaller Sojourner rover used. After landing, it has to unfold like a contortionist
Rolling out
Dismounting, as NASA is discovering, can be hard. Spirit's forward petal is partly obstructed by an air bag. The rover will either have to roll over it or choose a less accessible ramp
GOING FOR A STROLL ON MARS
Getting a rover up and rolling is a lot more difficult than simply backing a car out of a garage. Maneuvers are planned far in advance and computer commands are beamed up in blocks. The first steps are the hardest

Illustration for TIME by Daniel Maas/Maas Digital LLC

Sources: NASA/JPL, Cornell University

ried in by crashing comets and then quickly evaporated.

The experiments that put that theory to rest were largely conducted by Opportunity on an outcropping in the Meridiani Planum nicknamed El Capitan. The surface of the formation is made up of fine layers—called parallel laminations—that are often laid down by minerals settling out of water. The rock is also randomly pitted with cavities called vugs that are created when salt crystals form in briny water and then fall out or dissolve away. But the real persuader was the presence of "blueberries" in El Capitan *(see sidebar)*. Their discovery led NASA to describe Mars as having been "drenched" in water in the past.

As if not to be outdone, a few weeks later the Spirit rover found hematite in a rock dubbed the "pot of gold" on the other side of the planet. Hematite is usually, but not always, formed in water. Spirit, however, was hindered by a balky front wheel as it moved some two miles across the Martian surface. The solution: in July mission scientists turned it around and drove it in reverse.

The twin rovers were designed to last only three months on the surface of Mars. But by mid-August, with the Martian winter setting in, they had doubled their expected life, and Opportunity was descending into Endurance Crater, a depression the size of a football stadium, about 1.5 miles from the craft's landing site. In September NASA extended the funding for the two vehicles' mission for the second time. While the rovers hadn't solved the biggest riddle of all—was there ever life on Mars?—they had certainly made for a lively 2004 on the Red Planet. ■

THE BLUEBERRIES OF MARS

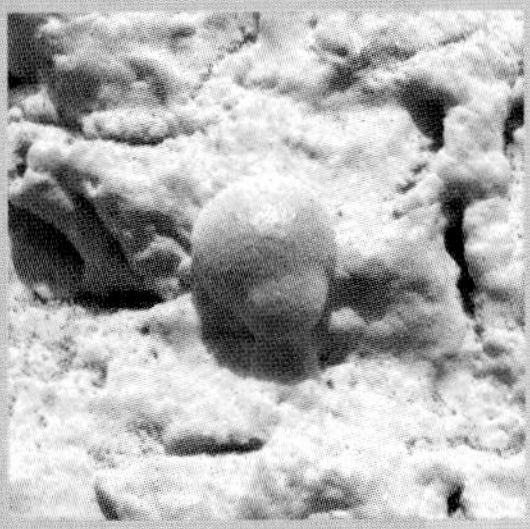

The most intriguing evidence that there was once water on Mars comes in the form of BB-size spherules—or "blueberries," as NASA calls them—scattered throughout a 10-in.-high, 65-ft.-wide rock outcropping that mission scientists dubbed El Capitan. Spheres like these can be formed either by volcanism or by minerals accreting under water, but the way the blueberries are mixed randomly through the rock—not layered on top, as they would have been after a volcanic eruption—strongly suggests they are not volcanic in origin. Chemical analyses of El Capitan show that it is rich in hematite, a sulfate known to form in the presence of water, as well as a mineral called jarosite, which not only forms in water but also contains a bit of water trapped in its matrix.

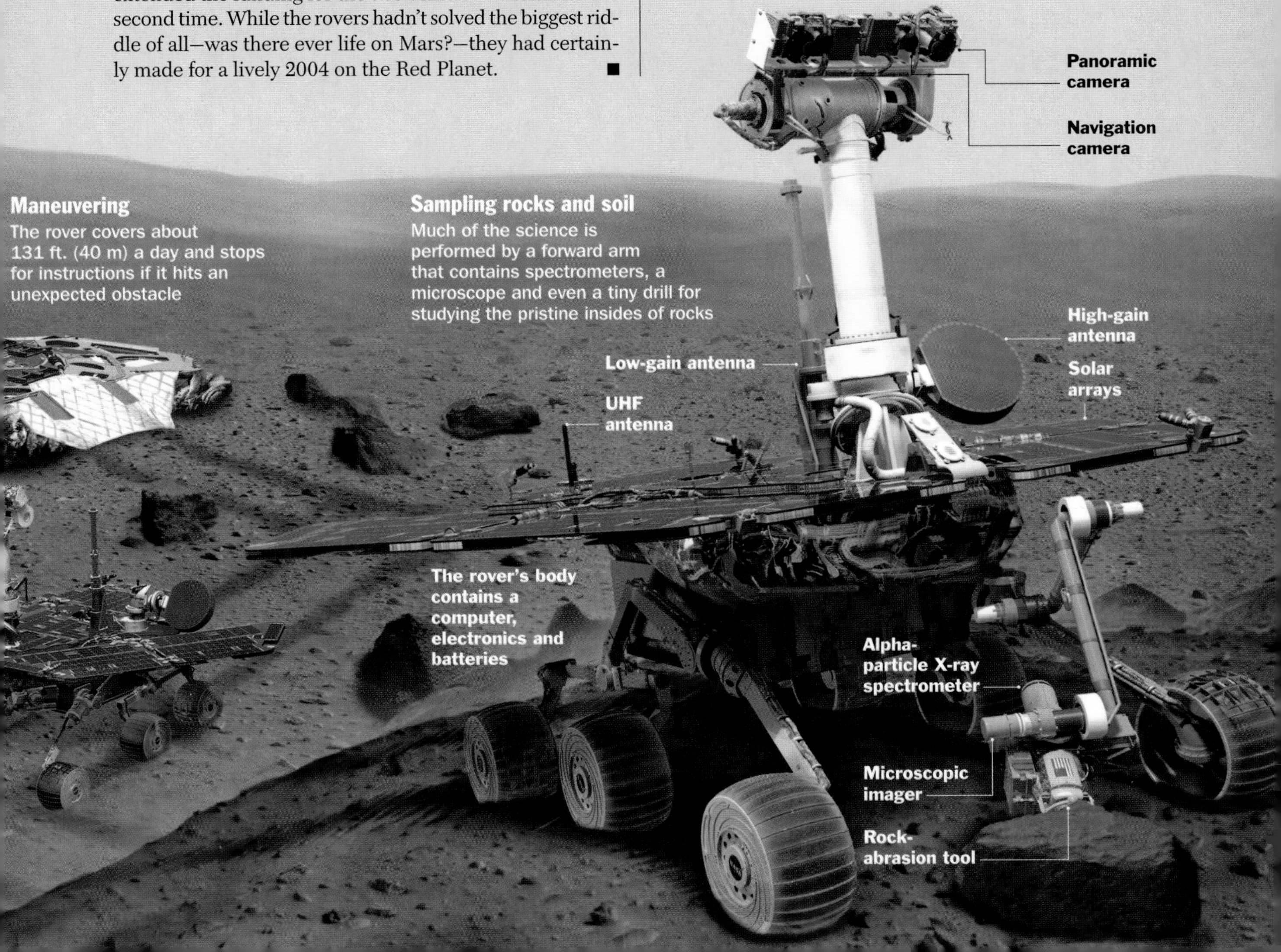
Panoramic camera
Navigation camera
Maneuvering
The rover covers about 131 ft. (40 m) a day and stops for instructions if it hits an unexpected obstacle
Sampling rocks and soil
Much of the science is performed by a forward arm that contains spectrometers, a microscope and even a tiny drill for studying the pristine insides of rocks
High-gain antenna
Low-gain antenna
Solar arrays
UHF antenna
The rover's body contains a computer, electronics and batteries
Alpha-particle X-ray spectrometer
Microscopic imager
Rock-abrasion tool

Transits and Transitions

Venus keeps a rendezvous with the sun, a rocket plane goes out of this world, and a NASA mission ends with a thud

BEHOLD THE TRANSIT OF VENUS across the face of the sun, a sight last seen when Chester A. Arthur was President, John L. Sullivan was the heavyweight champion of the world, and Jesse James was gunned down. Fortunately, optical technology has advanced a bit since 1882, allowing millions of us to see the orbital encounter in gorgeous detail. But 2004 also brought bad news about one of our most advanced telescopes, the orbiting Hubble platform: it may end its mission in a few years.

BEAUTY MARK
In 1627, the great German astronomer Johannes Kepler first predicted a transit of Venus across the face of the sun, but he died before he could witness the 1631 event. In 1874 more than 50 expeditions were launched from the U.S., Britain, Russia and other nations to every corner of the earth to see the transit. Reason: by recording the precise time a transit began and ended from different vantage points around the globe, 19th century astronomers could use trigonometry to calculate the distance from Earth to the sun. Another transit is coming June 6, 2012. If you miss that one, you're out of luck. There won't be another transit until 2117

FREDERIC NEEMA—GAMMA

PRIVATE SPACE FLIGHT LIFTS OFF

Paging Buck Rogers! On June 21, when *SpaceShipOne* returned to Earth with Michael Melvill, 63, at the controls, he became the first person ever to fly a civilian craft into space. His top altitude of 328,491 ft. was about a quarter of the way to the International Space Station. Designed by Burt Rutan, the impressively small and lightweight rocket plane (it's about the size of an SUV) is also relatively cheap: it cost about $20 million, compared with the $400 million-plus that NASA drops on each space shuttle launch. In October, *SpaceshipOne* completed two more journeys into the stratosphere, winning the $10 million Ansari X prize, designed to jump-start a new age of space flight for civilians.

NASA—JPL—REUTERS—LONDON

HERE COMES THE SUN—NOT!

Well, it seemed like a good idea: NASA would team up with Hollywood helicopter stunt pilot Cliff Fleming to attempt a daring mid-air catch of a falling satellite. NASA launched the $260 million Genesis satellite into Earth orbit in August 2001 to harvest solar wind on collector plates. The goal: to allow scientists to study the mysterious particles, which might lead to an understanding of how the planets first formed. But on Sept. 8, when Genesis came down from orbit, its parachutes failed to open. Fleming and a backup chopper didn't get a chance at making the catch, as the 450-lb. craft slammed into the Utah desert at 200 m.p.h. Ouch.

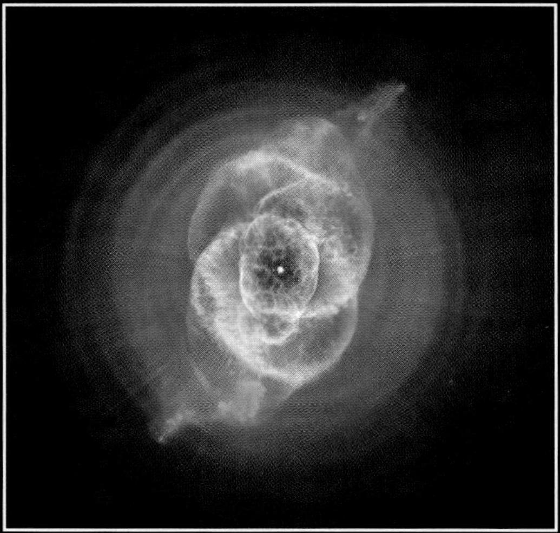

NASA—ESA—HEIC AND THE HUBBLE HERITAGE TEAM

THERE GOES HUBBLE?

This image of the galactic formation dubbed the Cat's Eye Nebula is typical of the entrancing views of deep space taken by NASA's Hubble Space Telescope, which was launched in 1990 and repaired in a 1993 mission. NASA distressed millions of amateur sky gazers—and a clutch of celebrated astronomers—when it said it would cancel scheduled service missions to Hubble and would dispatch a space tug in the next few years to guide it out of orbit to fall into the ocean. The January announcement caused an uproar, and Hubble fans vowed to save the craft. Stay tuned.

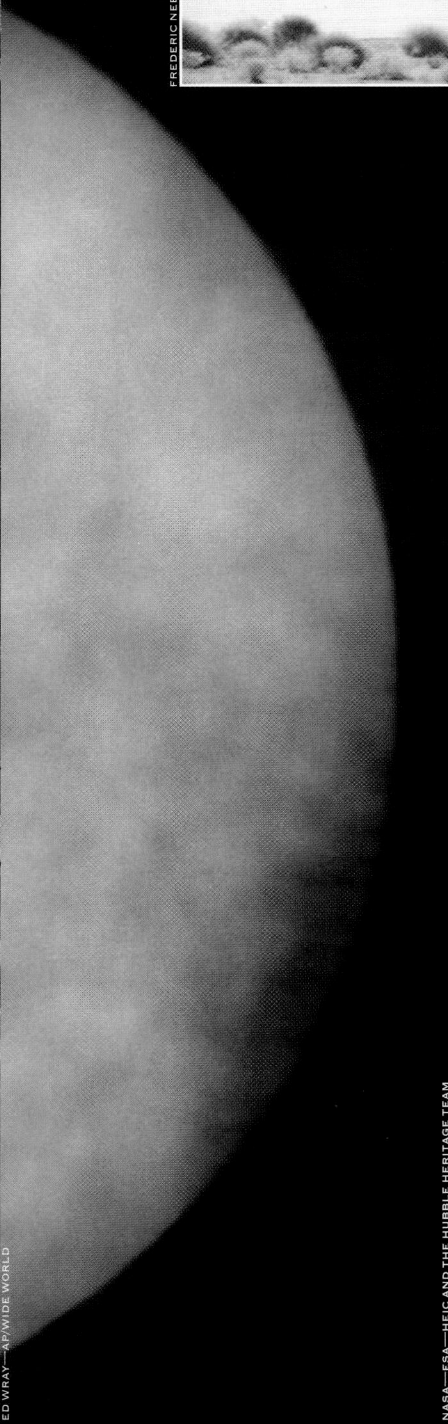

ED WRAY—AP/WIDE WORLD

ANNUAL CHECKUP

In a year of wonder drugs and blunder drugs, the cruelest month was October, when the nation's flu supply came up short and a widely used painkiller was pulled from the market

MARK HUMPHREY—AP/WIDE WORLD

Depression Drugs and Teens

It's a quandary: antidepressant drugs that alter brain chemicals (such as Paxil and Zoloft) are effective in treating depression in many teens but can cause suicidal thoughts in others. After studies showed young antidepressant users were about 1.8 times as likely to have suicidal urges or behaviors as patients given a placebo, the FDA said it would issue stronger advisories against prescribing the drugs for teens.

Flu Vaccine Shortage

Lines of the elderly seeking precious flu shots became a sadly familiar sight in the fall, after federal health officials said the nation's expected supply of flu vaccine would be halved. Reason: the British government suspended a major drug factory's license due to concerns about unsterile conditions. Health officials asked that most Americans give up their shot in favor of the very old and the very young.

STEVE LISS

Oldest American Dies

When she died on Dec. 1 in Worthington, Ohio, Verona Johnston was the oldest person in America, at age 114. Johnston was one of the world's growing numbers of the superold, who are increasingly a subject of study by scientists seeking to learn why some people remain robust and active into extreme old age while others age far more quickly. Johnston never smoked, but she did begin drinking—at age 98.

Viagra Has Company

Viagra's got the blues. In their first full year in wide release, two new drugs that treat erectile dysfunction, Levitra and Cialis, took away a chunk of the pioneer's market. Cialis, below, whose maker, Eli Lilly, boasts that it is effective far longer than Viagra, won some 14% of the market; Levitra, made by Bayer and GlaxoSmithKline, had a market share of 12%. Physicians say the three drugs are increasingly popular with younger men.

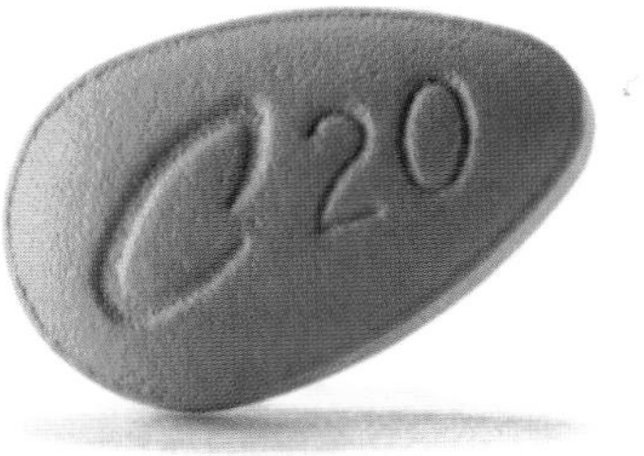
C 20

ELI LILLY

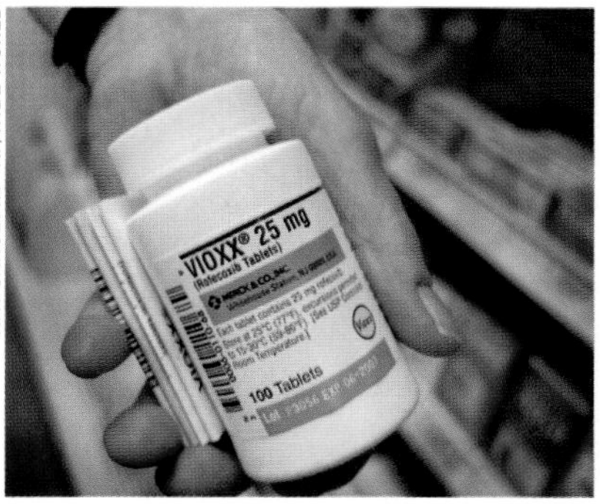
VIOXX® 25 mg
100 Tablets

AMY SANCETTA—AP/WIDE WORLD

Vioxx Withdrawn

On Oct. 1, after a new study found that the arthritis and pain medication Vioxx might double a patient's risk of a heart attack or stroke, the drug's maker, Merck, pulled it from the market. Vioxx earned $2.5 billion for Merck in 2003 alone. The sudden decision caused an uproar, raising questions as to how long before the announcement Merck and the U.S. government had been aware of the drug's harmful side effects.

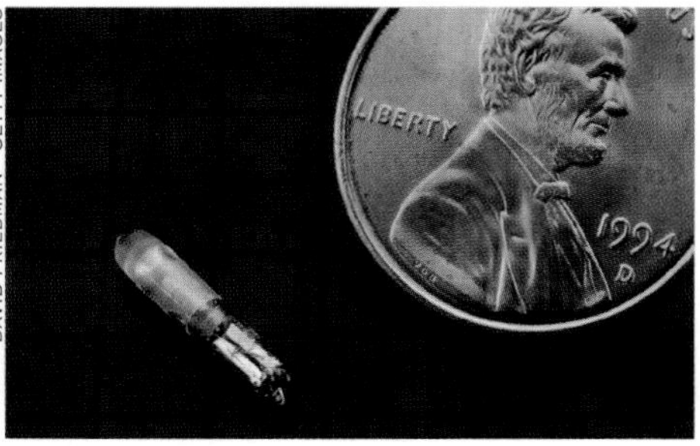
LIBERTY
1994

DAVID FRIEDMAN—GETTY IMAGES

VeriChip Approved

In October the FDA gave the go-ahead for maker Digital Solutions to begin selling the VeriChip, a tiny computer chip that is implanted beneath one's skin and carries coded health data that can be read by a scanner. While some health professionals praised the minichip as a potential life saver in emergency situations, privacy advocates charged that the chip could undermine confidentiality or even be used to track one's movements. To jump-start use of the product, Digital Solutions said it would donate $650 scanners to 200 of the nation's busiest trauma centers.

Asia's Avian Flu

Epidemiologists are greatly worried by the outbreak of avian (bird) flu that struck nations of Southeast Asia in 2003-04. The highly lethal disease killed 31 of the 43 people known to have caught it in 2004, all in Thailand and Vietnam. Some 200 million chickens and other fowl either died of the disease or were killed to prevent its dissemination. This strain of avian flu has shown a rare ability to spread between different animal species.

VINCENT YU—AP/WIDE WORLD

Statin Power

Statins, originally developed to lower cholesterol levels, are poised to become what aspirin has been for decades: an all-purpose miracle drug used to treat dozens of ailments. Now research shows that statins may help prevent heart disease and various types of cancer (including breast cancer) and that diabetes patients who take the drugs could cut their risk of both stroke and heart attack. Statins also cause few side effects and show promise as a therapy for more than a dozen other serious diseases. Britain has already approved the sale of statins without a doctor's prescription.

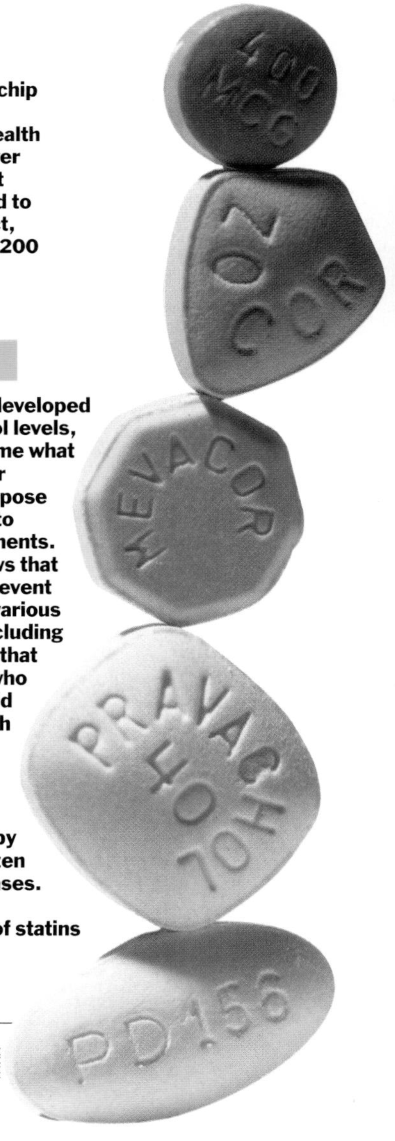
ZOCOR
MEVACOR
PRAVACHOL

TAKA

Science Notes

PROFILE

Hawking Thinks Twice

For more than two decades, Stephen Hawking has been one of the most famous scientists on earth. The brilliant physicist, whose ALS disease has confined him to a wheelchair, is heir to the revered Cambridge professorship once held by Isaac Newton. Best sellers like the 1988 blockbuster *A Brief History of Time* and a guest appearance on a *Star Trek* episode are certainly more familiar than Hakwking's highly recondite work as a cosmologist, but most of us are aware of his work on black holes, those mysterious remnants of collapsed stars whose gravity is so strong that nothing, including light, can escape them.

Well, that was Hawking's story, anyway, and he was sticking to it—until now. In July, before an array of TV cameras and hundreds of colleagues at the ordinarily obscure International Conference of General Relativity and Gravitation in Dublin, Hawking recanted. Black holes, he declared, do not forever annihilate all traces of what falls into them; some information does escape in the form of radiation. Conceding defeat, Hawking also paid off a long-standing bet with Caltech astrophysicist John Preskill. The stakes of the decades-old wager: a hefty baseball encyclopedia—from which, of course, it's easy to extract information.

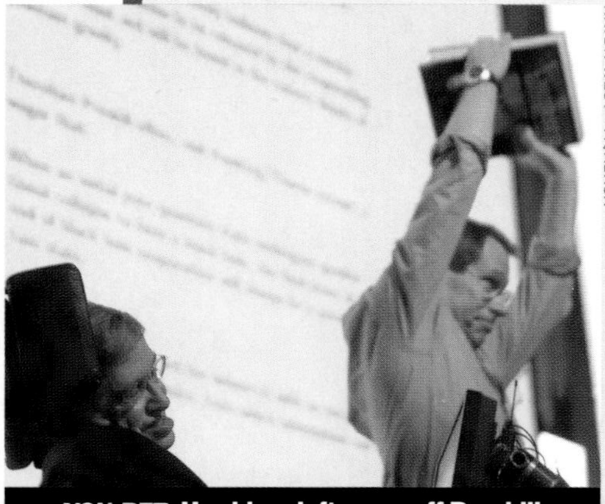

HAYDN WEST—PA/ABACA

YOU BET: Hawking, left, pays off Preskill

LEFT: AP/WIDE WORLD; BELOW: PETER BROWN

HOBBIT HOME? Liang Bua cave on Flores

Island of the Lost Hobbits

Not-so-big news! A team of Australian and Indonesian scientists announced in October in the science journal *Nature* that they had found remains of a tribe of tiny humans, only about 3 ft. tall, that lived on Flores, a Pacific island 350 miles west of Bali. In a cave called Liang Bua, above, the team found bones from seven individuals, including the nearly intact skeleton of an adult female they nicknamed the Hobbit. Unlike African pygmies, these were not simply short versions of *Homo sapiens.* Dubbed *Homo floresiensis,* they are an entirely new twig on the human family tree. Although their brains were tiny, the mini-folk used fire, made tools and hunted. They are believed to have died out some 13,000 years ago.

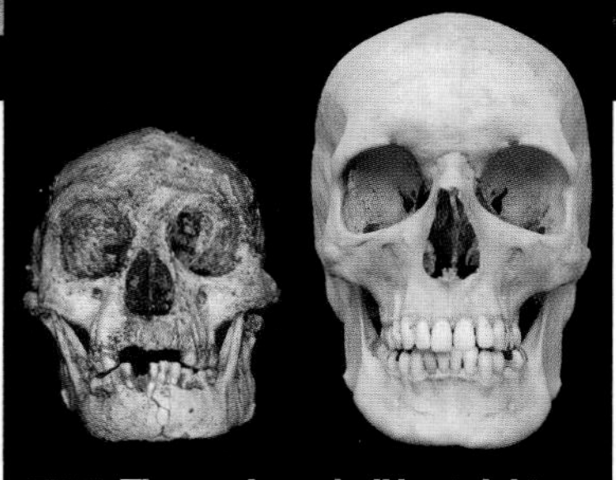

TINY: The modern skull is at right

Fine Feathered Friend

Watch your step with that annoying pigeon in the park; it may have had an ancestor that once ruled the earth. Writing in *Nature* in the fall, Chinese and U.S. paleontologists announced the discovery of one dinosaur that evidently slept curled up in a posture identical to that of a sleeping duck, and another that is the first tyrannosaur ever found with feathers. That's significant because that family of dinosaurs is believed to be among the closest relatives of modern birds. The new specimens were unearthed in a geological formation in northeastern China's Liaoning province that has become one of the world's most renowned fossil beds.

Another team, meanwhile, published an analysis showing that *Tyrannosaurus rex* grew (and thus metabolized) at an impressively fast rate—suggesting that it might have been warm-blooded like birds.

PORTIA SLOAN—IVPP—AMNH

QUACK! A feathered *Tyrannosaurus*

STEVE SCHILLING—USGS

■ IMAGE

Fixin' to Blow?

Look who's back: the volcano at Mount St. Helens, 100 miles south of Seattle in Washington State, began belching smoke in September, and a large lava dome appeared in its crater. When last heard from, the volcano erupted in 1980, blowing off the top 1,300 ft. of the mountain, destroying tens of thousands of acres of forest and killing 57 people. Its massive plume reached 80,000 ft. in less than 15 minutes.

JOE MCDONALD—DRK PHOTO

HANG ON: Leopards are now sparse in Asia

Death Knell for Big Cats?

As the word's human population grows, its supply of wild felines is dwindling. Ten years ago, scientists thought there were as many as 100,000 lions in Africa, but a new appraisal says there may only 23,000 left in the wild. Tigers are even scarcer; only 7,000 may walk the earth today. Leopards, more widely dispersed, may number 300,000.

A Cloning Milestone

In a breakthrough in human cell cloning, researchers Woo Suk Hwang and Shin Yong Moon, from Korea's Seoul National University, announced in February that they had created more than 200 embryos by cloning mature human cells and had grown 30 of them to the blastocyst stage of development, each more than 100 cells strong. The news was significant on two fronts. The first is simply that their embryos didn't die, though many experts were convinced that they would be impossibly fragile. Second, the scientists extracted embryonic stem cells from the blastocysts and coaxed some of them into a self-perpetuating colony. Some of the stem cells evidently turned into bone, muscle and immature brain cells. Such stem cells could in theory supply replacement tissues to treat any ailment involving cell damage—including heart disease, diabetes, spinal-cord injury, Parkinson's and Alzheimer's.

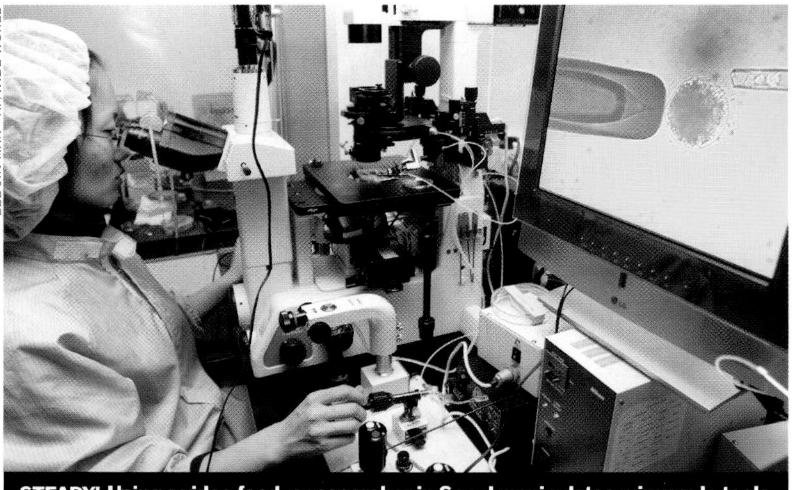

LEE JIN-MAN—AP/WIDE WORLD

STEADY! Using a video feed, a researcher in Seoul manipulates minuscule tools

A Grand New Face For the Windy City

Towering like Big Brother over a reflecting pool, a 50-ft. video image of a Chicagoan's face projected on glass bricks is a focal point of Crown Fountain, designed by Spanish sculptor Jaume Plensa for the city's new Millennium Park. The fountain is bookended by two monoliths that face each other; their giant changing visages purse their lips at intervals, and water shoots from their mouths. *Voila!* The City of Big Shoulders is now the City of Big Spouters. The $475 million park occupies 24 acres adjoining Grant Park and facing Lake Michigan. Although it opened four years after its name declared it would, the new park was worth the wait. Other highlights include a 110-ton, lozenge-shaped sculpture in highly reflective stainless steel by Anish Kapoor that was instantly dubbed *"The Bean,"* and a curvilinear bridge and shimmering outdoor concert space designed by Frank Gehry, shown on the next page.

SCOTT OLSON—GETTY IMAGES

FOR ART THAT'S NEW, ROOMS WITH A VIEW

Frank Gehry adds to Chicago's great legacy of design, while New York City gets an elegant aerie for jazz and a massive MOMA makeover

JAZZ ASCENDING
In New York City, Jazz at Lincoln Center opened its skyscraper home in the glitzy new Time Warner Building, just across from Central Park and a few blocks down the street from Lincoln Center (don't ask). With three separate halls—including the Allen Room, which seems to suspend the musicians in midair above a smashing urban view—the $128 million complex reflects the towering ambitions of its director, Wynton Marsalis. The New Orleans–born trumpeter has long sought to elevate the profile of America's indigenous musical form. He's got the elevation part down; bring on the noise!

EXIT

SCOTT OLSON—GETTY IMAGES

CHICAGO AL FRESCO

Chicago's eye-catching new Millennium Park is a fitting addition to a city that is proud to have been a cradle of great modern architecture. Gleaming along the city's "front porch" facing Lake Michigan, the new park includes a typically exuberant outdoor concert space designed by Frank Gehry. With its swooping, melting ribbons of metal and its nifty cross-ribbed "ceiling" (which holds suspended speakers), Gehry's outdoor "hall" succeeds in one of its main goals: making all the right-angled skyscrapers behind it look, well, *so* 20th century.

MOMA ON STEROIDS

Curators around the world envy the rich holdings of New York City's Museum of Modern Art almost as much as they envy the deep pockets of its benefactors. After a two-year period of exile in Queens, MOMA returned in November to renovated new digs in Manhattan. The $858 million reconstruction, designed by Japanese architect Yoshio Taniguchi, is a crisp exercise in modernism (no surprise there), which updates MOMA's beloved sculpture garden, rendered at right. The addition doubles the space MOMA can devote to showing off its unparalleled collection of Picassos, Mirós and Serras.

COURTESY MUSEUM OF MODERN ART

THE EYES OF AN ERA

The year 2004 saw the passing of a number of groundbreaking photographers, pioneers who helped turn the camera into a new kind of recording device with a surprisingly broad array of uses: to capture history, to probe identity, to celebrate style and to create desire

740

CARL MYDANS—TIME LIFE

1907-2004

Carl Mydans

MYDANS WAS PRESENT AT THE CREATION. WITH ALFRED EISENSTADT AND MARGARET Bourke-White at LIFE magazine, he helped transform news photography from a parade of static head shots and ceremonial poses into the supple narrative art we call photojournalism. When he joined LIFE in 1936 as its first issue was just going to press, Mydans was fresh from the fabled team of photographers for the U.S. Farm Security Administration—Walker Evans and Dorothea Lange among them—whose pictures would become our collective memory of the Depression. From them, he learned the moral dimension of photography and its power to turn life into theater. Captured by the Japanese in World War II, he was released in time to take his famous shot of General Douglas MacArthur sloshing onto a beach in Luzon in the Philippines—a picture of victory as both moral triumph and the ultimate photo opportunity.

CARL MYDANS—TIME LIFE

CALL OF DUTY: Mydans in Korea in 1951. He and his wife Shelley, a LIFE reporter, were captured in Manila in 1942 and spent two years in Japanese prison camps

JACK MANNING—NEW YORK TIMES CO.—GETTY IMAGES

1923-2004

Richard Avedon

AVEDON STARTED HIS CAREER IN THE MERCHANT MARINE, TAKING identity-card shots. Years later, in a breakthrough aesthetic insight, he appropriated the bare format of an ID for his mature portrait style, a high-focus inspection of unsmiling faces against an arctic-white background. Under that light, the body capitulates. Each line and facial sag announces itself. But these pictures were not cruel: they were fearless, lucid and unsentimental. Avedon knew that every portrait was a performance but that the performance could be a passage to something true. Before becoming famous for his portraits, Avedon energized fashion photography, replacing chic with cheek. In one giddy series of pictures from 1962, he had model Suzy Parker high-stepping it around Paris with Mike Nichols, a funny young couple on the run, at a time when fashion photography was still largely a matter of subdued, immobile poses. As a fashion photographer, Avedon took human vanity to new heights; as a portraitist, he brought us all back down to earth.

DAVID SEYMOUR—MAGNUM PHOTOS

ICONS: The stylish Avedon was the template for Fred Astaire's portrayal of fashion photographer Dick Avery in *Funny Face* (1957); above, the two clown around in Paris. At left, Avedon poses with one of the portraits from his 1985 book *In the American West.* Below, Avedon's 1980 shot of a 15-year-old Brooke Shields hawking jeans became an icon of the era

Calvin Klein Jeans

1933-2004

Eddie Adams

WHAT IS THE PRICE OF AN ICON? ASSOCIATED PRESS PHOTOGRAPHER Eddie Adams was haunted for three decades by a single picture he took in Saigon—the picture above. As Adams told the story, he had hitched a ride with a crew from NBC News on Feb. 1, 1968, the second day of the Tet offensive. The crew followed the sound of weapons firing and ended up in Cholon, Saigon's Chinese neighborhood, where they found no combat. Then a group of policemen came walking out of a building with a bound prisoner in custody. "All of a sudden, out of nowhere, comes General [Nguyen Ngoc] Loan, the national police chief," Adams recalled. "I thought he was going to threaten the prisoner. So as quick as he brought his pistol up, I took a picture. But it turned out he shot him."

The photograph encapsulated the brutality of the war in a single indelible image, and it brought Adams fame and the Pulitzer Prize for news photography in 1969. Thirty-five years later, it remains one of the most familiar images of the Vietnam era. But Adams grew to hate the photo. "In taking that picture," he once told *Parade* magazine, "I had destroyed [Loan's] life ... [he] had become a man condemned both in his country and in America because he had killed an enemy in war. People do this all the time in war, but rarely is a photographer there to record the act." Loan claimed that his victim was a Viet Cong captain responsible for many murders. In an eerie postscript, Adams visited the former South Vietnamese officer in the 1980s, when Loan was running a pizza parlor outside Washington. "He told me, 'You were doing your job, and I was doing mine,'" Adams said.

EDDIE ADAMS—AP/WIDE WORLD

EDDIE ADAMS—AP/WIDE WORLD

HAUNTED: Adams on the trail of a story in South Vietnam, above, in 1965. He covered 13 wars and took many portraits of world leaders, but he came to loathe his most famous picture. "Photographs, you know, are half-truths," he said the day after General Loan, the executioner in his famed image, died in 1998

1908-2004

Henri Cartier-Bresson

WHEN THE GREAT FRENCH PHOTOGRAPHER DIED, AT 95, *TIME* invited veteran photojournalist James Nachtwey to write an appreciation. "He made us see," Nachtwey wrote. "He spent his life reconciling opposites, not laboriously but in an instant, with the grace of an athlete, on the run. Through his eyes we see the universal in the specific, large issues in small things, mystery in the obvious, poetry in the mundane. We see infinity in the blink of an eye.

"He was the foundation of contemporary photography. He made an image in Spain of a band of children playing on a street [*shown below*], a heavyset man in a suit and fedora walking through their midst and, in the background, a constellation of windows scattered across the wall of a building. It wasn't a picture about anything. It was a moment most of us would never notice, but in his eyes it became an enigma, so full of suspense, you could almost hear the click of a detonator. Cartier-Bresson was mercurial, synchronized to the changing tides of history. He was in China on the eve of revolution and with Mahatma Gandhi 15 minutes before his death. But Cartier-Bresson was not a reporter. The world in process was his raw material."

GEORGE HOYNINGEN-HUENE—MAGNUM PHOTOS

SNAP! Cartier-Bresson described his impromptu photographs as a search for "the decisive moment" of illumination. He used a simple Leica camera, allowing him to capture life's fleeting details. He was photographed above in 1935

HENRI CARTIER-BRESSON—MAGNUM PHOTOS

Arts Notes

PROFILE

Time Traveler

"Fun, Fun, Fun" it wasn't: when Beach Boys genius Brian Wilson, obsessed with topping his musical rivals the Beatles, tried to record his visionary epic *Smile* in 1965-66, his bandmates found it inchoate and overly obscure (although they may have not have used those precise terms to express their dismay). Already troubled with the mental and substance-abuse problems that would derail his career for decades, Wilson shut the lid on *Smile,* killing the project and releasing it only in such tantalizing snatches as the No. 1 single, *Good Vibrations,* the shimmering *Surf's Up* and other fragments.

Fast-forward 38 years: Wilson, now 61, happily married for nine years and back in the groove, thanks to treatment for depression by a team of UCLA doctors, has been touring to great acclaim. After successfully performing the Beach Boys' classic 1965 album *Pet Sounds* in its entirety on the road, Wilson went into the studio and finally recorded his original version of *Smile,* complete with shifting time signatures, stunning harmonies and sonic collages that employ bells, whistles, sirens and glockenspiels. In February, after Wilson debuted the work in Britain's Royal Festival Hall, the London *Times* declared, "Leonard Bernstein said Brian Wilson was one of the greatest composers of the 20th century. He was not wrong."

JIM MONE—AP/WIDE WORLD

WILSON: A masterpiece restored

RUSTY KENNEDY—AP/WIDE WORLD

VOCAL: R.E.M.'s Michael Stipe joins Springsteen at a Vote for Change show

Vote, Yes; Change, No

Aroused by a divisive presidential election, pop musicians turned into advocates in the fall. Bruce Springsteen, R.E.M., John Fogerty and the Dave Matthews Band took to the road under the banner Vote for Change, performing 33 concerts in support of Democrat John Kerry. The shows were short on political discourse but long on music and moolah, taking in some $15 million. Meanwhile, rap impresario Russell Simmons' Hip-Hop Summit Action Network worked to fire up minority voters. Both groups succeeded in registering voters, but when the fat lady sang, Mr. Bush was still Boss.

Two Who Laughed Last

They may be an odd couple, but filmmakers Michael Moore and Mel Gibson each stunned Hollywood bigwigs by turning movies from oft-scorned genres into box-office gold. Moore, the gadfly of the left who scored critical acclaim, if not big numbers, with *Bowling for Columbine* in 2002, proved that documentaries could fill seats with his attack on the Bush Administration, *Fahrenheit 9/11,* which raked in $250 million by December.

Actor-director Gibson, a Roman Catholic, showed that religious movies could work wonders at the box office with *The Passion of the Christ.* Released just before Easter, the film earned a total of $625 million around the world by late fall.

LEFT: JOHN FLESHER—AP/WIDE WORLD; RIGHT: MUNAWAR HOSAIN—GETTY IMAGES

HIT MEN: Moore and Gibson

Mark Your Calendar Now

Battling cable networks, video games and the Internet for viewers' attention, TV networks are

KEVIN WINTER—GETTY IMAGES

HEIR APPARENT: O'Brien sizes up his next perch

MARY ALTAFFER—AP/WIDE WORLD

IMAGE

Taymor's Triumph

She has directed Wagner, Strauss and Shakespeare, but Julie Taymor, 51, remains best known for her resplendent visual production of Disney's Broadway smash *The Lion King*. When Taymor's Asian-influenced version of Mozart's *The Magic Flute* debuted at New York City's Metropolitan Opera in October, critics hailed its hallucinatory look. "Utterly enchanting," said the *Daily News;* "Spectacular," agreed *Newsday*.

looking far ahead as they seek to keep their late-night and morning shows—key profit centers—viable. Even so, NBC stunned Hollywood when it revealed in September that it had signed late-late star Conan O'Brien to replace Jay Leno has host of *The Tonight Show*—in 2009.

SIDSEL DE JONG—AFP—GETTY IMAGES

GONE: A Munch snatched

Old Yeller

Easily one of the most iconic images in fine art, Norwegian painter Edvard Munch's portrait of a soul in anguish, *The Scream* (1893), has been ripped off to create blow-up dolls, political cartoons and album covers. On Aug. 22, it was ripped off for real: in a brazen daylight heist, two masked bandits threatened a guard with a gun, then removed the painting (one of several versions of the image) from the wall of Oslo's Munch Museum. If you see it ... holler.

A TRIO OF SITCOMS RIDE INTO THE SUNSET

FRIENDS Long the second pillar in NBC's vaunted "must-see TV" lineup on Thursdays, *Friends* cashed it in after 10 years. Matt Le Blanc's cute but dim hunk *Joey* is hoping to catch some of *Frazier's* spin-off magic

Who needs friends, family or lovers, when you can get by on a virtual diet of relationships, thanks to your trusty TV set, which never asks for a night out or even a birthday card? Yet even TV shows have a sell-by date, and in 2004 viewers bade farewell to three beloved sitcoms. Our pals at *Friends* tabled their flings, the *Frazier* cast chugged their last lattes, and the *Sex and the City* gals hugged their last hotties.

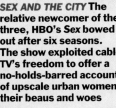

SEX AND THE CITY The relative newcomer of the three, HBO's *Sex* bowed out after six seasons. The show exploited cable TV's freedom to offer a no-holds-barred account of upscale urban women, their beaus and woes

FRASIER Some said Kelsey Grammar's Dr. Crane from *Cheers* couldn't carry his own show, but *Frasier* sent him off to Seattle and became one of the most successful spin-offs in TV history after its 1993 debut

CLOCKWISE FROM TOP: WARNER BROTHERS; HBO; JUSTIN LUBIN—NBC

Milestones

Mourning In America

When Ronald Reagan became President in 1981, America was a dispirited nation, humiliated abroad and uncertain at home, with a hunger for heroes but little faith that even a President could make a difference. The burdens of the Oval Office had killed John F. Kennedy, destroyed Lyndon Johnson, corrupted Richard Nixon and overwhelmed Gerald Ford and Jimmy Carter. Reagan restored the belief that an ordinary American raised in the heartland could give his nation a sense of direction and purpose. "We have every right to dream heroic dreams," he declared in his Inaugural Address. Though he was nearly 70 when he took office, this Dreamer in Chief managed to make the country feel young again, its mission not yet completed, its glory days ahead. Hope is contagious, and Ronald Reagan was a carrier.

THE

THE WHITE HOUSE

GIPPER

ON DUTY: Reagan admitted he got goose bumps when he first entered the Oval Office as President

ARNOLD NEWMAN—GETTY IMAGES

1911-2004

The Life and Times of an American Optimist

Ronald Reagan merged passion, politics and perceptions to change the world

"I LOVED THREE THINGS: DRAMA, POLITICS AND SPORTS, and I'm not sure they always come in that order," Ronald Reagan once said. His picture in the high school yearbook bore the caption "Life is just one grand sweet song, so start the music." He was born Feb. 6, 1911, in Tampico, Ill.; nothing about his origins augured any remarkable success. His father Jack, who had never reached high school, was a shoe salesman and an alcoholic. The family moved often; money was short.

Sports gave Reagan a chance to get an education. He won a scholarship to tiny Eureka College, where he discovered his gift for public speaking when he helped organize a student strike, and also began his love affair with theater. He spent much of his time in student theatricals as well as in football and swimming, only to emerge into the Depression-stricken America of 1932 to find there were very few jobs for actors and fewer still for football players. So he wandered through nearby towns, looking for work at local radio stations. A station manager in Davenport, Iowa, asked him to narrate an imaginary football game, and Reagan poured into the fakery all the enthusiasm of desperation. He was hired for $5 a game.

By 1937 he was broadcasting from Des Moines, where he persuaded radio station WHO to send him to California to cover the spring training of the Chicago Cubs. A Des Moines friend sent him to see her agent, who called the casting director at Warner Bros. and said, "I have another Robert Taylor sitting in my office." Warner gave him a screen test, then signed him for $200 a week.

Reagan's early films, as many as nine a year, were forgettable. But he struck paydirt playing legendary Notre Dame halfback George Gipp in *Knute Rockne, All-American* (1940) and with a turn as a double amputee in *Kings*

AP/WIDE WORLD

GOOD SPORT: As a youngster, Reagan, second from left, already wore a big smile

GEORGE TICE

WARNER BROTHERS

WHO
MICHAEL ROUGIER—TIME LIFE

EARLY YEARS: Reagan as a lifeguard in his college years, top left, and as "the Gipper" in his 1940 signature role. He was a popular sportscaster on an Iowa radio station in the 1930s

Row, which made him a star. But by now it was 1942, and there was a war on. Reagan could see very little without eyeglasses; barred from combat, he spent the war years making training films for soldiers.

In the postwar years Reagan became involved in Hollywood union politics. "I was a near hopeless hemophilic liberal," Reagan said later. "I had followed F.D.R. blindly ... " But by 1947 he was president of the Screen Actors Guild and found himself embroiled in the union wars ravaging Hollywood. Reagan came to believe that the bitter strikes in 1945 and 1946 by stagehands of the Conference of Studio Unions represented a communist attempt to take over Hollywood, and that belief changed his political views forever. His union activity may have damaged his career as an actor: he stopped getting offers of good parts.

By 1953 Reagan was reduced to doing a nightclub routine in Las Vegas, but he was soon offered a position as host and occasional star of a weekly television drama series for General Electric; he also became a goodwill ambassador to GE plants around the nation. *The General Electric Theater*, with Reagan as host from 1954 to 1962, was a success. Yet what changed Reagan was his tours of the GE plants.

RALPH CRANE—TIME LIFE

BARRY! Reagan first entered the political arena as a Goldwater delegate to the 1964 Republican Convention

There he polished his delivery: the intimate confiding tone, the air of sincerity, the wry chuckle, the well-timed burst of fervor. He also listened. As he zigzagged across the country, he acquired a strong sense of what ordinary people thought and hoped and wanted. The hemophilic liberal was becoming steadily more conservative.

Reagan became so vocally critical of such sanctified New Deal creations as Social Security that GE abruptly dropped him in 1962, but he was by now much in demand on what he liked to call "the mashed-potato circuit." In 1964, Reagan's gift for oratory provided an unexpected highlight to the doomed campaign of Barry Goldwater, when a nationally televised speech turned the actor into a G.O.P. star. Backed by a group of wealthy California conservatives, he ran for Governor in 1966. Exploiting a new issue—middle-class discontent over disturbances at the University of California—he won in a landslide over incumbent Democrat Pat Brown. He was a pragmatic and successful Governor, who, surprisingly, imposed the biggest tax hike in state history.

Reagan's successes came during the years when his party was falling into disgrace nationally because of President Nixon's Watergate scandal. Yet to Reagan the optimist, spreading his message was just a matter of patience and marketing. He began a weekly radio commentary broadcast on some 200 stations and a biweekly column in 175 newspapers. It was almost unheard of to run against an incumbent President from one's own party, but in 1976 Reagan took the risk, challenging Gerald Ford, but losing at the

GLOBE PHOTOS

FRIENDS IN HIGH PLACES: Reagan brought star power to politics with his first race, for Governor of California in 1966

MARINES
REAGAN
BUSH
EXIT
REAGAN
COUNTRY

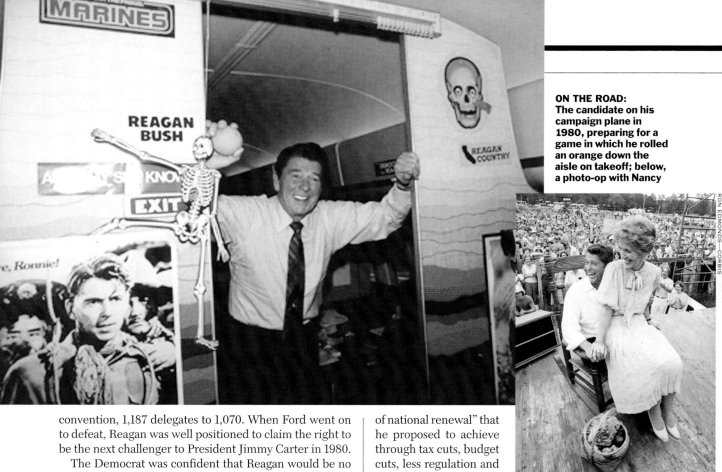

ON THE ROAD:
The candidate on his campaign plane in 1980, preparing for a game in which he rolled an orange down the aisle on takeoff; below, a photo-op with Nancy

RON EDMONDS—CORBIS

convention, 1,187 delegates to 1,070. When Ford went on to defeat, Reagan was well positioned to claim the right to be the next challenger to President Jimmy Carter in 1980.

The Democrat was confident that Reagan would be no match. But the Republican scored with his repeated question to the voters, "Are you better off than you were four years ago?" The answer was, 50.7% of the votes for Reagan, with 41% for Carter and 6.6% for independent John Anderson. Reagan took the vote as a mandate for an "era of national renewal" that he proposed to achieve through tax cuts, budget cuts, less regulation and less welfare. But first he had to endure a shattering murder attempt by John Hinckley, a young man whose only motive for the attack was his desire to impress a movie actress he had never met. Five of six bullets missed the President, but one apparently ricocheted off his car, spun below his armpit and punctured a lung. The stoic Reagan quipped to doctors as he entered surgery: "Please tell me you're Republicans."

ADMINISTRATION

HE'S BACK: Bringing his message to his hometown, Tampico, Ill., in 1980. Reagan was born in the apartment above the bank just behind him

CORBIS BETTMANN

The new Congress gave the new President what he most wanted, a 25% tax cut over three years and a $35 billion cut in the budget. Meanwhile, Reagan reappointed the tough Paul Volcker as Chairman of the Federal Reserve Board and supported Volcker's war on inflation despite withering attacks and considerable domestic pain. The economy swooned into a recession: unemployment reached 10.8%, the highest since the Depression, and the poverty rate grew faster than it had in decades. Reagan rejected predictions of doom. Everything would soon get better, he kept saying. And to the surprise of most professional economists, just about everything did.

By 1984, in time for his re-election campaign, the GNP was growing a robust 6.8%, while inflation had dropped to 4.3%. And from then on, despite the spectacular but brief stock-market crash in 1987, the boom kept right on booming. Those gains, however, were unequally distributed: for the first time since the Depression, U.S. streets were filled by huddled figures who became known as "the homeless." And Reagan turned his back on AIDS sufferers when the deadly new medical plague appeared.

When Reagan took office, the Soviet Union was crumbling. The rot in its marrow, while still hidden to the outside world, was metastasizing. Reagan's great contribution to the end of the cold war was first understanding that

CLOSE CALL: Reagan waves just before being hit by a bullet in 1981

MICHAEL EVANS—ZUMA

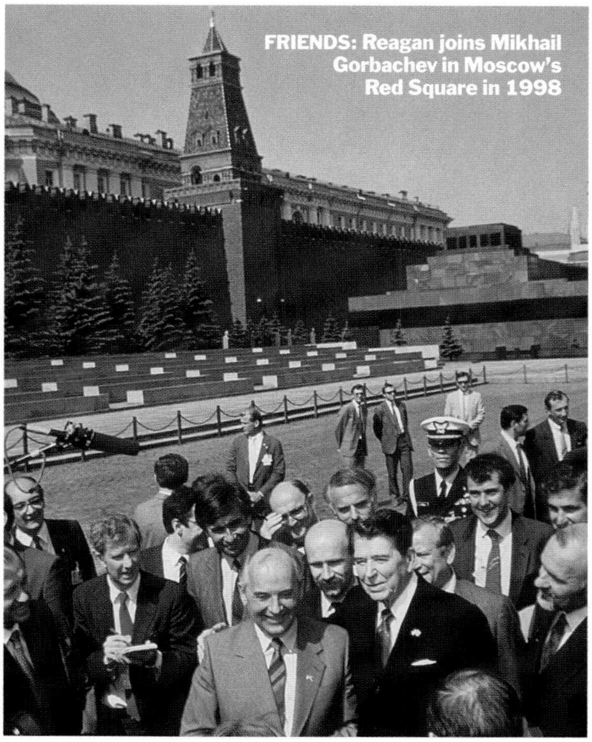
FRIENDS: Reagan joins Mikhail Gorbachev in Moscow's Red Square in 1998

TASS—SOVFOTO

Moscow's cancer was terminal and then working to ensure that the end would come about, peacefully but inexorably. After a decade of Presidents' carefully talking détente, Reagan denounced the Soviet Union as the "evil empire." To armor such rhetoric, Reagan nearly doubled defense spending during his first term while deploying medium-range nuclear missiles in Europe and battling communists in Central America; he also rattled the Kremlin by proposing a defensive Star Wars antimissile shield. He covered up one serious fumble in foreign policy—the deaths of 241 Marines on an ill-advised mission to Lebanon in 1983—by sending U.S. troops into Grenada only days later.

Yet Reagan's final years in office were overshadowed by scandal. Committed to finding a way to free American hostages held in Lebanon, he allowed Marine Lieut. Colonel Oliver North, a gung-ho assistant to National Security Adviser John Poindexter, to carry out a sorry scheme in which illegal arms were sold to Iran, and the profits were used to buy more illegal arms for Nicaraguan rebels. When this official smuggling and dissembling came to light shortly after the summer of 1986, it was a cruelly self-inflicted wound to the whole Reagan Administration. Yet many Americans seemed to forgive the President as easily as he forgave himself. When he left office just a year later, his approval rating stood at 63%.

If anything, the public's admiration for the 40th President grew in the years after he left office—not least because of a fervent effort on the part of his admirers to exalt him. Popular affection and admiration ultimately mixed with sympathy once he revealed his battle with Alzheimer's in 1994. "When the Lord calls me home, whenever that day may be," he wrote in a letter revealing his condition, "I will leave with the greatest love for this country of ours, and eternal optimism for its future." ■

PETE SOUZA—THE WHITE HOUSE

WINDING UP: Above, British P.M. Margaret Thatcher shares a stroll with the President at Camp David in 1986. At right, Reagan waves a farewell to the White House and Capitol from his helicopter on his last day in office, Jan. 20, 1989

AT EASE: The actor at
his Hollywood home, 1954

1947: A STREETCAR
NAMED DESIRE,
ON BROADWAY

1931-2004

Hostage of His Own Genius

TIME film critic Richard Schickel recalls the complex career of Marlon Brando

"THERE'S NO ROOM FOR GENIUS IN THE THEATER," Laurence Olivier once remarked. "It's too much trouble." He was right. For all the Sturm und Drang and general lunacy that so often attend the production of a play—or a film, for that matter—the aim is to mobilize genial craft and polished technique to make something that clutches the audience's heart but does not send it spiraling into cardiac arrest. For an important time in his life—and ours—Marlon Brando was touched by genius, by which we mean that he did things in his art that were unprecedented, unduplicable and, finally, inexplicable. And sure enough, for a much longer time, he was "too much trouble" for everyone to bear—including, possibly, himself.

But let's not talk about that—not yet. Let's think instead about brutal Stanley Kowalski in *A Streetcar Named Desire*, about yearning Terry Malloy in *On the Waterfront*, about the rough voice and silky menace of Don Corleone in *The Godfather* and the noble and ignoble ruin of Brando's Paul in *Last Tango in Paris*. Sometimes in those movies, and in others too, he gave us moments of heartbreaking behavioral reality in which he reached through whatever fictional frame surrounded him and gave us not just the truth of his character but also the truth about ourselves.

No wonder the devotees of Method acting so eagerly claimed him. They believed he was pulling all that conflict out of himself, out of his troubled and rebellious past (cruel and drunken father, wistful and drunken mother). They had long needed a star to lead their revolution—against the well-spoken, emotionally disconnected acting style that had long prevailed on stage and film, indeed against the whole slick, corrupt Broadway-Hollywood way of doing show business. Brando was their stud, possibly the most gorgeous (and authentically sexy) male the movies had ever seen. But he was in his nature ill suited to superstardom. Maybe he didn't want to be anyone's figurehead. Besides, Brando made the leap from Broadway to Hollywood just as movies changed. In the 1950s, the screen widened to CinemaScope proportions while the audience shrank more than 50% and a panicky Hollywood pretty much abandoned small, tight character-driven dramas.

But Brando didn't change. He remained an adolescent idealist, loving the art that had redeemed his incorrigible flakiness but becoming increasingly lost and miserable in this new context. He threw himself distractingly into the great causes of his time, like civil rights. He chose bad movies in which he hid in plain sight under pounds of makeup, talking in weird accents. That led directly to the greatness of *The Godfather.* But it was his one full, belated embrace of the Method that led to *Last Tango,* in which he improvised yards of dialogue, based on his own history, to explain his desperately sad character.

That was in 1972. He had 32 more years to live, encased in fat and cynicism, enduring personal tragedies (notably the killing of his daughter's lover by one of his sons), emerging occasionally to grab some bucks for reading a few lines off cue cards. No, he never did Hamlet or Lear or Uncle Vanya—those were someone else's dreams, not Brando's. He did, without quite knowing it, something grander than that. He gave generations of actors permission to make metaphors of themselves, letting their public find something of themselves in those private moments that, before Brando, no one dared bring forth. Maybe his greatest legacy is named Sean Penn. Or Johnny Depp. Or some nutsy kid whose name we don't yet know. In the end, most acting careers consist of no more than half a dozen great performances and an equal number of near-misses. Those he gave us. The work will abide—while the often foolish and more often misspent life will fade away. ■

1953: THE WILD ONE

1954: ON THE WATERFRONT

1972: THE GODFATHER

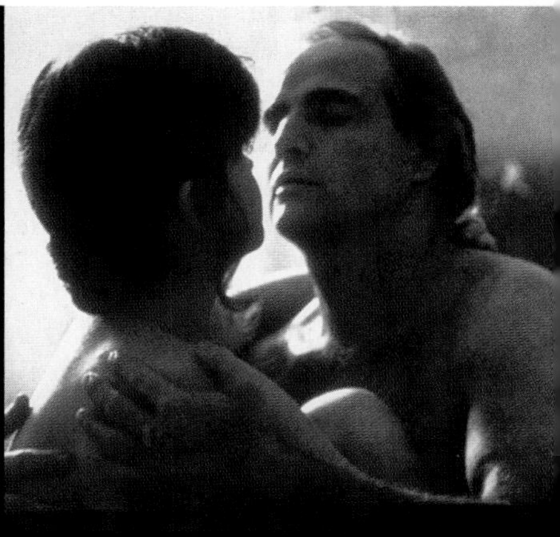

1972: LAST TANGO IN PARIS

HULTON ARCHIVE—GETTY IMAGES; PARAMOUNT PICTURES; COLUMBIA PICTURES

RAY OF LIGHT: The exuberant performer adopted a stage name to avoid being mistaken for boxer Sugar Ray Robinson

KELLY A. SWIFT—RETNA

1932-2004

He Had the Whole World in His Hands

Never mind what to call it: when Ray Charles played, the feelings came first

BORN TO A POOR TEENAGE MOTHER, RAY ROBINSON NEVER knew his father. But he got to know hard times. He was 5 when he watched his younger brother George drown. Two years later a bout with disease, probably glaucoma, left him blind. Enrolled as a charity student at the Florida School for the Deaf and Blind, he learned to read music in Braille. At age 15 he changed his name and hit the road as a singer and pianist, and he didn't slow down for 59 years.

In the 1950s Ray began to create his unique sound, a shotgun wedding of gospel and groove. On hits like *What'd I Say* (1959), he used the call-and-response of a church choir to spark musical drive and sexual tension. He was called the father of soul music, but he was too gifted to be restricted: he mastered jazz and country, imbuing each with his singular grit and charm, and his electrifying take on the patriotic warhorse *America the Beautiful* made it seem just-minted. Many of his hits were suffused with despair, but he delivered them with a fortitude that made them inspiring. Indomitable in life (he overcame a 20-year heroin habit and fathered 11 children) and in song (he won 12 Grammys), he raised money not for the blind but for the hearing impaired. "I can't imagine being deaf," he said. "Imagine never being able to hear music." ■

EVA SERENY—CAMERA PRESS/RETNA

TIMOTHY GREENFIELD SANDERS—CORBIS OUTLINE

SUPER: Reeve stunned his doctors by regaining sensation in parts of his body

1952-2004

A Body Confined, a Spirit That Soared

Christopher Reeve made heroism seem effortless—but there were strings attached

WHEN WE FIRST SPOTTED HIM, CHRISTOPHER REEVE was defying gravity, hurtling through the air as Superman in the hit 1978 movie that spawned two sequels. But the chiseled star won more lasting renown when he came down to earth, emerging as a medical activist after a 1995 horseback-riding accident left him a quadriplegic. He spent his immobile years in constant motion, raising money for paralysis research, speaking out for stem-cell funding, even using his body as a proving ground for new therapies. His efforts helped accelerate paralysis research, while his example fired the dreams of his fellow paraplegics around the world. When he died at 52 of heart failure brought on by pressure sores, a common affliction of the paralyzed, he was mourned as a great spirit and a powerful voice for change.

If his role seemed effortless, it wasn't. "I'm tired of being noble," he confessed to TIME in 2002. "I try to go about this with as much dignity as I can, but not a day goes by when I don't make some effort to get out of this situation." Dignity and effort are good words to describe this man, who offered the greatest of gifts—hope—to those who need it most. ■

MORE WINE! Child adds a favorite ingredient to a pot of stock in 1989

JIM BOURG—NEW YORK TIMES—GETTY IMAGES

1912-2004

The Class Clown of Classic Cuisine

Julia Child turned our kitchens into temples—and playgrounds—of great cooking

SHE WAS RAISED IN CALIFORNIA BY A MOTHER WHO WAS SO New Englandy that she registered her daughter at Smith College the day she was born. But Julia McWilliams, later Child, was never a snob—and that's why Americans fell in love with her. Julia wasn't much of a cook to begin with, but when her diplomat husband Paul was stationed in Paris in the '50s, she enrolled at France's Cordon Bleu. With two French colleagues, she went on to write *Mastering the Art of French Cooking;* published in 1961, the magisterial cookbook launched a revolution in American kitchens. Two years later, at age 51, Child became the host of *The French Chef,* a weekly program on Educational Television (now PBS).

Americans had never seen anything like it. A 6-ft. 2-in. matronly woman with a warbly Boston accent, Child swigged wine, hefted a meat cleaver with extreme prejudice and occasionally picked up ingredients she'd dropped on the floor, explaining, "You're all alone in the kitchen, and no one can see you." A sworn enemy of health food, junk food and all forms of pomposity, she fought against everyone who believed in living correctly instead of living well. If you seek her monument, look around your kitchen, or visit hers—it was installed at the Smithsonian Institution in 2002. *Bon appétit,* Julia! ■

A.C. BARRINGTON BROWN—SPL/PHOTO RESEARCHERS

TINKERING: Crick, who trained as a physicist, not a biologist, toys with a model of the double helix in 1953

1916-2004

Decoder of the Secret Structure of Life

Francis Crick, co-discoverer of the double helix, is recalled by partner James Watson

THE DEATH OF FRANCIS CRICK DEPRIVED THE WORLD OF a remarkable scientist and conversationalist whose forceful voice and overpowering laugh made him the focal point of any room that he chose to occupy. From the morning of Feb. 28, 1953, when he and I discovered the double-helical structure of DNA—and showed that the secret of life was a large molecule—he held court over the new field of research that this discovery unleashed.

Exuding an Edwardian elegance of logic as well as dress, Crick instantly brought to mind the good-natured arrogance of Henry Higgins in George Bernard Shaw's *Pygmalion*. From early adolescence, Crick had no truck with truths arrived at by religious revelation, as opposed to observation and experimentation. Upon learning that Cambridge University's science-dominated new college was planning to build a Christian chapel, he resigned from the ranks of its Fellows. "Perpetuating mistakes from the past" was not Crick's way to move forward. ■

G. COOPER

BETTMANN CORBIS

Gordon Cooper

1927-2004

One of NASA's original seven astronauts, "Gordo" was famously casual in his approach to pilot training—and famously brilliant at it nonetheless. Cooper flew twice into orbit, as the sole pilot of the last *Mercury* mission in 1963 and as commander of *Gemini 5* in 1965. The most colorful of the *Mercury* crew, he nodded off in his capsule on the launch pad before his first spaceflight; claimed to believe in alien encounters; and, visiting a booster rocket under assembly, scrawled an arrow pointing up on its side and wrote, "Launch this way!" For a time, Cooper held the world record for time logged in space, 222 hours, but his strap-it-on-and-go approach served him less well in the lunar program, when NASA preferred more by-the-book pilots. He never got a trip to the moon—a loss more for NASA, many space historians believe, than for Cooper.

Elisabeth Kübler-Ross

1926-2004

The Swiss-born psychiatrist's research in the 1960s demolished medical taboos against discussing death with the dying and helped establish hospice care in the U.S. "Few books have had as profound an effect on public dialogue as did her 1969 blockbuster, *On Death and Dying*, written at a time when the topic was rarely discussed in public and studiously avoided at the bedside," wrote Dr. Sherwin Nuland in TIME. "Fear not, she reassured the tens of millions who would read and then quote her teachings: the human mind has the wondrous capacity to prepare itself for dying, by a progressive series of five steps—denial, anger, bargaining, depression and, finally, acceptance—that ultimately lead to a peaceful resolution."

AP/WIDE WORLD

SOPHIE BASSOULS—CORBIS SYGMA

Czeslaw Milosz

1911-2004

The Polish poet and essayist came to world notice with his earnest, politically charged writing in the shadow of communism; in 1980, his body of work earned him the Nobel Prize for Literature. Born in the Lithuanian capital of Vilnius, he began writing poetry in the 1930s and spent World War II writing for the anti-Nazi underground in Warsaw. In 1951, after a stint as a diplomat, he broke from the Polish government and settled in France, where he wrote about the plight of intellectuals under communism in his challenging 1953 essay collection, *The Captive Mind*. After immigrating to the U.S. in 1960, he taught Slavic literature at the University of California at Berkeley for more than 20 years.

Tony Randall
1920-2004

The actor will always be associated with his role as fussy Felix Unger on TV's *The Odd Couple,* but he was far more than that: a veteran of Hollywood and show biz; a fine raconteur; a smart, capable man who cherished the family he started late in life. *Odd Couple* co-star Jack Klugman wrote in TIME, "His dream was to bring classic theater to America through repertory companies. He was outraged that it was not subsidized by the government. He said he would set up the National Actors Theater in New York, and nobody believed him, including me. And by God, he did it ... During his last few years, he was the happiest actor I ever knew."

PHOTOFEST—RETNA LTD.

Paul (Red) Adair
1915-2004

The legendary oil-field fire fighter put out an estimated 2,000 blazes around the world with a rather strange brew: water and dynamite. After World War II, the native Texan returned home from a two-year stint in the Army's bomb demolition unit to take a job with Myron Kinley, a pioneer of well-fire and blowout control. Adair later started his own business, and his exploits, which included the time an explosion in South Texas propelled him 50 ft. in the air and he emerged unscathed, inspired the 1968 John Wayne film *Hellfighters.* Adair got a taste of hell in the wake of Operation Desert Storm in 1991, when he quenched 119 burning wells in Kuwait torched by retreating Iraqi soldiers. In his biography, Adair recalled that he would often walk up to a burning well accompanied by 10 men: "Pretty soon, though, I'd look around and there'd only be five left."

WOWE—NETWORK

the
EVENING MAKE-UP
COLLECTION
by
Estée Lauder

DALLAS MORNING NEWS

Estée Lauder
1908-2004

The woman born Josephine Esther Metzer struggled mightily to ascend from her parents' apartment above the family hardware store in Queens, N.Y., to preside over a global cosmetics company. The daughter of Jewish immigrants from Eastern Europe, she was enthralled by beauty and glamour, and her talent lay in convincing other women she could help them attain those qualities. After being granted counter space at Saks Fifth Avenue in 1948, she hatched what is today a promotional mainstay in the industry, the "gift with purchase." When she died at 97, the company she founded was worth $10 billion.

Spalding Gray
1941-2004

Gray was the master of a theatrical form he helped pioneer: the confessional monologue *(Swimming to Cambodia; Monster in a Box).* His body was found floating in New York City's East River two months after his disappearance in January. Gray had a history of depression, exacerbated by a 2001 car accident.

©DAN DION—RETNA LTD.

PHOTOFEST—RETNA LTD.

Rodney Dangerfield

1921-2004

Born Jacob Cohen, he struggled to make it as a young Catskills comic, using the stage name Jack Roy, then left show business for 12 years and sold aluminum siding. But he made a comeback in his 40s, with a new name (suggested by a club owner) and a new catchphrase, "I don't get no respect." He got his first big break with a spot on *The Ed Sullivan Show* in 1967. His tie-tugging tics and depressive one-liners became a staple on TV in the '70s and '80s; and as a late-blooming movie star in films like *Caddyshack* and *Back to School*, he made his old-style comedy seem eternally young.

©RB—REDFERNS—RETNA LTD.

Rick James

1923-2004

The early '80s funk icon was perhaps best known for his outrageous fashion sense and a troubled personal life that included a five-year prison sentence for assault and a 10-year addiction to cocaine. His infectious 1981 single *Super Freak* launched him to superstardom—and did the same trick for M.C. Hammer, who sampled it, note for note, years later in *U Can't Touch This*.

Alistair Cooke

1948-2004

©SNOWDON—CAMERA PRESS—RETNA LTD.

To most Americans, Cooke was the baronial M.C. of *Masterpiece Theatre*, a genial, avuncular visitor to the living room. But his role as a TV host was a sideline for the British journalist who knew everyone and remembered everything, from Charlie Chaplin to Michael Jackson. His weekly BBC chat series, *Letter from America*, mesmerized millions of listeners on five continents and ran for 58 years—the world's longest-running series with a single person as host.

Geoffrey Beene

1927-2004

The Louisiana native first landed on Seventh Avenue in the 1950s and started his line in 1963, raising the standards of American design with technical innovations, sumptuous fabrics and minimalist creations whose streamlined silhouettes belied their complicated construction. Widely admired for his facility with cut and his uncompromising creative vision, Beene was a contrarian among his peers; he did not follow trends or play the fashion game, often rejecting the notion of fashion as commerce in favor of it as art.

GLOBE PHOTOS

Jack Paar

1918-2004

You don't hear much talk on the network talk shows these days—not much real conversation to broaden the mind, upset the rigid format or challenge guests and viewers. In TV's robust youth it was different, owing in large part to Jack Paar. Though his tenure as host of *The Tonight Show* lasted only five years, from 1957 to '62, the former disc jockey and B-movie actor made late-night TV both a habit and an event. He visited Cuba to talk to Castro, and Berlin when the Wall went up. More often, Paar made news by being himself—a softy quick to anger, quick to cry—and by keeping his audience guessing what mood he would be in tonight.

GETTY IMAGES

Janet Leigh

1927-2004

The coolly seductive Hollywood star earned immortality as the cinema's prime slasher victim in Alfred Hitchcock's *Psycho.* She could have settled for being Tony Curtis' wife (for 11 years) and Jamie Lee's mother. But Leigh had a gaze as alert and sexy as any in movies. It bored into Frank Sinatra's frazzled psyche in *The Manchurian Candidate* and mixed fear and fire as a captive in Orson Welles' *Touch of Evil.*

Pat Tillman

1976-2004

The tough linebacker walked away from a $3.6 million three-year contract with the N.F.L.'s Arizona Cardinals because there was another uniform he wanted to wear in the wake of 9/11: that of a U.S. Army Ranger. Refusing to capitalize on his act, Tillman denied interview requests after he signed up. His decision wasn't a publicity stunt or a career move—it was patriotism. Sent to Afghanistan, he took part in Operation Mountain Storm, a campaign launched in March by U.S.-led forces against Taliban and al-Qaeda fighters along the border with Pakistan. He died in a fire fight on April 22; the cause is thought to have been friendly fire.

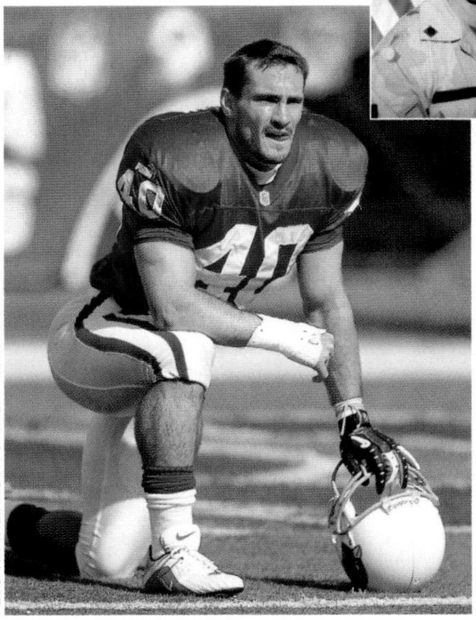

REUTERS—LANDOV. INSET: BOB WILLIAMSON—PHOTOGRAPHY PLUS VIA WILLIAMSON STEALTH MEDIA SOLUTIONS

JONATHAN BLAIR—CORBIS

Fred Whipple

1906-2004

The inventor and rocket scientist correctly proposed in 1950 that comets may be regarded as "dirty snowballs," making it easier to track them. The core of a comet, Whipple said, consists of ice, ammonia, methane and carbon dioxide; its tail is formed by particles that break off from the mass as it approaches the sun. Over seven decades at Harvard University and the Smithsonian Astrophysical Observatory, Whipple also discovered that the source of meteors is not far-flung stars but Earth's solar system. Earlier, Whipple saved the lives of countless Allied flyers in World War II by inventing a device that cut aluminum foil into thousands of fragments; when released from planes, the shards fooled German radar by showing tens of thousands of planes were attacking.

FRANK DRIGGS COLLECTION—GETTY IMAGES

Illinois Jacquet

Abu Abbas, 56, mastermind of the 1985 hijacking of the Italian cruise ship *Achille Lauro;* he died in U.S custody after being captured in Baghdad in April 2003.

Elmer Bernstein, 82, composer who created both jazzy and gentle scores for more than 200 Hollywood films, including the themes for *The Magnificent Seven* and *The Great Escape.*

Jan Berry, 62, of the duo Jan & Dean, who produced a string of 1960s surf-music hits. The singer of *Surf City* and *Dead Man's Curve* sustained brain damage and paralysis after a 1966 car accident.

Daniel J. Boorstin, 89, historian and public servant who served for 13 years as Librarian of Congress and won a Pulitzer Prize in 1974 for *The Americans: The Democratic Experience.*

Lloyd Bucher, 76, former U.S. Navy commander of the U.S.S. *Pueblo,* whose crew was held captive by North Korea for 11 months in 1968.

Cy Coleman, 75, veteran composer for such Broadway musicals as *Sweet Charity* and *City of Angels.*

Ken Caminiti, 41, the National League's most valuable player in 1996 who later admitted to steroid use and battled substance abuse.

Iris Chang, 36, historian whose landmark 1997 best seller *The Rape of Nanking* chronicled the torture and murder of hundreds of thousands of Chinese civilians in the former capital by Japanese soldiers in the late 1930s. Hospitalized for depression early in 2004, she took her own life later in the year.

Archibald Cox, 92, Harvard professor and Watergate special prosecutor whose insistence that Richard Nixon hand over tapes of Oval Office conversations got him fired in 1973.

David Dellinger, 88, antiwar activist who helped organize the 1967 march on the Pentagon and was one of the Chicago Seven tried for inciting a riot at the 1968 Democratic Convention.

Jacques Derrida, 74, French philosopher who was the godfather of deconstruction, a critical approach that emphasizes ambiguity, self-reference and multiple, shifting meanings.

Carmine de Sapio, 95, who ruled New York City politics as the last boss of Tammany Hall and hand-picked mayors and Governors. By the late 1960s he had been convicted of petty bribery and defeated in local elections.

Fred Ebb, 76, lyricist who, in partnership with composer John Kander, created the brassy, cynical-but-sweet scores of such Broadway musicals as *Cabaret* and *Chicago.*

Illinois Jacquet, 81, innovative tenor saxophonist and bandleader. A master of the style known as screeching, he was was equally adept at slow ballads.

EVERETT COLLECTION

Bob Keeshan

©PETER SMITH—RETNA LTD.

Russ Meyer

Howard Keel, 85, beefy baritone star of such premier 1950s musicals as *Show Boat* and *Kiss Me Kate.* He came back with flair on TV's *Dallas* in the 1980s.

Bob Keeshan, 76, TV's Captain Kangaroo, who aimed his CBS (and, later, PBS) children's show to counter small-screen violence and hyperstimulation. He was also the original Clarabell the Clown on *Howdy Doody.*

Frances Shand Kydd, 68, who had an often turbulent relationship with her daughter Princess Diana. When she and Edward John Spencer divorced in 1969, the future princess, then 8, stayed with her father.

José Lopez Portillo, 83, who, as President of Mexico from 1976 to 1982, led a free-spending, corruption-ridden government that took the nation to the brink of economic collapse in the midst of an exuberant oil boom.

John E. Mack, 74, controversial Pulitzer-prizewinning psychiatrist and Harvard professor who was best known for studying people who claimed to have had alien encounters.

William Manchester, 82, scrupulous author of thrilling narratives on military and political power whose works include two volumes of *The Last Lion,* a brilliant yet sadly uncompleted biography of the life of Winston Churchill.

Alicia Markova, 94, British ballerina who popularized ballet in Britain and beyond. In 1925 she became the youngest member of Ballets Russes, then the world's finest company; she later worked with George Balanchine and Frederick Ashton.

Alberta Martin, 97, the last living widow of a Confederate soldier. In 1927 she married William Jasper Martin, then 81. After he died in 1931, she married his grandson.

Tug McGraw, 59, whose relief pitching helped the New York Mets and Philadelphia Phillies win the World Series; the intense left-hander coined the '73 Mets' battle cry, "You gotta believe!"

©DAVID CORIO—RETNA LTD.

Johnny Ramone

Norris McWhirter, 78, who with his identical twin brother Ross founded the *Guinness Book of Records* after being asked by the head of the Guinness brewery to create a reference for settling bets between drinking buddies.

Mary McGrory, 85, liberal, no-nonsense Washington newspaper columnist who won a Pulitzer Prize in 1974 for her work on Watergate.

Robert Merrill, 87, powerful singer whose baritone made him a favorite at the Metropolitan Opera for 30 years.

Russ Meyer, 82, World War II combat cameraman and later a soft-core porn director whose movies set the tone for late 20th century pop culture at its most cheerfully leering.

Marvin Mitchelson, 76, Hollywood divorce lawyer whose advocacy of the right to alimony sans marriage ("palimony") earned riches and fame.

Paul Nitze, 97, formidable diplomat and negotiator who was one of the principal architects of America's cold war policies toward the Soviet Union; he later became better known for his efforts at conciliation.

F. Booker Noe II, 74, former master distiller of Jim Beam bourbon. A grandson of Jim Beam's, Noe created Booker's Bourbon, a small-batch whiskey that established a new market for upscale bourbon.

Princess Juliana, 94, revered Queen of the Netherlands for 32 years. Shy and informal, she recognized Indonesia's independence after being crowned in 1948 and abdicated to her daughter Beatrix in 1980.

Johnny Ramone, 55, guitarist and paternal driving force behind the Ramones, the seminal rock band that defined the 1970s punk movement.

Laurance Rockefeller, 94, one of five grandsons of oil baron John D. Rockefeller, the reserved visionary made his mark as a philanthropist, venture capitalist and conservationist.

Marvin Runyon, 79, onetime auto-factory worker who, as Postmaster General from 1992 to 1998, pulled the U.S. Postal Service into the black. The first U.S. employee of Japanese carmaker Nissan, he became CEO of its U.S. subsidiary and chaired the giant Tennessee Valley Authority.

Roger Straus, 87, dominant force in the publishing house Farrar, Straus & Giroux, whose roster of celebrated authors included T.S. Eliot, Nadine Gordimer and Isaac Bashevis Singer.

Pierre Salinger, 79, debonair press secretary during the Kennedy and Johnson administrations; an archliberal, he left the U.S. when George W. Bush became President; he died in France.

Marge Schott, 75, controversial philanthropist and former owner of the Cincinnati Reds, whose insensitive ethnic and racial comments overshadowed her numerous good deeds.

GORDON ANTHONY—GETTY IMAGES

Peter Ustinov

Timothy the Turtle, approximately 160, British navy mascot that witnessed the bombing of Sevastopol in 1854 during the Crimean War. To the navy's distress, an ill-fated 1926 mating attempt revealed that he was, in fact, a she.

Peter Ustinov, 82, actor, wit and inexhaustible raconteur who spoke six languages and won his greatest movie renown as Agatha Christie's detective Hercule Poirot.

Fay Wray, 96, shriek-tacular heroine of the original *King Kong* and other thrillers of the movies' early talkie era.

Paul Winfield, 62, actor who brought an imposing demeanor and human-size emotions to roles ranging from Martin Luther King Jr. to the sharecropper father in the 1972 film *Sounder.*

HULTON ARCHIVE—GETTY IMAGES

Fay Wray